Mac

In *Macroeconomics: An Introduction*, Alex M. Thomas provides a lucid and novel introduction to macroeconomic issues. The book introduces the reader to an alternative approach of understanding macroeconomics, which is inspired by the works of Adam Smith, David Ricardo, Karl Marx, John Maynard Keynes and Piero Sraffa. It also presents the reader with a critical account of mainstream marginalist macroeconomics.

The book begins with a brief history of economic theories and then it takes the reader through three different ways of conceptualising the macroeconomy. Subsequently, the theories of money and interest rates, output and employment levels, and economic growth are discussed. This is followed by a chapter on why economic theory matters. The book ends by providing a policy template for addressing the macroeconomic concerns of unemployment and inflation.

The conceptual discussion in *Macroeconomics* is situated within the context of the Indian economy. Besides using publicly available data, the contextual description is instantiated using excerpts from works of fiction by Indian authors.

Other key features of the book:

- A critical pedagogy
- A problem-setting approach as opposed to a problem-solving one
- In-text questions that mimic the format of an interactive lecture
- Illustrations to convey key points
- Figures and tables to complement the text
- An annotated list of further readings at the end of each chapter

This book will be of interest to anyone looking for an alternative macroeconomics framework, a critique of mainstream marginalist macroeconomics and an understanding of the Indian macroeconomy.

Alex M. Thomas is Assistant Professor of Economics at Azim Premji University, Bengaluru, India. His primary research is in the area of history of economic thought, with a special focus on classical economics. His research has been published in both national and international journals, including the *Economic and Political Weekly*, *History of Economic Ideas*, *History of Economics Review* and *Journal of Interdisciplinary Economics*.

Macroeconomics

An Introduction

Alex M. Thomas

CAMBRIDGE
UNIVERSITY PRESS

University Printing House, Cambridge CB2 8BS, United Kingdom

One Liberty Plaza, 20th Floor, New York, NY 10006, USA

477 Williamstown Road, Port Melbourne, VIC 3207, Australia

314–321, 3rd Floor, Plot 3, Splendor Forum, Jasola District Centre, New Delhi–110025, India

79 Anson Road, #06–04/06, Singapore 079906

Cambridge University Press is part of the University of Cambridge.

It furthers the University's mission by disseminating knowledge in the pursuit of education, learning and research at the highest international levels of excellence.

www.cambridge.org
Information on this title: www.cambridge.org/9781108486941

© Alex M. Thomas 2021

First published 2021

Printed in India by Thomson Press India Ltd.

A catalogue record for this publication is available from the British Library

Library of Congress Cataloging-in-Publication Data

Names: Thomas, Alex M., author.
Title: Macroeconomics : an introduction / Alex M. Thomas.
Description: Cambridge, United Kingdom ; New York, NY : Cambridge
    University Press, 2021. | Includes bibliographical references and index.
Identifiers: LCCN 2021005355 (print) | LCCN 2021005356 (ebook) | ISBN
    9781108486941 (hardback) | ISBN 9781108731997 (paperback) | ISBN
    9781108764919 (ebook)
Subjects: LCSH: Macroeconomics.
Classification: LCC HB172.5 .T4695 2021 (print) | LCC HB172.5 (ebook) |
    DDC 339--dc23
LC record available at https://lccn.loc.gov/2021005355
LC ebook record available at https://lccn.loc.gov/2021005356

ISBN 978-1-108-48694-1 Hardback
ISBN 978-1-108-73199-7 Paperback

To Appacha,
who always encouraged me to ask questions

Contents

CONTENTS

Illustrations

Figures

Tables

Preface

At the very outset I must confess that I did not want to write a textbook. This is because all economics textbooks, except for a few, are essentially the same in their core content and presentation. In particular, there is no recognition of pluralism in theoretical approaches. My engagement with economics in varying capacities—as a student, a teacher, a researcher, a blogger and a commentator—has mostly dealt with a critical appraisal of mainstream economics and the strengthening of an alternative approach inspired by Adam Smith, David Ricardo, Karl Marx, John Maynard Keynes and Piero Sraffa. Both my interest in this alternative approach and the need to present the same to a wider audience persuaded me to organise and document my approach to macroeconomics in a written form.

Besides my desire for documentation, another motivation for writing this book arises from the need to provide good texts (even in the form of a short extract) to students studying in Indian colleges and universities where libraries are not well stocked. I vividly remember, as an M.Phil student at the University of Hyderabad (which has a reasonably well-stocked library), how I had struggled to obtain the materials I required for my research on the economics before Adam Smith. Fortunately, I received help from friends who were in other Indian universities and from historians of economic thought based in foreign universities. I hope that the short extracts, book suggestions in the chapters and the suggestions for further reading at the end of each chapter will provide an impetus to the readers not only to read original texts, but also to demand well-stocked libraries.

I strongly recommend and encourage the use of various texts (books, journal articles, government reports, fiction, newspaper articles and textbooks) in the teaching of any course in economics. This stems from my rather modest experience of just over 15 years as a student and teacher of economics. While the use of varied texts is challenging for both the teacher and the student, I firmly believe that the long-term benefits far outweigh the short-term costs, and that it truly contributes to good learning as it enables the students to become better arbiters of knowledge. After all, we live in the age of information abundance, and perhaps the most valuable skills are the ability to identify credible sources of information and the ability to evaluate, with sufficient confidence, contending arguments, perspectives and standpoints.

In keeping with the above spirit, in *Macroeconomics: An Introduction*, I have tried to provide the reader with an assortment of texts, most notably from books of economics and fiction. However, as H. G. Jones writes in the preface to his excellent 1975 textbook on economic growth, it is crucial to keep in mind that "no textbook, however comprehensive, can ever be a substitute for the enlightening and rewarding process of struggling with the original books and articles" (p. iii).

A brief comment on how I have chosen the texts is now in order. First, I have tried to minimise the need for the reader to look up any extra material to follow the basic argument so as to not place the burden of seeking out a book or an article on the reader or her institution. To provide the flavour of the text, I have excerpted passages (sometimes long ones) from it. Second, this textbook possesses a distinct 'Indian' character—in terms of the examples and selection of literature. And the reader will find hardly any reference to examples from the American economy and works of fiction by American/British writers. It is in Raja Rao's foreword to his 1938 novel *Kanthapura* that I first came across an explicit recognition of this standpoint: "The tempo of Indian life must be infused into our English expression" (p. v). Not surprisingly, almost all the economic theories you will come across in this textbook have non-Indian origins. But the Indian context has been infused into *our* non-Indian economics concepts, as it were, to rephrase Rao. Another criterion underlying the choice of fiction, besides my own very limited exposure, is that they engage with at least one of the following themes: caste, ecology, gender or land.

Finally, this book adopts a problem-setting approach rather than a problem-solving one, as is the case with most economics textbooks. To put it more clearly, this text helps you to identify, conceptualise and discipline a macroeconomic problem. Therefore, this book does not contain exercises in problem solving, but it contains discussions and questions that make you think about the nature of assumptions, the logic of the theory, the limits of the theory, the interface between theory and policy, a little bit about the gaps between theory and data, and, occasionally, the nature of past and present economic thought.

Therefore, this book aims to provide you with an (introductory) immersive experience in macroeconomics.

Bengaluru
July 2020

Acknowledgements

The origins of this book can be traced to my macroeconomics lectures to the first-year undergraduates at Azim Premji University from 2016 to 2018. Other courses I taught since then have also immensely helped in the writing of the book; in particular, I should mention 'History of Economic Thought' and 'Quantitative Reasoning for Humanities', for reaffirming my belief in the intellectual benefits of pluralism in theory and the power of descriptive statistics.

I had no plans of writing a textbook when I started teaching introductory macroeconomics; for the inception of the idea in July 2017, I am indebted to Anwesha Rana. Her editorial support throughout the writing of the book has been outstanding. I am grateful to the four anonymous reviewers who, on behalf of Cambridge University Press, read some of the chapters of the first draft and provided extremely useful suggestions. I am much obliged to Aniruddha De for his care in overseeing the production of the book and accommodating my unconventional requests regarding style. I am thankful to Amit Prasad for preparing the index.

The book has taken close to three years from inception to completion—a rather long time for a work like this. Each year, I managed to complete the first drafts of roughly three chapters. This was because I found it difficult to find time to write at a stretch, given the immediate demands of teaching and other pressing research and speaking commitments. Despite the delay, I am quite certain that my teaching and research engagements have contributed positively to the making of this book. Additionally, the talks I have given at various Indian universities and colleges on aspects of the Indian economy and history of economic thought provided me with several opportunities to think about particular issues in a focused manner; several of those issues figure in this book. I remain grateful to all those who invited me to give these talks.

My understanding and articulation of economic matters have improved from the questions posed by my students and our subsequent discussions both inside and outside the classroom. In particular, I wish to record my gratitude to the following students: Mridhula Mohan and Niveditha G. D. for having readily agreed to type out my handwritten first draft, which suffered from poor penmanship; Anushka Kale and Indu Periodi for their encouraging comments on some chapters of the first draft; Ashwath R. for his astute comments on the entire final draft; and Sahana

Subramanyam for her wonderful illustrations that complement the discussion of some of the key ideas in this book.

I must place on record my deep appreciation for all my colleagues at the Azim Premji University Library for promptly sourcing the books I needed throughout the three years. I am indebted to the following colleagues and friends—in the alphabetical order of their surnames—for having provided helpful comments on some chapters of the first draft: Tony Aspromourgos, Rahul De, Sunandan K. N. and Bhavya Sinha. Mohib Ali read two chapters of the revised draft and provided invaluable suggestions. The entire revised manuscript benefited from the critical observations of Syed Atif, Varadarajan Narayanan and Limakumba Walling. Needless to mention, I have not heeded all the advice I received, and I alone am responsible for any remaining errors.

For providing me with intellectual and emotional succour during the three years of writing this book, I am indebted to Abhigna, Atif, Chaitra, Divya, Lima, Neeraja, Nilesh, Rahul, Sharmadip, Sunandan, Tarangini, Varada, Varun and Varuni. I am grateful to my parents and my grandmothers for their unwavering support and my sister Elizabeth for her presence during the final stages of writing the book, and also for proofreading the final draft. The subsequent meticulous editing of the manuscript by Abhigna Arigala improved its quality significantly— and for this too, I remain indebted. I owe a special debt of gratitude to Anjana Thampi for carefully going through the typeset manuscript and providing helpful suggestions.

As with any intellectual endeavour, I have benefited immensely from the discussions I have had with several of my peers, teachers, students and especially those with my two research mentors. Many of the elements of my approach to economics are those I have imbibed from my mentors during the course of my studies at the universities of Hyderabad and Sydney. Consequently, my greatest intellectual debts are to Goddanti Omkarnath and Tony Aspromourgos.

Note to the Reader

Macroeconomics: An Introduction assumes some familiarity with economics—at least, a year of undergraduate economics education. It is not a big book and has been written with a view that it will be read in its entirety. However, if you are interested only in conceptual or theoretical aspects of macroeconomics, you can focus on Chapters 3, 4 and 5 after having read Sections 1.4, 2.4 and 2.5. To obtain a broad policy perspective aimed at improving employment levels and stabilising inflation (with special reference to India), reading Chapters 7 and 8 is adequate. Finally, if you are particularly interested in the history and philosophy of macroeconomics, you can read Chapters 1, 2, 6 and 9.

The table of contents provides only an outline of the book's contents. A more rewarding approach to understanding the perspective and intentions of the book/ author is by *reading* the index. It is not only helpful in locating the occurrence of a word, but also provides you with a map to understand the various interconnections between macroeconomics concepts, contexts, accounting, policies and sources that are discussed in this book. That is, the index provides you both the obvious and not-so-obvious links present between theories, within a theory, between concepts and context, between accounting and theory, and so on. For instance, if you wish to know what the book has to offer on 'consumption', look for its entry in the index; you will find obvious entries such as 'autonomous', 'induced' and 'and theory of output', but you will also find not-so-obvious entries such as 'and index numbers' and 'versus investment'. If you are reading the e-book format, note that electronic keyword searches may not tell you about the nature and instances of such not-so-obvious interconnections between the ideas in the book.

While I have used quantitative data to capture relevant features of the Indian economy, they need not be the latest available ones. This is so because the figures and charts that display quantitative economic characteristics are being used as vehicles for communicating relevant aspects of the Indian economy and for providing readers with the broad orders of magnitude relating to the Indian economy, and not to supply you with the most up-to-date statistics.

If you are a teacher who wishes to use this book, each chapter can be transacted in the classroom in at least four hours. I have weaved in questions alongside the explanation of concepts and not placed it at the end of the chapter, as is the convention. This has been done partly to recreate the experience of an interactive lecture and to underscore the fact that normally questions arise at specific points during the course of an argument or discussion.

To obtain an immersive experience of macroeconomics, this book has to be used in the company of other texts and experiences. In order to facilitate such conversation, I have posed questions intended for both individual contemplation and discussion in groups. At several points in this book, you might perhaps wish that I provided an answer to a question or carried out an elaborate discussion. However, such a pedagogy is deliberate, and, in fact, this book would have attained its purpose if it motivates discussions both inside and outside the classroom on conceptual and contextual issues in macroeconomics. In other words, it is intended to serve as a critical companion.

Although this book's primary audience is undergraduate economics students, I think that it will be of interest to other social science students, and also to general readers interested in gaining an understanding of macroeconomic issues.

1

What Is Economics

1.1 Introduction

A cursory glance at your daily newspaper for an entire week might tell you about: how the Indian farmers are struggling, how the manufacturing sector is not creating enough jobs, the nature of India's economic growth, the changes made by the Reserve Bank of India (RBI) to the interest rates, the stubbornly wide socioeconomic inequalities across caste and gender, how growth in manufacturing is causing ecological damage, and/or how the Bombay Stock Exchange (BSE) reacted with cheer to a recent government notification. All these listed issues are economic in nature because they deal with employment, economic growth, interest rates and economic inequalities, and they affect the livelihood of individuals, entire communities, sectors as well as the nation. But why spend time trying to understand these economic issues? Of course, if you are enrolled for a bachelor's or master's course in economics, you are required to study them. To pose the earlier question slightly differently, what is it that motivates you to enroll for an economics course or to spend time studying them independently?

To an economist, all the above-mentioned issues will appear related. Although Indian farmers are struggling, they are unable to find jobs in the manufacturing sector because it has not been creating adequate jobs and because the farmers do not have access to the skills/education that are required in the manufacturing sector. India's economic growth is mainly driven by the growth of the services sector; here too, not many jobs are being created and nor do the Indian farmers have the requisite skills/education. The fact of unequal access to education is explained mostly by the historical inequalities arising from the ownership of land and capital. Since agricultural output is insufficient (due to which the farmers' livelihoods are adversely affected), agricultural prices rise. To tackle this price rise (or inflation), the RBI decides to increase the rate of interest to mop up excess money (more accurately, liquidity) from the economy; this is done because it believes that inflation is caused by too much money chasing too few goods. The investors of stocks listed in the BSE are happy because this rise in interest rate is going to attract an inflow of foreign capital to India as the rate of return in India is higher than that in their own country. What are the mechanisms that cause these outcomes? What determines the levels and growth rates of these macroeconomic variables such as money, interest rates and employment? Studying macroeconomics helps you make sense of these seemingly disparate events. And it is hoped that any engaged reader of this textbook will become equipped with the necessary concepts required to make such connections and explain them.

Most of us live in societies where the governments are democratically elected, that is, directly or indirectly, by *our* votes. The efficacy of government functioning is, therefore, largely contingent on how we cast our votes. You might have noticed how political parties, coalitions and independent candidates all have some vision of how to improve the existing availability and distribution of material goods and services. Additionally, they promise us better wages, greater employment opportunities and low inflation. But how do we decide what is the 'best' based on their manifestos or vision documents? Such vision documents and plans are also released by the government; examples include the annual economic surveys and the union budgets. How do you evaluate the claims made in these public documents? The study of economics can help with making an informed judgement. Besides this reason, you might want to see to it that everyone in your community and/or country gets a good life. If this is your motivation, your natural choice of occupation might be a policy maker in the government, an independent consultant for ecological issues, a socioeconomic journalist, a teacher, a social entrepreneur or a trade union leader. Whichever occupation you aspire to be in, the knowledge of economic matters is necessary.

However, be mindful of the fact that the study of economics, especially of the current university kind, is never *sufficient* to fully understand our societies. Therefore, as students of economics, it is recommended that you read widely. Read good books of fiction that convey to you the realities about your surroundings in a manner no economics book does (or can). This book hopes to make a slight difference to that state of affairs by including excerpts from relevant fiction. Read history. Understand the operation of the political systems in your community and country. Listen to those who have experienced socio-economic hardships. Finally, remember that any economics textbook, including this one, should be seen only as a stepping stone and should be used in the good company of other kinds of texts and experiences.

This is the right time to read a motivating passage by John Maynard Keynes on the kind of skills an economist ought to possess.

> … the master-economist must possess a rare *combination* of gifts…. He must be mathematician, historian, statesman, philosopher—in some degree. He must understand symbols and speak in words. He must contemplate the particular in terms of the general, and touch abstract and concrete in the same flight of thought. He must study the present in the light of the past for the purposes of the future. No part of man's nature or his institutions must lie entirely outside his regard. (1924, pp. 173–4)

Keynes wrote the above sentences in his obituary for Alfred Marshall, his economics teacher. But, as I tell my students in class, the male pronoun ought to be changed. Closer in space and time, Jean Drèze draws our attention to what he terms 'research for action' in a 2002 article in the journal *Economic and Political Weekly*, where he stresses the "value of personal experience as a source of knowledge" (p. 819). He subsequently clarifies this approach to doing economics in his 2017 book *Sense and Solidarity: Jholawala Economics for Everyone*, which is a collection of previously published essays.

Since we have now touched upon the various motivations to study economics, the future possibilities arising from the study of economics, and, very importantly, the limits to the formal study of economics and how to overcome those by reading widely, the path is now clear to begin our study of economics.

1.2 A brief history of economics

Before I present the definition of economics used in this book, it is useful to provide you with a brief outline of the evolution of economic ideas. When do you think economics as a distinct subject/discipline emerged? Also, do you notice any correspondences between the emergence of capitalism as a way of organising society and the emergence of economics as a distinct subject of study? (Capitalism is a mode of economic organisation wherein the capitalists own all the means of production and the workers have nothing but their labour.)

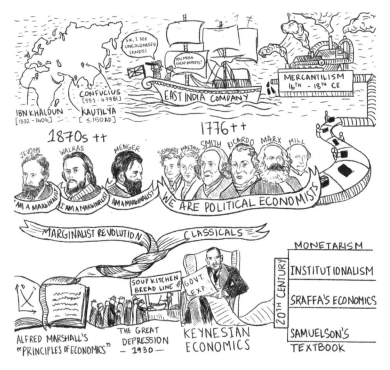

Most historians of economic thought (that is, economists who study the history of their discipline) identify William Petty as the first 'political economist', as they were then called. Petty was also a surgeon and a surveyor. In 1662, he published a book titled *A Treatise of Taxes and Contributions* which puts forward a way of accounting for aggregate output and a proposal of how much of that ought to be taxed. That is, as some of you might already be thinking, economics has a short history (a little over 350 years) vis-à-vis the natural sciences. However, is it true that no one before Petty wrote about economic issues? Of course not! Just a little before and around Petty's time, there were a group of merchant-economists, loosely called mercantilists, who wrote about money, wealth and foreign trade. Of this motley group, Thomas Mun is the most famous. They identified the stock of gold reserves in the nation, which flowed in when exports exceeded imports, as an indicator of economic health. Also, Petty and Mun are both from the European continent. Were there no economic discourses elsewhere?

Some notable non-European economic discourses are: *Muqaddimah* by Ibn Khaldun (1332–1406), a North African Arab thinker; *Arthashastra* by Kautilya written no later than 150 AD; and works by Confucius (551–479 BC) in China. However, you will not find anything resembling a theory in these works. Kautilya is not the name of a single person but perhaps a title and, therefore, some Kautilya scholars argue that it is a compilation by several individuals over time.

While many of the economic concepts (such as the division of labour) in Adam Smith's *Wealth of Nations* (1776) were already prevalent in the extant literature, Smith deserves credit for conceptualising political economy, the science of wealth, as a distinct field of inquiry (but note that Smith uses wealth interchangeably with income). Subsequent economists like David Ricardo, Thomas Tooke, Robert Malthus, J. C. L. Sismondi and J. S. Mill further developed the science of political economy. It is in Karl Marx's work that classical political economy (or classical economics, as it is also called today) receives a very mature treatment. In particular, Marx lays bare the exploitation of workers by capitalists in our epoch. Ricardo had already highlighted the conflict over income distribution between workers and capitalists when he demonstrated the inverse relationship between wages and the rate of profit (this idea will be discussed further in the chapter on inflation). The classical economists used concepts such as the social surplus, (customary) subsistence wage and social classes in their theories of value, distribution and economic growth.

Subsequently, in the 1870s, there was a revolution in economic thinking, pioneered by Léon Walras, William Stanley Jevons and Carl Menger, independently of each other. It was a revolution because it supplanted the concepts and ideas proposed by the classical economists. This is referred to as the marginalist revolution owing to their use of and reliance on marginal concepts and principles such as marginal utility, marginal product, marginal cost and the marginal productivity theory of income distribution. According to the marginal productivity theory of (income) distribution, in a competitive economy (that is, there is free mobility of labour and capital across industries), workers will be paid the marginal product of labour and capitalists the marginal product of capital. The marginal product of labour denotes the addition made to the total product when one additional labourer is employed (and similarly for capital). Note that this theory implies a kind of harmonious income distribution in a capitalist society, whereas the political economy of the classical economists and Marx explicitly highlights conflict, especially between workers and capitalists.

Alfred Marshall, in his *Principles of Economics* (1890), attempts to establish a continuity between classical political economy and marginalist economics, two distinct theoretical or conceptual frameworks. First, while the starting point of marginalist economics is an individual, that of classical political economy is a class/group. Second, in classical political economy or classical economics, the real wage is determined by social and political forces, and, therefore, it is irreversible to a large extent, whereas in marginalist economics, wages are determined by the marginal product of labour and is, therefore, reversible. Recall from introductory (marginalist) microeconomics that the equilibrium wage is determined at the intersection of labour demand and supply, and shifts in these curves can push down or pull up the equilibrium wage rate. For example, classical economists would argue that the daily wage of a bus driver in Kerala is INR 1,000 as a consequence of wage bargaining and government policies. Marginalist economists would argue that the wage reflects the productivity of the bus driver and, therefore, if the productivity falls, the wage can fall to INR 800. And this reduction in wages could be considered economically *fair*. However, classical economics would point to the irreversibilities associated with consumption (particularly of the workers) and consequently deem it unjust. Third, according to classical economists, competitive economies do not possess an intrinsic/natural mechanism of ensuring that *all* workers who are willing to work at the going wage rate will find employment. In other words, there is no tendency to the full employment of labour (except in the *very* long run where the supply of labour adapts to the demand for labour, a causation opposite to that found in marginalist economics).

Marginalist economics, on the contrary, argues that a competitive economy will tend towards a state with full employment of labour.

Amidst the Great Depression of the 1930s, John Maynard Keynes published his revolutionary book *The General Theory of Employment, Interest and Money* (1936) wherein he argued that the tendency to full employment found in the then-dominant economics (Marshall and Arthur Pigou mainly) was flawed. And that the only solution for reviving the depressed level of aggregate income and employment is through an expansion in government expenditure. This was because Keynes rightly noted that private investment is volatile (as it is driven by the profit motive) and depends on 'expectations' which further depend on a large set of variables unamenable to theorising. However, government expenditure was (and is) not constrained by such expectations. The Polish economist Michał Kalecki, independent of Keynes, also made essentially the same point in his 1933 article.

In the 20th century, economics witnessed five other significant developments: (*a*) monetarism led by Milton Friedman which challenged Keynes's notion of the 'monetary production economy' by arguing that 'monetary' forces have no impact on 'real' variables such as aggregate real output and employment; (*b*) institutionalism as developed by Thorstein Veblen, John Kenneth Galbraith and Gunnar Myrdal which underscored the importance of social and institutional norms in determining economic outcomes; (*c*) the application of game theory, particularly to understand strategic interactions between countries, firms, groups of people and individuals; (*d*) Piero Sraffa's devastating critique of marginalist economics, followed by the capital theory debates of the 1960s which challenged the marginal productivity theory of distribution due to the problems associated with the conception and measurement of capital in economic theory; and (*e*) the textbook culture of teaching (marginalist) economics pioneered by Paul Samuelson.

I shall end this section after making one important point. Textbooks often portray economics as a *settled* science but this is far from the truth. The preceding narrative, albeit a linear one, on the history of economic thought was to communicate the fact that despite the dominance of certain ideas during certain periods of time, all the different theories and concepts still continue to be employed, in varying degrees, to make sense of our economic surroundings. A majority of the textbooks, especially the introductory microeconomics and macroeconomics variety, communicate the idea of a largely settled domain of inquiry to the students. By now, you must have gathered that there exist multiple perspectives and schools of thought in economics. Two significant schools of thought absent in our discussion are ecological economics and feminist economics. I would like to end this section with a quote from the philosopher of science Paul Feyerabend's chapter 'Rationalism, Relativism and Scientific Method' in the 1999 book *Knowledge, Science and Relativism*.

> The questions "What shall we do? How shall we proceed? What rules shall we adopt? What standards are there to guide us?" however, are answered by saying: "You are grown up now, children, and so you have to find your own way." (p. 211)

While mainstream textbooks adopt the dominant (marginalist) economics framework to understand economic issues, this textbook follows a different path and highlights the pluralistic nature of economics through the presentation of contending economic theories. It is hoped that such an approach, to paraphrase Feyerabend, will help you better in your journey of learning.

1.3 Our definition of economics

As some of you might already know from the economics you learnt in school/college, there exist several definitions of economics. In any case, if you reflect on the discussion in the preceding section about the different perspectives in economics, the (co)existence of competing definitions might become apparent. And if it does not, it will, after you complete reading this section and then read Section 1.2 again.

Recall that Section 1.1 had outlined the different ambitions, aims and persuasions for studying economics. This section will make clear to you that it is the aim, in a way, that determines the definition. It is because of this reason that we discussed 'why economics' before 'what is economics'.

Adam Smith was particularly interested in finding out the "nature and causes of the wealth of nations". In textbooks, this is often referred to as the 'wealth definition'. Let us now read Smith's definition of economics, or political economy, as it was then called; this is found in the introduction to Book IV of *The Wealth of Nations*.

> Political economy, considered as a branch of the science of a statesman or legislator, proposes two distinct objects: first, to provide a plentiful revenue or subsistence for the people, or more properly to enable them to provide such

a revenue or subsistence for themselves; and secondly, to supply the state or commonwealth with a revenue sufficient for the public services. It proposes to enrich both the people and the sovereign. (p. 428)

Alongside acknowledging Smith's contributions, Ricardo states in the preface to his *Principles of Political Economy and Taxation* (1817) that "the principal problem [remaining] in Political Economy" is to "determine the laws which regulate" the distribution of the aggregate output between rents, profits and wages (p. 5). Broadly, the classical economists were interested in explaining how economies grow and how the surplus, that is, the aggregate output net of replacement requirements, is distributed between landowners, capitalists and workers. In other words, economics was defined and understood as a science of wealth/income by the classical economists.

With the advent of the marginal revolution in the 1870s, the emphasis shifted from viewing the fundamental unit of analysis as a 'class' to an 'individual'. This represents a shift in the method of doing economics—from methodological holism to methodological individualism. Those readers of this book who have some prior economics knowledge (from school or the first semester of your undergraduate degree in economics) will find the marginalist economist Jevons's definition similar to what you have already studied. For Jevons, "Pleasure and pain are undoubtedly the ultimate objects of the Calculus of Economics" (p. 37), as he writes in his 1871 book *The Theory of Political Economy*. In other words, economics is about maximisation of pleasure and minimisation of pain. Marginal revolution also marks the extensive use of the mathematical branch of calculus in economics, owing to the theoretical needs of maximising utility and profit functions of the individual consumer and the firm, respectively.

Alfred Marshall, in his attempt to see marginalist economics as a continuation of classical economics, defines economics as "a study of mankind in the ordinary business of life; it examines that part of individual and social action which is most closely connected with the attainment and with the use of the material requisites of wellbeing" (p. 1) in chapter 1 of his highly influential book *Principles of Economics*, first published in 1890. And finally in his 1932 book *An Essay on the Nature and Significance of Economic Science*, Lionel Robbins provides the definition of economics which I think is closest to most people's understanding of economics: "Economics is a science which studies human behavior as a relationship between ends and scarce means which have alternative uses" (p. 16). Today, the dominant understanding of economics is that it is a science of choice. The science of choice was taken to its peak, or literally maximised, in the way that marginalist principles were employed by Gary Becker in his 1976 book *The Economic Approach to Human Behavior.*

In this book, we adopt the 'science of wealth' definition of economics because of its emphasis on production, as opposed to allocation, which is central to the 'science of choice' definition. The rationale behind this choice will become clearer as you advance through the book and a compact statement can be found in Section 6.3. To use Keynes's phrase, our theoretical object of study is the 'monetary production economy' and the knowledge arising therein is applied to the monetary production economy of India. (Keynes [1933, p. 408] uses this phrase in a *Festschrift* for Arthur Spiethoff, an important figure within the German Historical School.) That is, in this book, we will study how the levels of aggregate output, money and employment are determined in a competitive economy. To put it differently, we will study the pure theory of aggregate levels and growth of macroeconomic variables. When this conceptual framework is applied to the Indian economy, it will be done in conjunction with the relevant contextual characteristics. Hence, for instance, we will learn about the financial architecture in India, including the informal moneylenders (Section 3.2), and the significance of agriculture in the Indian economy (Section 6.4).

For Smith and other classical economists, the questions of what determines the production, distribution and disposal of the surplus were central. The 'science of wealth' definition incorporates discussions around the disposal or utilisation of the surplus based on the wishes of the populace. This openness to politics and policies found in classical economics provides another reason for adopting the 'science of wealth' definition of economics because, whether in India or elsewhere, we wish to live in an ecologically clean and socially equal economy with full employment of labour, low inflation, decent wages and good working conditions. This warrants an important role for the government at all levels—centre, state and local. Therefore, this book discusses the effects of the utilisation of the surplus by the government (commonly known as public expenditure) in connection with employment and inflation via the creation of physical and social infrastructure such as roads, lakes, trains, houses, schools, hospitals and toilets. In our study of economics—the science of wealth—we also need to enquire as to how the existing distribution of wealth has come about. For instance, how did we end up in a situation where 1 per cent of the population owns 80 per cent of the land? Was it through the arbitrary use of power (and privilege) or through some kind of 'merit' (whatever that means)?

On the question of land ownership, Hansda Sowvendra Shekhar writes the following in his 2015 short story 'The Adivasi Will Not Dance':

> Which great nation displaces thousands of its people from their homes and livelihoods to produce electricity for cities and factories? And jobs? What jobs? An Adivasi farmer's job is to farm. Which other job should he be made to do? Become a servant in some billionaire's factory built on land that used to belong to that very Adivasi just a week earlier? (p. 185)

It is because of similar concerns that many of you might have decided to learn economics. This book is a modest attempt to help you articulate such concerns and find solutions to them. Of course, the translation of economic theory into action warrants good politics (and ethics) too. To sum up the preceding discussion, much like Adam Smith and other classical economists and Keynes, this book also views economics as a policy science. Viewing economics as a subject that is intended to aid policymaking is well aligned with the aim of ensuring a good life for all (Section 1.1). Consequently, as noted already, a brief understanding of Indian socio-economic institutions becomes necessary.

Finally, I must alert the readers that despite the name change from 'political economy' to 'econom*ics*' (with an intent to appear scientific like 'phys*ics*'), the knowledge of politics and history is indispensable to the study of economics. After all, the decisions to distribute wealth have been political, and the distribution of material resources is always and everywhere an expression of politics, that is, of power, ethics and our collective aspirations for the future. The evolution of the distribution/ownership of land is clearly political. The average hourly minimum wage (adjusted for exchange rate differences) in India is less than USD 1 and that in the United States (US) is more than USD 7 because of the historical differences in our respective approaches to politics and policy. The point I wish to make is this: any economics that claims to be ahistorical and apolitical needs to be treated with extreme caution. Our definition of economics as a science of wealth explicitly acknowledges the role of history and politics in making sense of economic phenomena.

1.4 A note on our approach

Now that you have an understanding of the brief history of economics— the different schools of thought with contending perspectives—and of the definition of economics adopted in this book, it is the right time to provide you with a glimpse into the nature of economic theorising (see Chapter 6, which undertakes a detailed discussion of economic theorising). By definition, theorising implies the careful selection of *relevant* aspects of economic processes and the (temporary) jettisoning of the rest. Let me use an analogy to scrutinise the 'relevant' aspects. When we go with an ailment to the doctor, we are very often asked to get a blood test done. The test conveys to the doctor whether the relevant components of the blood fall in the 'normal' range or outside it. How is this normal determined? Does the normal not vary according to the body constitution? Does the normal not vary according to the place where you live (and the associated environment)?

Similarly, will the Kochi (a cosmopolitan city in Kerala) economy be the same as the Madenapalle (an agricultural town in Andhra Pradesh) one? Or will the nature of Uttarkashi (a town in hilly Uttarakhand) and Gokarna (a coastal town in Karnataka) economies be the same? In this section, we shall discuss the method of theorising that will allow us to talk of the 'normal' in the context of a macroeconomy. Another way to think of the 'normal' is to pose the following question: what is the standard of reference when we discuss the macroeconomy? While some of you might find the foregoing analogy to medicine slightly fanciful, it is not quite. The founders of political economy, William Petty and François Quesnay, were medical doctors. In fact, present-day commonplace terms in economics such as 'circulation' and 'inflation' are imports from the medical lexicon.

Object of analysis

While the object of analysis for some of you might be the 'Indian' economy, some of you might want to understand how the Nagaland or Telangana economy functions. Some of you may also wish to know how the Kalaburgi (a town in Karnataka) or Rourkela (a city in Odisha) economy works. The chief purpose of this book is to provide you with an apparatus, a framework, to help you make sense of any economy. And as pointed out in the previous section, a proper understanding of any economy requires you to possess a reasonably good knowledge of that economy's history, culture and politics. In other words, shallow and shabby applications of economic theories on actual economies cannot, and should not, be done.

Our object of analysis, at the first level, is an economy with free mobility of labour and capital. Many a time, students lose interest at this very point because the economies we have seen and grown up in are not ones where labour and capital are freely mobile. To move your business (which comprises capital equipment and workers) from Tamil Nadu to Telangana, you need to incur additional costs (not just money but also time and, therefore, the business income foregone ought to be included). Labour is even more immobile. Owing to the Indian caste system, those from the marginalised castes and those outside the caste system are not free to do any work they wish to. Hence, B. R. Ambedkar (who made important contributions to monetary economics and centre–state financial relations) points out in his book *Annihilation of Caste* (1936) that the caste system is not just a division of labour but a division of labourers (p. 47). As a matter of fact, the caste system dictates that you should milk cows because you are born into a caste which is supposed to do that. Forget actual mobility, you cannot even *dream* about it. Imayam, a Tamil school teacher and author, poignantly describes this in the introduction to his 2015 book *Pethavan* (*The Begetter*), a novella about the story of a father who is being forced by the community to kill his own daughter because she dared to dream of marrying a Dalit man:

> My characters are not great thinkers or rebels. They belong to the land.
> They are labourers. Theirs is a constant struggle with land and nature.... My
> characters do not even dream. Even if they dream, it is about eating well.
> (pp. xv–xvi)

Additionally, in India, it is not easy for women to dream of mobility either, owing to the patriarchal expectations and norms. In the 2012 novel *The Taming of Women*, P. Sivakami captures evocatively the social constraints faced by Anandhayi, a Dalit labourer who harvests coriander: "Anandhayi could not help feeling bitter. She was fed up with this life. She was reduced to being just a mother to her children" (p. 80). Thus, the extent of labour immobility varies depending on the specificities of their caste, gender, community and region. At the initial level of theorising, we do not accommodate these realities. This is done by keeping in mind that when we apply (pure) theory to understand any economy, we ought to engage with its socio-cultural specificities. To put it differently, a good economic understanding warrants the coming together of both concept and context (for a concluding statement, see Section 9.2).

13

Another reason for viewing a competitive economy as the standard of reference or the normal is that it enables us to say something definitive or precise (of course, given the assumptions) about the economic phenomena under study. The assumption of free mobility of labour and capital implies that the rates of return across sectors will tend to be uniform. Since each sector has its own specific technological requirements and skills, the rate of profit across sectors is necessarily different. That is, if we keep aside sector-wise differences in skills and risks, the rate of profit across sectors will be uniform; you can visualise this profit as a 'pure' rate of return. The following passage in Ricardo's *Principles of Political Economy* provides a nice description of the free mobility of capital.

> Whilst every man is free to employ his capital where he pleases, he will naturally seek for it that employment which is most advantageous; he will naturally be dissatisfied with a profit of 10 per cent, if by removing his capital he can obtain a profit of 15 per cent. This restless desire on the part of all the employers of stock, to quit a less profitable for a more advantageous business, has a strong tendency to equalize the rate of profits of all.... (p. 88)

Once we study the properties and tendencies of a competitive economy, we are better equipped to study non-competitive economies, a central feature of the actual world (I prefer using 'actual' to 'real' as the theoretical world is also real). Since this book is pitched at an introductory level, there will be no substantial theoretical discussions on non-competitive economic arrangements such as monopoly or oligopoly. However, we will engage with these features when applying the analytical framework of the competitive economy to understand the Indian macroeconomy.

After noting two further reasons for choosing the competitive economy as our object of analysis, we move on to discuss the *level* of analysis adopted in most parts of this book. First, irrespective of the school of thought, almost all economists up until the 1930s 'imperfect competition revolution'—pioneered by Joan Robinson and Edward Chamberlin in their books *The Economics of Imperfect Competition* and *The Theory of Monopolistic Competition*, respectively— conducted their investigations within the framework of a competitive economy. However, there is still merit to treating the competitive economy as the object of analysis because it helps us see clearly the interdependencies and sometimes lays bare the consequences of an economic action. Second, since the emergence of capitalism as a way to organise societies, much has been written about its merits and demerits. A key merit is the belief that competitive economies (more specifically, competitive markets for commodities and labour) bring about the full employment of labour. Moreover, most economic 'reforms' seem to be undertaken with an implicit belief that a competitive economy is better for *all*. Since such an implicit belief exists and will continue to exist, it is important for all of us to thoroughly understand how a competitive economy operates in theory, the economist's laboratory, as it were. Thus, an understanding of a competitive economy is a prerequisite for understanding the past, present and future of India's economic vision.

In India, we have wage labour, alongside caste labour, and private property. Think of why about 1 per cent of Indians own the majority of the 3,287,263 square kilometres of Indian land.

Level of analysis

Now that we have identified our object of analysis, let us move on to discuss the various possible levels of analysis before we state the level adopted in this book. Extending our earlier examples, we could look at the Indian economy, Manipur economy, Kerala economy, Gujarat economy, Palanpur economy, Dharwad economy or Vidarbha economy. While the Indian economy is constituted by Manipur, Kerala, Gujarat, Palanpur, Dharwad and Vidarbha economies, it is not a simple aggregation of all of them. In any case, how does it make sense to aggregate the Kerala and Gujarat economies? What kinds of economic information can you meaningfully aggregate? That is, we could study the national, state, region or local economy. We could also study the formal and informal economies or the rural and urban economies. The level of analysis depends on the issue or topic we are interested in.

Besides these 'macro' ways of organising and studying an economy, we could adopt a 'micro' approach and examine how an individual makes economic decisions or how a firm decides how much to produce and what technology to adopt. In between the macro and micro approaches to studying an economy, there exists what I call the 'meso' approach. This approach examines different sectors in the economy. Questions relating to the economic health of agricultural, manufacturing and service sectors fall within this approach. Hence, if you are interested in knowing how the agricultural sector is faring vis-à-vis the manufacturing sector, you would adopt the meso approach. To put it differently, if you study the terms of trade between agriculture and manufacturing, it would come under the meso approach.

Much of the analysis in this book is macro in approach, although this is occasionally complemented by meso and micro approaches. And, of course, it is not as if the macro, meso and micro economies exist per se in the actual world. Just as the 'economy' is an abstraction, so are the 'macro', 'meso' and 'micro' economies. And it is important to remember that most of us are studying economics not only to understand our economic surroundings but also to better them *for all*. Amidst all the abstraction, equations, graphs and numbers, we must not forget what it is that we are studying—the economic condition of each and every person in the Indian macroeconomy. This powerful poem by Abhay Xaxa (2011), a former national convener of the National Campaign on Adivasi Rights, is a constant reminder of the aim of our study. It also teaches us to remain humble about our approaches to understand the world.

> I am not your data, nor am I your vote bank,
> I am not your project, or any exotic museum object,
> ...
> Nor am I the lab where your theories are tested,
> ...
> I am not your field, your crowd, your history,
> ...
> I refuse, reject, resist your labels,
> ...
> Because they deny me my existence, my vision, my space,
> ...
> So I draw my own picture, and invent my own grammar,
> ...
> For me, my people, my world, my Adivasi self!

Precision in analysis

The previous discussions have clarified the object and level of analysis undertaken in this book. It is now time to talk a little bit about the nature of precision in economics and the need for it. As noted earlier, we wish to make some definitive and precise statements about economic phenomena. Let us suppose that you want to understand the main determinants of employment. There are several options—you could examine wages and employment, aggregate output and employment, inflation and employment, government expenditure and employment, or private investment and employment. And when you, say, examine aggregate output and employment, you keep all the other variables constant. This is done in order to understand how two economic variables are related and, more importantly, to understand what causes what. In economic theorising, we use the Latin phrase *ceteris paribus*, which means 'everything else remaining the same'. You can think of the ceteris paribus assumption as a girdle on a horse or a scaffold on our thoughts, a way to theoretically discipline or control the concurrently occurring multitudinous economic activities. The use of the ceteris paribus assumption is most ably described by Marshall in his *Principles of Economics*.

> The element of time is a chief cause of those difficulties in economic investigations which make it necessary for man with his limited powers to go step by step; breaking up a complex question, studying one bit at a time, and at last combining his partial solutions into a more or less complete solution of the whole riddle. In breaking it up, he segregates those disturbing causes, whose wanderings happen to be inconvenient, for the time in a pound called *Caeteris Paribus*. The study of some group of tendencies is isolated by the assumption other things being equal: the existence of other tendencies is not denied, but their disturbing effect is neglected for a time. The more the issue is thus narrowed, the more exactly can it be handled: but also the less closely does it correspond to real life. Each exact and firm handling of a narrow issue, however, helps towards treating broader issues, in which that narrow issue is contained, more exactly than would otherwise have been possible. With each step more things can be let out of the pound; exact discussions can be made less abstract, realistic discussions can be made less inexact than was possible at an earlier stage. (p. 304)

The ceteris paribus assumption is not sufficient to make definitive statements. Remember that our object of analysis is a competitive economy that exhibits a tendency to a uniformity of rates of return across sectors. Furthermore, if an external event raises the rate of return/profit in one sector, there will be an inflow of labour and capital in that sector until the rates become uniform, as the excerpt from Ricardo showed. This tendency, in an economy, underpins our notion of equilibrium because any change in the economic system eventually leads to a state with a uniform rate of return across sectors. Equilibrium in economics, as in physics, is a state of rest. But suppose you do not assume ceteris paribus; in this case, do you think you can identify an equilibrium tendency?

Economists make assumptions such as ceteris paribus so as to say something precise or definitive about the phenomenon we are studying. There is another area wherein precision is fundamental—the definitions of concepts in theory. For instance, how do you define the rate of profit? Or how do you define capital? Or technology?

In statistical analysis, due to the unavailability of relevant data, approximate measures can be used. However, in theory, imprecision is unacceptable. For example, is capital defined as a heterogenous bundle of commodities or as a value magnitude in economic theory? To use an example, is capital a collection of seeds, ploughs and tractors or a sum of money? While we are discussing the importance of precision in economics, it is apt to quote Sraffa, the Italo-Cambridge economist who made significant and revolutionary contributions to economic theory. Sraffa made this observation at a 1958 conference, the proceedings of which were published in 1963 as *The Theory of Capital: Proceedings of a Conference Held by the International Economic Association.*

> The theoretical measures required absolute precision. Any imperfections in these theoretical measures were not merely upsetting, but knocked down the whole theoretical basis. (p. 305)

In sum, we need to be very precise in our definitions of variables in theory. You can find more on measurement issues in Sections 7.2 and 8.2, which deal with the nature of employment and inflation in India, respectively. Let me end this section with a question: can you come up with multiple (theoretical) definitions of capital?

1.5 Conclusion

This chapter began with several motivations for taking up the study of economic phenomena. Subsequently, we took a brief tour of the evolution of economic thought, which included works such as the *Arthashastra*. Then we laid down the possible ways of studying economics, and we stated that this book adopts the *science of wealth* definition. The final substantive section of this chapter provided you a peek into the approach to theory in *Macroeconomics: An Introduction*. In particular, we discussed the object and level of analysis adopted in this book—a macro approach to study the economic properties of a competitive system—and the need for precision in theory.

Suggestions for further reading

For obtaining a good overview of the history of economic thought, consult Heinz Kurz's 2016 book *Economic Thought: A Brief History* (New York: Columbia University Press). While Kurz's book will be of interest to a general reader as well, for a keen economics student, I recommend Alessandro Roncaglia's 2017 book *A Brief History of Economic Thought* (Cambridge: Cambridge University Press). If the discussion on theoretical measurements in this chapter intrigued you, you can follow up by reading pp. 168–70 of Kurz (2016) or pp. 237–9 of Roncaglia (2017). However, if you do not have access to either of these books, you can read my review of Kurz (2016) in *Economic and Political Weekly* (2016, vol. 54, no. 33, pp. 47–8) and of Roncaglia (2017) in *Artha Vijnana* (2019, vol. 61, no. 4, pp. 364–72). A more advanced treatment of the evolution of economics from classical to marginalist economics that offers the readers with several critical pointers is Krishna Bharadwaj's 1986 revised edition of her 1978 classic *Classical Political Economy and the Rise to Dominance of Supply and Demand Theories* (Hyderabad: Universities Press). If you wish to be introduced to the economy and economics found in *Arthashastra*, a good accessible starting point is Thomas R. Trautmann's *Arthashastra: The Science of Wealth* (New Delhi: Penguin Books) published in 2012. And if you are interested to learn more about the relationship between medicine and economics, look at Peter Groenewegen's collection of essays published as *Physicians and Political Economy: Six Studies of the Work of Doctor Economists* in 2001 (London: Routledge). An advanced discussion on the rationale behind studying a competitive economy with uniform rates of profit can be found in John Eatwell's entry on 'imperfectionism' in *The New Palgrave: A Dictionary of Economics*, a four-volume set, published in 1987 (London: Macmillan). However, given the state of our libraries, for an Indian student, it might be easier to access a restatement of it in chapter 8 of John Eatwell and Murray Milgate's 2011 book *The Fall and Rise of Keynesian Economics* (Oxford: Oxford University Press).

2

Conceptualising the Macroeconomy

2.1 Introduction

What do you think are the relevant aspects of a macroeconomy that can be utilised in the first stage of theorising? Should we try to classify households as rich and poor or treat them as if they are a single homogenous unit? Should we distinguish between local governments and the central government? Should we begin with a classification of firms as capital intensive and labour intensive? Or should we distinguish firms that cater primarily to the rest of the world from those that cater to the domestic economy? While all these are indeed important aspects of a macroeconomy, in this chapter you will soon see that these are not treated as relevant in the first stage of theorising.

This chapter takes you through a quick chronological tour of both the past and present of conceptualising the macroeconomy starting with William Petty in England and ending with V. K. R. V. Rao and P. C. Mahalanobis in India. After introducing you to three distinct ways of conceptualising the macroeconomy, the macroeconomy itself is conceptualised as being embedded within the larger domains of society and ecology. Subsequently, the economy is treated as a web of dual flows of commodities and money moving across the following key sectors: households, financial, non-financial and government. The chapter ends by making explicit the nature of abstraction employed in this book. And as with any theory which is necessarily abstract, its application to the actual world must be undertaken with great caution.

2.2 Conceptualising the macroeconomy: past and present

Understanding the macroeconomy requires that it be conceptualised. This calls for the identification of its boundaries and the relevant organs/parts. Since this book defines economics as the science of wealth and adopts a macro approach, certain forms of conceptualising the macroeconomy and the measurement of wealth and income are warranted. Henceforth, I shall use 'the macroeconomy' and 'the economy' interchangeably because the usual way of expressing the idea of a macroeconomy is through the term 'the economy'. The economy has been and can be conceptualised and understood by focusing on the following relevant aspects: (*a*) aggregate income and expenditure, (*b*) inter-sectoral relations and (*c*) the flow of funds across sectors. As with the macro, meso and micro distinctions, these are merely three ways of 'seeing' the same economy. In reality, a single economic transaction may be seen through all the three lenses.

In a way, conceptualising is similar to accounting. Both are done to meet certain predetermined objectives, and there are multiple ways of doing both. The importance of precision in theory has been highlighted and discussed in the previous chapter. Accounting, owing to its adherence to the system of double-entry bookkeeping, allows us to identify mistakes easily. Theory can improve from better accounting, and the outcomes from accounting can improve from the *demands* for certain kinds of accounts made by theory (for more on this, see Section 6.5).

Historically, social accounts were a by-product of the administrative machinery, be it the King, the Church, or the State; therefore, such data captured a society's number of births, deaths, area of land owned and amount of gold and silver in circulation. Much of our economic data today is collected as a part of the regular administrative processes. Think about *why* we are required to register the birth of a child at a government office. Moreover, the Indian government collects data on our incomes while levying the personal income tax. Recently, in 2014, the economist Thomas Piketty used income tax data from France, Germany, Great Britain, Japan and the United States to compute income inequality in these countries, which are well documented in his book *Capital in the Twenty-First Century*. This is a bit like Karl Marx using factory records to criticise the capitalists; in fact, Friedrich Engels, his friend and political economist, remarked: "I delight in the testimony of my opponents" (as cited in Wheen 2006, p. 51). In a democratic society, it is important that the government publishes timely socio-economic data (a quantitative testimony, so to speak) in a transparent manner because it helps us voters in critically evaluating the performance of the government.

How do you think wealth and incomes were defined and measured in the *Arthashastra* and *Muqaddimah*?

Aggregate income and expenditure

Our current method of computing the gross domestic product (GDP), which employs the aggregate income and expenditure conceptualisation, can be traced all the way back to Petty, the 'father of political economy' (as labelled by Marx in his first volume of *Capital* [p. 259], published in 1867). The Government of England tasked Petty to survey the lands it had acquired in Ireland so that it could impose taxes and use that income to meet its debt obligations. Subsequently, he used the Bills of Mortality, which contained information on births and deaths, to make a quantitative assessment of housing, furniture, cattle, shipping, and so on, to arrive at estimates for the population and the aggregate income of England. Petty's statement in his 1690 pamphlet on economic accounting, or 'political arithmetick', as he called it, deserves to be quoted in full.

> The Method I take to do this, is not yet very usual; for instead of using only comparative and superlative Words, and intellectual Arguments, I have taken the course (as a Specimen of the Political Arithmetick I have long aimed at) to express myself in Terms of Number, Weight, or Measure; to use only Arguments of Sense, and to consider only such Causes, as have visible Foundations in Nature; leaving those that depend upon the mutable Minds, Opinions, Appetites, and Passions of particular Men, to the Consideration of others.... (p. 224)

From the above extract, it is clear that quantitative expressions for socio-economic matters were not commonplace. So Petty is proposing a new method—that of political arithmetick—which is restricted to only those kinds of information that can be expressed in terms of 'number, weight, or measure', that is, quantitatively. Thus began systematic economic accounting.

Although an embryonic version of modern-day national accounts statistics (NAS) was present in Petty's work, it is only with the pioneering works by Colin Clark, Simon Kuznets and Richard Stone in the first half of the 20th century that 'modern' national income accounts was developed. And Stone received the 1984 Nobel Prize in Economics for his contributions to national income accounting; in particular, he is given credit for having employed the double-entry bookkeeping to national income accounting (NIA). He aptly titled his Nobel lecture 'The Accounts of Society' in which he recounted the history of national income accounts since Petty. (It may be noted that the Prize in Economic Sciences was only added later to the list of subjects by the Sveriges Riksbank, the Swedish bank which instituted the prize, and was not part of Alfred Nobel's list.)

In order to ensure that the NAS of different countries are comparable over time, the United Nations (UN) developed a framework called the System of National Accounts (SNA); the first SNA was published in 1953. The government agency responsible for compiling and publishing India's national income accounts is the Central Statistical Organisation (CSO), under the aegis of the Ministry of Statistics and Programme Implementation (MOSPI). Much like Clark and Stone who made significant contributions to England's NAS, Dadabhai Naoroji, V. K. R. V. Rao and P. C. Mahalanobis pioneered the estimation of India's national income (Section 7.3 contains a brief description of some of the contributions made by Rao and Mahalanobis to Indian economic thought).

The NAS records the value of the economy's aggregate income, output, consumption, saving and investment over the period of, usually, one financial year. There are two serious dissatisfactions with India's (and other countries') NAS, which, in turn, reflect poorly on our economic understanding *and* vision. First is the significant undervaluation of women's value addition to the economy. This undervaluation is owing to the fact that household activities like cooking, cleaning, fetching water and firewood, and taking care of children and the elderly, which are primarily undertaken by women, are not paid activities. Second, our NAS does not take into consideration the ecological costs arising from production. While there have been occasional attempts to remedy these in the form of conducting time-use surveys to estimate the extent of women's unpaid labour and in the developing of a 'green' national income accounts that includes data on the rate of utilisation of natural resources, they remain far from satisfactory. Although the economic historian Phyllis Deane through her village surveys and work on national income accounts in the 1940s and 1950s had highlighted the problem of excluding women's unpaid labour, it was not included in the SNA 1953 and it still remains excluded.

Do note that the demand for better systems of accounting with richer details is not merely an academic need but a political need. Let me explain. In countries like India, where the government invests in physical and social infrastructure like roads, railways, hospitals and schools, correct and timely information enables the better delivery of government services and better targeting of welfare beneficiaries (be it the quasi unemployment insurance scheme like the Mahatma Gandhi National Rural Employment Guarantee Scheme [MGNREGS], pensions or ration shops). But of course, it is not necessary that good accounts imply good policies.

Inter-sectoral relations

Treating the economy as an interconnected system is the second of the three ways of conceptualising the economy. François Quesnay, the author of *Tableau Économique* (1765), built upon Petty's economics, and examined the inter-sectoral relations between agriculture and manufacturing, a sector that was just emerging in Europe. At the core of the inter-sectoral conceptualisation is the idea of *interdependence*. That is, no sector in the economy, be it agriculture or manufacturing, can function on its own and, therefore, all economic sectors are structurally interdependent. Agriculture requires tools and machinery from manufacturing and manufacturing requires food (grains) from the agricultural sector. After Quesnay's explicit diagrammatic representation of inter-sectoral relations, this idea returns to economics in Karl Marx's volume I of *Capital*, first published in 1867. By the way, Marx was familiar with Quesnay's work. Marx, in volume II of *Capital* (1885), divides the economy into departments; department I produces consumption goods and department II produces investment goods. In Marx too, the interdependence between departments I and II, or investment and consumption goods, was explicitly put forth. More than half a century later, in 1936, Keynes uses the terms 'consumption' and 'investment' in his book *The General Theory of Employment, Interest and Money*, which, as noted in our Chapter 1, had a revolutionary impact on economic thinking at that time. Keynes well understood the interdependence present in an economy and wrote the following insightful sentence as a response to those (marginalist) economists who believed that investment is independent of consumption: "[C]apital is not a self-subsistent entity existing apart from consumption" (p. 106). This brief history of the economic thought of Quesnay and Marx highlights that the origins of macroeconomic thinking go way before Keynes's *General Theory*. Additionally, it also demonstrates an affinity of thought between Quesnay, Marx and Keynes.

Around the same time as Keynes, in the 1930s, the Russian-American economist Wassily Leontief was working on what is now called the 'input–output (I–O) framework', which can be used to examine the structure/nature of interrelationships between sectors or industries in the economy. As the name suggests, this framework shows the interdependence between inputs and outputs in an economic system. Even a quick glance at the I–O table (see Table 2.1) is instructive because it is a visual representation of the economy as an interconnected system—an obvious enough insight one might think—but often glaringly absent in several discussions in economics. In particular, it tells us that shocks to a key sector (like the primary sector) can affect other sectors both directly and indirectly.

The Government of India compiles the Input–Output Transactions Table (IOTT) quinquennially. In India, the first IOTT consistent with the NAS was published by CSO in 1978. Table 2.1 shows the inter-sectoral relationships for the year 2007–08.

Table 2.1 Inter-sectoral relations in the Indian macroeconomy

Sector \ Commodities	Primary	Secondary	Tertiary	Others	Intermediate Consumption	Final Consumption	TOTAL (% of total sectoral output)
Primary	17%	51%	5%	0.1%	73.6%	26.4%	100%
Secondary	2.4%	40%	7.2%	2%	51.8%	48.2%	100%
Tertiary	4.9%	31.6%	11.3%	3.4%	51.2%	48.8%	100%
Others	1.4%	16.3%	6.3%	6.8%	30.8%	69.2%	100%

Source: Input–Output Transactions Table 2007–08, Chapter 3, Table 3.3, Ministry of Statistics and Programme Implementation (MOSPI), Government of India.

25

The output of the primary sector includes crops, livestock and fish. Secondary sector output is mainly manufactured products such as sugar, textiles, footwear, newsprint, fertilisers, cement and machine tools. The tertiary sector's output comprises trade, hotel, transport and communication services. And 'others' includes financial and real estate services. The proportion of final consumption of output is close to 50 per cent of the total for both secondary and tertiary sectors. In agriculture, it is just slightly over 25 per cent. In the 'others' sector, the final consumption makes for close to 70 per cent of the total output. Examining the entries/cells diagonally from left to right gives us the proportion of intra-sectoral use of respective sectoral output. For instance, 40 per cent of total output of the secondary sector is used up as input in the secondary sector itself. The 'others' sector is the one that uses its own output the least (6.8 per cent). Around 56 per cent (51 per cent + 5 per cent + 0.1 per cent) of primary sector output is used by other sectors, whereas only around 11 per cent (2.4 per cent + 7.2 per cent + 2 per cent) of secondary sector output is used by other sectors. The secondary sector, as a whole, is highly dependent on itself for its input. Now, what do you think will happen to the economy if there is an ecological shock to the primary sector and its total output gets halved? Also, trace out the effects cascading through the economy.

Sectoral flow of funds

The third and last conceptualisation of the economy proposed in this section is that of the economy as a system of money flows. When you reach Section 2.4, you will notice that this conceptualisation of the economy as a system of money flows bears strong similarities with conceptualising the economy as a web of (commodity) flows. The idea that commodities and money circulate in the economy is found in the *Essay on the Nature of Trade in General* (1755) by Richard Cantillon, an important predecessor to Quesnay. According to Cantillon,

> Whatever be the case, it will always be found, when an inhabitant's means of subsistence are examined and traced back to their source, that they originate from the owner's own land.... (p. 22)

Cantillon divides the economy into those who owned land and those who did not. The latter were dependent on the former for subsistence, and the source of their subsistence was the agricultural surplus. It is perhaps no coincidence that the physician-economists Petty and Quesnay conceptualise the economy as a circular flow, with the agricultural surplus as the fountainhead. Interestingly, the idea that blood circulates in the body, with the heart as the centre, underpins their idea of commodities and money circulating in the *body politik*.

In the 20th century, the credit for conceptualising the economy as a system of money flows goes to Morris Copeland. In the aftermath of the Keynesian revolution, Copeland published the seminal article 'Social Accounting for Moneyflows' in *The Accounting Review* in 1949. If I–O is a representation of commodity flows in the economy, Copeland's flow of funds (FoF) represents money flows in the economy. As he writes,

> Because we live in a money economy where moneyflows play an important role in organising economic activity, a better understanding of moneyflows should help us toward a better understanding of the problem of maintaining full employment. (p. 245)

Recall Keynes's object of analysis: the 'monetary production economy'. Moreover, Keynes had already identified the cause of unemployment as the deficiency of aggregate demand—the sum of aggregate expenditures on consumption and investment by the government and the private sector—and the solution was to increase government expenditure (for a detailed discussion, see Section 4.2). Copeland's improved accounting framework for the money flows helps us better understand the macroeconomy and, therefore, enables us to formulate superior policies for the unemployment problem (a detailed discussion of money flows is provided in Chapter 3).

The Reserve Bank of India has been publishing the FoF reports for the Indian economy since 1964. While the IOTT divides the economy into primary, secondary and tertiary sectors, the FoF divides the economy into the household, private corporate business, government, banking and foreign sectors. The NAS provides the value of the total output of primary, secondary and tertiary sectors, and the value of aggregate consumption, investment, government expenditure and net exports. The money flows in India take place through financial instruments such as currency, bank deposits, 'investments' (for example, mutual funds), small savings and life funds (for example, insurance policies by the Life Insurance Corporation) (see Table 3.1 in Chapter 3).

In the introductory paragraph of this section, it was pointed out that the conceptualisations of the macroeconomy follow from our analytical standpoint: the macro approach. To understand the factors that determine aggregate economic magnitudes such as aggregate output and employment, the three lenses of conceptualising the economy are complementary. For instance, your purchase of this book will be included in the aggregate consumption and aggregate output in NAS, will also figure in the 'final consumption' of the tertiary sector in IOTT, and will be captured as a money flow (via currency) from households to the private corporate business sector in the FoF. Furthermore, IOTT and FoF help with obtaining a meso understanding of the economy.

2.3 The macroeconomy as an embedded system

In the previous section, we outlined three ways of conceptualising the macro economy. And the previous chapter underscored the limits of economics and its need to be in the good company of anthropology, history and politics (Section 1.3). The aim of this section is to situate our study of the economy in the larger context, notably, as embedded in a society. We had already alluded to this in our discussion of labour immobilities due to caste in Section 1.4. For instance, in Imayam's *Pethavan* (*The Begetter*), the protagonist's daughter's decision to start a family and set up a household is opposed by the villagers and the caste *panchayats* because the person she wishes to be with is a Dalit. Sometimes, owing to community norms, the outflow of services may not receive an equivalent money flow or vice versa. Due to caste differences, Dalits and members of marginalised caste groups may not be able to obtain the desired commodities and services despite advancing adequate money. While this might be labelled an unequal exchange by economists, such exchanges in reality are not fully 'capitalistic' and are part economic and part social. Moreover, this reinforces the fact that economic outcomes are strongly mediated by social or community norms.

Saadat Hasan Manto brings out this social character of the economy in his short story 'Ram Khilavan', which revolves around the interactions between the narrator and Ram Khilavan, his *dhobi* (washerman). Below, I reproduce the passage where the narrator's wife (much like many present-day marginalist economists) finds the dhobi not keeping 'accounts' as irrational, even untrustworthy, and Khilavan's response.

> One month, a hundred and fifty pieces of clothing went to the wash. To test the dhobi, my wife said, "Dhobi, this month sixty items of clothing were washed."

He said, "All right Begum saab, you wouldn't lie." When my wife paid him for sixty clothes, he touched the money to his forehead and headed out. My wife stopped him. "Dhobi, wait, there weren't sixty pieces of clothing, there were a hundred and fifty. Here's the rest of your money. I was just joking."

The dhobi only said, "Begum saab, you wouldn't lie." He touched the rest of the money to his forehead, said "salaam", and walked out. (p. 94)

The above excerpt underscores the idea of trust in society which influences economic transactions. Both *Pethavan* and 'Ram Khilavan' point to the social nature of economic decisions and transactions. Thus, while we do not undertake a systematic study of societal norms of communities in this introductory book, such information is essential for anyone who wishes to understand their economic surroundings. To obtain such information, read stories such as the ones mentioned above, written in any of the local languages or in English.

The key point of the extracts from Shekhar and Xaxa in the previous chapter was to highlight the problems with (economic) policymakers who assume that they know what is best for everyone (Sections 1.3 and 1.4). Therefore, before undertaking any economic intervention—via the market, government or the community—it is extremely important that the economic policy be evaluated after taking into account all the costs as well as benefits, both economic and social, not just for 5 years or so, but over, say, 20 years or so, incurred not only by the various castes and classes who are stakeholders, but also by the environment.

In his 2017 book *Islands in Flux: The Andaman and Nicobar Story*, Pankaj Sekhsaria, the environmental journalist, articulates the scary ill-effects of the *myopic* economic expansion in the Andaman and Nicobar Islands; an extract from the book follows.

The forests were 'wastelands' that needed to be tamed, settled and developed. It did not matter that these forests were the home of myriad plants and animals that had evolved over aeons. It did not matter that ancient tribal people were living here for centuries, neither that they were physically and spiritually sustained by these forests…. The Nehruvian dream of massive industrialization was calling and the rich evergreen forests of the islands promised abundant timber to feed it. The tribals too had to be civilized, brought into the Indian mainstream. There was no question of inquiring, let alone bring to understand and factor in, what it was that the Onge, the Andamanese or the Jarawa themselves wanted. (pp. 4–5)

To reiterate, as economists, on what basis do we decide the sort of economic 'development' the Andamanese should want? Furthermore, there are strong binding ecological constraints on the capacity of an economy to grow. As Amitav Ghosh tellingly puts it in his 2016 book *The Great Derangement*: "Every family in the world cannot have two cars, a washing machine and a refrigerator—not because of technical or economic limitations but because humanity would asphyxiate in the process" (p. 124).

From the preceding discussion, it is clear that our study of the economy ought to be embedded in wider societal norms and within an ecological system. For purposes of theorising, we do treat the macroeconomy as a distinct and separable entity, but always keep in mind that this is an abstraction. This section can be concluded once we visually summarise the ecological and social embeddedness of the economy (see Figure 2.1).

Figure 2.1   The macroeconomy as an embedded system

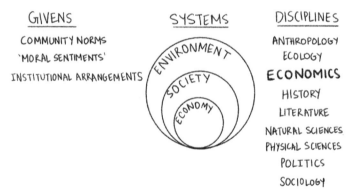

The social and ecological embeddedness of the economy ought to put a break on the tendency to universalise economic predictions and interventions made based on those predictions. Not all actions are based on *incentives*, especially monetary ones. To put it differently, incentives vary across communities owing to the different cultural norms, 'moral sentiments' (Smith's term) and institutional arrangements (classified under 'givens' in Figure 2.1). As Smith notes in *The Theory of Moral Sentiments* (1759), society flourishes when its members possess good moral sentiments: "All the members of human society stand in need of each other's assistance, and are likewise exposed to mutual injuries. Where the necessary assistance is reciprocally afforded from love, from gratitude, from friendship, and esteem, the society flourishes and is happy" (p. 85). Other moral sentiments Smith considers favourable to society are benevolence, care, sympathy and virtue.

Finally, the actual world—consisting of the ecology of which (human) society is a part, and of which the economy is a part—can be conceptualised, theorised, studied and documented by several 'disciplines', of which economics is just one. While studying macroeconomics, the community norms, 'moral sentiments' and institutional arrangements are taken as given, that is, no attempt is made to explain these 'givens' by taking recourse to macroeconomic theory. But recall from Section 1.2 that the sub-discipline of institutional economics does substantively incorporate these 'givens' in their explanations.

Economics becomes richer the more it converses with ecology, anthropology, literature and other disciplines. However, a warning must now be issued: in the attempt to move theorising closer to reality, there is sometimes a tendency to eschew disciplinary boundaries and a simultaneous embracing of interdisciplinarity. Without a conceptual core, such an approach might not be very fruitful and, in fact, might even turn counterproductive. For further understanding, look up an interdisciplinary study that includes economics and identify its fundamental unit of analysis, its core assumptions, its givens and its central explanatory mechanisms. Are the majority of them taken from economics or from the other discipline? Or are you able to identify elements that transcend the knowledge of all the relevant individual disciplines?

2.4 The macroeconomy as a web of flows

We discussed the three ways of conceptualising the economy in Section 2.1. They are NIA, I–O method, and FoF analysis. The latter two together, particularly, aid our understanding of contemporary economies, which are monetary production economies. And in Section 2.3, we pointed out the scope of economics in relation to the divergent views between economists' wishes for the community and the wishes of that community and the boundaries presented by the social and ecological systems. In this section, we visualise the macroeconomy as a web of commodity and money flows.

An early representation of this, as noted earlier, is found in Quesnay's *Tableau Économique*—a zig-zag of value-sums travelling across the proprietary, agricultural and manufacturing classes. For you to appreciate Quesnay's work better and to get a flavour of his conceptualisation, I present an abstract from his *Tableau Économique*.

The 300 livres of revenue which have passed into the hands of the [manufacturing] class are spent by the artisan, as to one-half, in the purchase of products for his subsistence, for raw materials for his work, and for foreign trade, from the [agricultural] class; and the other half is distributed among the [manufacturing] class itself for its maintenance and for the redistribution of its *advances*. This circulation and mutual distribution are combined in the same way by means of sub-divisions down to the last penny of the sums of money which mutually pass from the hands of one class into those of the other. (pp. ii–iii)

From Quesnay's conceptualisation, it is clear that to study the macro economy (and meso economy), we need to examine sectoral flows. The sectors could be agriculture, manufacturing or services as in IOTT or households, private corporate business or government as in FoF.

Marx, writing 100 years after Quesnay, also possessed a depiction of commodity and money flows: M–C–C'–M'. In a capitalist society, the capitalists, who are the owners of the means of production, exchange money (M) for commodities (C). Workers are employed to increase the value of C to C'; the difference between C' and C is owing to the value added by the workers. If all of C' is sold (or exchanged for money) in the market, the capitalists obtain M', a sum of money greater than M. We can identify three phases in the above "general formula for capital", as Marx calls it. The M–C is the investment phase, C–C' the production phase where value gets added, and C'–M' the consumption (or selling or exchange) phase. If a disruption occurs in the selling phase, the capitalists need not obtain their advances or investment back, and the circular flow in the economy is disrupted. In other words, if there are inadequate sales, insufficient profits are made and the aggregate output contracts (this is conceptually equivalent to a contraction of the circular flow).

Roughly another century later, Piero Sraffa, in his 1960 book *Production of Commodities by Means of Commodities*, credits Quesnay's *Tableau Économique* for containing "the original picture of the system of production and consumption as a circular process" (p. 93). Contemporary research in economics, which follows the classical tradition of Smith, Ricardo and others, is indebted to Sraffa's book, which revived the tradition of classical political economy. In Quesnay, Marx and Sraffa, we also find meso approaches to studying the economy.

It is now time to list the key sectors in our conceptualisation of the Indian macroeconomy. In order to study the commodity and money flows, we divide the economy—the Indian economy, to use a concrete example—into five sectors: households, non-financial businesses, financial businesses, government and foreign (or the rest of the world [RoW]). Before I present the sectoral commodity and money flows conceptualisation visually, let me remind you that while most of these transactions/flows occur within the Indian geographical space, this space is hardly homogeneous; it has 15 agro-climatic zones, which are further subdivided into regions based on soil types, climate, cropping patterns and topography. Yet we talk of this juggernaut of the Indian economy every day as if it were a concrete homogeneous entity. For visual ease, we omit the RoW sector in our diagrammatic representation (Figure 2.2).

Figure 2.2 Commodity and money flows in the macroeconomy

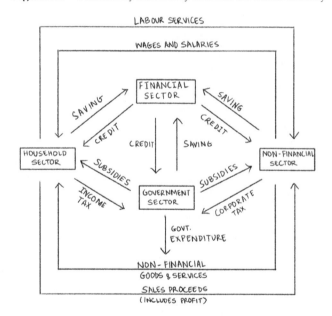

Some of you might recognise that our diagrammatic representation is similar in spirit to that of the idea of circular flow in Quesnay and Marx. Although the diagram is self-explanatory for the most part, some commentary is warranted.

The household sector offers its labour, a commodity in capitalist societies, in exchange for wages and salaries to the government, non-financial and financial sectors. But Figure 2.2 only depicts the flows between the household sector and the non-financial sector, to avoid clutter. On the basis of their estimates regarding current and future aggregate demand, the non-financial firms decide the size of investment (and production). Investment, in the context of macroeconomics, always refers to the additions to the capital stock and does not include the money that is 'invested' in financial instruments such as bank deposits or mutual funds. This is so because such economic transactions do not add to the capital stock (this issue receives further treatment in Section 5.3, when discussing the growth of financial services). In more precise terms, investment refers to the additions made to the physical means of production or capital, such as an increase in the tonnes of steel, food storage godowns, coverage of highways, furnaces, wind turbines, tractors, cables, computers, and so on. A portion of the funds for investment comes from internal sources (mainly, retained earnings—a portion of profits which are 'retained' for reinvestment), and a portion from external sources. (However, Figure 2.2 does not make reference to the internal sources of funds.) These external sources could be loans from the financial sector such as banks, or raising funds from the debt market by issuing bonds, or by issuing equity through initial public offerings. Both non-financial and financial firms (banks included) are interested in maximising profits through various means—strategic pricing, research and development and/or sales maximisation. When goods and services are sold as per their plans, the expected profits of the firms in the non-financial and financial sectors are said to be realised. The government sector does not try to maximise profit like the firms in the non-financial and financial sectors do; it provides public services such as education, health, roads, parks and street lights, which are partly defrayed by the revenue it collects from households (directly via income tax and indirectly via the Goods and Services Tax [GST]) and firms (directly via corporate tax). The firms in the financial sector make profits by intermediating between those who have money to spare (savings) and those who need money for investment or consumption needs (borrowing). Intermediation takes place through the issue of time deposits, equity shares, mutual funds and credit cards. Can banks offer loans without having the equivalent amount of deposits?

Before we conclude this section, let us spend a moment, or, more accurately, a paragraph, discussing the constituents of households, firms and the government, which we have thus far assumed to be homogeneous. The household sector includes all the self-employed individuals (for example, the *kirana* store, or the local grocery, the chicken shop, the barber shop and the farm household) and, therefore, a large proportion of agricultural workers. It also includes regular salaried workers. It may be further classified into rich and poor households. The I–O transactions, as already noted in Section 2.2, also happen *within* the primary, secondary and tertiary sectors. For example, take the case of the steel industry, which is a constituent of the secondary sector. It requires the transportation industry (also a constituent of the secondary sector) to help transport its product and the steel industry indirectly provides the transportation industry with the steel that goes into manufacturing vehicles. Finally, the government sector in India operates at three levels—local, state and central—with interdependencies and superfluities, although we treat them as if they are all similar. Thus, on closer inspection, it is clear that the homogeneous categories of the household, firm and government conceal a wide heterogeneity. This heterogeneity should particularly be borne in mind when economic theories are applied to understand our immediate economic surroundings and in the policymaking process.

2.5 A further note on our approach

Although we discussed the approach adopted in this book in Section 1.4, it was at a general level. From that discussion, we had concluded that precision in theory is important, that our level of analysis is macro and not meso or micro, and that our object of analysis is the competitive economy. Now that we have completed discussing the different conceptualisations of the macroeconomy, it is time to provide some additional commentary on the approach followed in this book. Specifically, we discuss the role of prices and the role of caste, ecology, gender and land in our 'general equilibrium' approach, and the conceptual jumps required to make sense of an actual macroeconomy, such as India's.

Throughout this book, we will be making one fundamental assumption: the economy is not close to a full-employment position. This implies that there exists, as is the case with the Indian economy, structural unemployment, underemployment and spare production (or productive) capacity. As a consequence, when aggregate demand increases, the aggregate price level (P) need not rise because more workers are available for employment at the going wage rate and spare productive capacity is available too. However, if the price of essential commodities such as wheat rises due to a bad monsoon or that of oil rises due to increased international oil demand, P will increase. Alternatively, consider the agricultural supply chain, which is made up of a sequence of activities starting from obtaining credit, sowing seeds, harvesting the crop, storing the produce, selling it to local traders, local traders selling it to retail traders, and the produce finally reaching the consumers. Even if other things remain the same, the general price level can rise due to disruptions in the agricultural supply chain. Before we conclude our discussion of prices, it should be understood that the 'general price level' is an abstract theoretical entity, just like the macroeconomy. In fact, Keynes finds P to be vague and highlights, like Sraffa, the importance of precision in theory in the chapter 'The Choice of Units' in *The General Theory*: "[T]he well-known, but unavoidable, element of vagueness which admittedly attends the concept of the general price-level makes this term very unsatisfactory for the purposes of a causal analysis, which ought to be exact" (p. 39). Price indices such as the consumer price index (CPI) and the wholesale price index (WPI) are statistical *approximations* of this theoretical entity (for a detailed discussion of P, CPI and WPI, see Section 8.2). (Perhaps some of you might have noticed this, but in case not: I italicise certain words for emphasis.)

In economics, there are two distinct approaches to study a particular economic phenomenon. For example, to understand the nature of the connection between the equilibrium price of 1 kilogram of *ragi* (a member of the millet family) and the quantity, we assume ceteris paribus. That is, we assume that there are no changes occurring simultaneously or sequentially in other markets. This is the partial equilibrium approach, extended and developed to maturity by Alfred Marshall. On the other hand, the general equilibrium approach also examines related markets, such as those for *jowar*, wheat, rice, the agricultural labour market, the agricultural tools market and so on. The general equilibrium approach studies the properties of the economic system when *all* markets are in equilibrium. Very crudely, one could respectively label them the 'narrow' and the 'holistic' approaches. A holistic approach is taken in this book wherein the importance of studying other relevant (not all) markets/sectors is incorporated, but the focus on all-around equilibrium is discarded. Therefore, our analyses of interest rates, employment and economic growth occasionally examine their effects on our natural environment.

Since our object of analysis is the competitive monetary production economy, the conclusions emanating from studying it should be 'applied' to the Indian economy with great caution. First, the insights and conclusions from theory only provide a *framework* to understand the Indian economy or Kerala economy or Madenepalle economy. A good policy requires both quantitative and qualitative information regarding the relevant population. For example, the norms of organising people for agricultural labour might be different in Madenepalle and Uttarkashi. Or, in one place, agricultural production might be mainly undertaken by large farmers and not small farmers. The first example provides information that is of a qualitative nature and cannot be reduced to quantitative information, while the second one provides information that is capable of being reduced to a quantitative nature. Second, to add to the discussion in Section 1.4, there are often gaps between theoretical and statistical measurements. Although we would prefer statistical measurements to correspond to theoretical measurements, rarely does it happen in practice. Almost always, statistical measurements are only approximate. Moreover, the quality of statistical data is also influenced by the methods of collecting/recording the data. Sometimes, the influence is not significant, but this is to be tested and is not to be assumed. For example, choosing the LIFO (last in, first out) or FIFO (first in, first out) method for measuring inventories yields different results. Or, if the data is collected through a lengthy questionnaire, how do we assess the reliability of such data? Third and finally, we need to understand the structure (the meso level) of the economy to be able to make good economic policies.

2.6 Conclusion

After outlining a brief account of the different ways to conceptualise the macroeconomy—NAS, IOTT and FoF—we visualised it as an entity, though abstract, that is intricately embedded in society and the natural environment. Subsequently, the interconnectedness of the economy was brought out after dividing it into four sectors—households, financial firms, non-financial firms and government—and marking the inter-sectoral commodity and money flows. Some of you might have wondered about the rationale behind my sandwiching the discussion on the embeddedness of the economy between the conceptualisations of the macroeconomy through three lenses and as a web of flows; it could have been easily positioned at the first or the last. But I felt that the back-and-forth in thinking and reflecting that the current arrangement generates is better for learning than the simpler alternative of a linear narrative. The final section further clarified the approach adopted in this book; most importantly, it was pointed out that a simple translation of theory into policy is not possible and must be resisted.

Suggestions for further reading

To obtain a good grasp of the nature and sources of India's national economic accounts—the estimation of the gross domestic product, private investment, workers' compensation, private saving, and so on—it is imperative to read the Government of India's 2012 document *National Accounts Statistics: Sources and Methods,* which is published by the Central Statistical Organisation (CSO) under the aegis of the Ministry of Statistics and Programme Implementation (MOSPI); it can be downloaded for free from the MOSPI website. An excellent reference book that describes both past and present official data collection procedures followed in India is M. R. Saluja's *Measuring India: The Nation's Statistical System* (New Delhi: Oxford University Press) published in 2017.

Money and Interest Rates

3.1 Introduction

This is the first of the three chapters in this book dealing with macroeconomic theory (the others being Chapters 4 and 5). But, given that one of the approaches adopted in this book is to combine both concept (or theory) and context, this chapter begins with an overview of India's financial architecture. Of the three ways of conceptualising the macroeconomy outlined in the previous chapter, the one pioneered by Copeland focuses on the flow of funds across sectors. Copeland's conceptualisation is complemented by the formulation in Section 2.4, where both the commodity and money flows in the macroeconomy are outlined (especially, see Figure 2.2). This chapter is an exposition of the money flows in a monetary production economy, carried out with specific reference to the Indian macroeconomy.

Revisit Figure 2.2 in the previous chapter and try to find answers to the following questions: What is the precise *form* in which money flows happen between the different sectors in the economy? What kinds of financial products or instruments connect you (as a member of a household) with non-financial firms? Similarly, what kind of financial instruments connect the non-financial firms with the financial firms? In what forms do the households receive wages and salaries in return for their labour? Is it in the form of cash (denominated in Indian rupee), bank deposit, company shares, foreign exchange or something else?

After answering the above-mentioned questions in Section 3.2, we move on to discuss 'what is money' and interest rates. Subsequently, the role of the central bank is explained with the spotlight on the Reserve Bank of India (RBI), India's central bank. The chapter ends with a section focusing on the money flows between India and the rest of the world.

3.2 The financial architecture of India

Many people rightly associate economics with the study of money and related variables like interest rates and inflation. As previously noted, the approach in this book is to understand the economic workings of a monetary production economy that is characterised by the free mobility of labour and capital. In a monetary production economy, it is imperative that the study of economics examines both money as well as commodity flows. Before we address the question of 'what is money' in Section 3.3, let us understand the institutions—both government and private—that enable the circulation of money within the Indian economy by linking the suppliers and users of funds. We have already sketched the web of money flows in Section 2.4, with the private financial firms undertaking the crucial role of financial intermediation in the economy. Do most Indians invest in mutual funds? Or do most of us park our meagre funds in post office savings accounts? And do we mostly borrow money from commercial banks?

Inter-sectoral financial flows

When a new firm wants to start production, the means of production (plant, machinery and labour) have to be purchased or hired. This presupposes access to financial resources. These firms have several options: use a portion of family funds, utilise a part of retained earnings, raise equity via an initial public offering (IPO), take a loan from a bank or issue debt securities. All these varied options, in different degrees, enable investment—the addition to an economy's productive capacity—to be undertaken. However, if the firm uses family funds or retained earnings, financial intermediation is not required (a mention of such internal sources was noted in Section 2.4). And if the firm resorts to one of the other options, financial institutions play the role of an intermediary between investors and the requisite funds. This, therefore, is a financial/fund flow between the financial and non-financial sectors.

It is not necessary that borrowing is undertaken only for purposes of investment. Households borrow in order to meet their consumption needs too—to buy a fridge, a television, a house, for their child's education or for a wedding function. They can borrow from moneylenders, pawnbrokers, chit funds or from banks. In this case, the flow of funds is between consumers and savers. The current consumption of households can exceed their current incomes in two distinct ways. They can either withdraw money from their past savings or take a loan. The latter has to be repaid from their future incomes. Economists term consumption loans as a dissaving (negative saving) because consumption can exceed current incomes *only* by decreasing past or future savings. Thus, is it possible to characterise a consumption loan as a financial instrument that smoothens your current consumption and future savings?

The government also borrows to meet its investment and consumption expenditures. It borrows primarily by issuing bonds to its citizens or to the rest of the world (RoW). In macroeconomic accounting, the former is termed internal debt and the latter external debt (a short discussion on public debt can be found in Section 7.3). A bond promises to pay the buyer a fixed interest rate and the entire face value at its maturity. Government bonds are also called sovereign bonds. Public sector undertakings (PSUs), very much like private firms, can borrow by issuing bonds. Examples of PSUs are National Thermal Power Corporation (NTPC), Oil and Natural Gas Corporation (ONGC), Steel Authority of India Limited (SAIL) and Bharat Heavy Electricals Limited (BHEL). If the Government of India borrows from citizens, it is a flow of funds between the government and household sectors.

What about the parking of surplus funds (a portion of their current income) by the various sectors? The household, non-financial and financial sectors may park their surplus funds in banks, equity markets (via IPOs), debt markets (via government bonds), insurance markets or with chit funds. Some of these financial instruments also work as collateral when funds are required in the future. For instance, an insurance policy with the Life Insurance Corporation (LIC) also can serve as a collateral for a loan as the following discussion between a husband and a wife from Volga's short story 'The Experiment' (1997) shows.

> "You only want money, don't you?—I'll get a loan on my LIC Policy. Will get PF Loan. I'll take a loan. I'll bring it somehow, okay? But I won't ask my father."

> "Take loans, go on paying interest and ruin the home. You can't touch the LIC and the PF. If you have an accident in the future, what will happen to me?" (p. 71)

PF refers to Provident Fund, a compulsory pension fund managed by the Government of India, to which every employee contributes a portion of their income. The above excerpt also indicates that the household is not a homogenous unit; as Bina Agarwal (2001), adopting a gender perspective, writes, the household is not "an undifferentiated unit in which members pool incomes and resources, and share common preferences and interests..." (p. 159).

Alternatively, the household, non-financial and financial sectors may park their surplus in mutual funds, whose managers maintain a portfolio of select equity and/or debt instruments. The managers of mutual funds maintain a portfolio so as to minimise the risk arising from the holding of an individual share or stock. Essentially, a mutual fund diversifies the risk and therefore tends to minimise it on the whole.

Financial institutions

India's financial architecture can be broadly classified into regulators, banks, money and capital markets, financial institutions and informal financial enterprises (see Figure 3.1). The key institutions within the secondary market for equities are the Bombay Stock Exchange (BSE) and National Stock Exchange (NSE). While most of the above architectural blocks are self-explanatory, non-banking financial institutions and informal financial enterprises warrant additional commentary. Non-banking finance corporations (NBFCs) include equipment leasing companies, housing finance companies, insurance companies, *nidhi*s or mutual benefit financial companies (MBFCs), and chit funds or miscellaneous non-banking companies (MNBCs). Bajaj Finance Limited, which provides funds/finance to consumers, is an example

Figure 3.1 The financial architecture of India

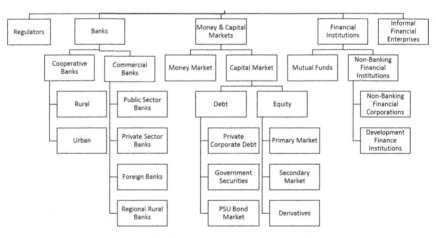

Note: In order to not clutter the figure, the markets within the money market—Repo Market, Call Money Market, and Treasury Bill Market—have not been drawn.

42

of an NBFC. Development finance institutions (DFIs) comprise the National Bank for Agriculture and Rural Development (NABARD), Industrial Development Finance Company (IDFC) and State Financial Corporations (SFCs). DFIs were established with the aim of providing funds to fulfill the unmet credit requirements of various sectors and sub-sectors of the economy. They were expected to accelerate private non-financial sector investment in capital goods; in other words, they provide funds to meet long-term financing needs of the private non-financial sector (especially manufacturing). The Industrial Development Bank of India (IDBI), set up in 1964 as a DFI, was transformed into a private bank in 2019; as an exercise, look up the history of IDBI and identify its role in India's development trajectory. Also, look up the role of co-operative banks on the RBI website. Where would you place them in Figure 3.1?

Informal finance

Before the First Five-Year Plan of India in 1951, it was the moneylenders who met almost all of the financial needs of rural Indians. The five-year plans, as their name suggests, emphasise the need for planned economic development, and the first one was almost entirely devoted to the primary sector (a brief discussion of the First and Second Five-Year plans is found in Section 7.3 in the context of discussing employment policy).

In order to bring most households and firms under the orbit of 'formal' (as opposed to 'informal' sources of finance like moneylenders and chit funds), the Indian government set up the Regional Rural Banks in 1975, created NABARD in 1982, and floated the Pradhan Mantri Jan Dhan Yojana in 2014. Despite these early initiatives, the 2003 All India Debt and Investment Survey (AIDIS) report by the National Sample Survey Organisation (NSSO) stated that, in 2002, out of the total rural debt, 20 per cent was advanced by professional moneylenders, 7 per cent by relatives and friends and 10 per cent by agricultural moneylenders (p. ii). And, according to the World Bank's *Global Findex Database*, in 2017, only 8 per cent of Indian adults borrowed from formal sources while 27 per cent borrowed from family or friends (p. 73).

The dependence on informal finance ought *not* to take you by surprise because in order to obtain formal credit, people need to undergo a maze of procedures and its volume is often inadequate and untimely. Interestingly, the word 'credit' has its origins in *credere*, 'to believe' in Latin. A good glimpse of this issue is found in R. K. Narayan's *The Financial Expert* (1952). The protagonist in Narayan's novel, Morgayya, makes his living from the hurdles generated by paperwork necessary to acquire formal credit. And the most important item in Morgayya's toolbox was the "loan application forms of the co-operative bank" (p. 9).

> He was to them [the peasants] a wizard who enabled them to draw unlimited loans from the co-operative bank. If the purpose of the co-operative movement was the promotion of thrift and the elimination of middlemen, those two were just the objectives that were defeated here under the banyan tree: Morgayya didn't believe in advocating thrift: his living depended upon helping people to take loans from the bank opposite and from each other. (p. 8)

In this fictional account, borrowers travelled on foot from villages 15 miles away (p. 13). The aim of financial inclusion programmes like the Jan Dhan Yojana is precisely this: to make finance more accessible not just in terms of paperwork and collaterals but also in reducing the physical distance to a bank (via the services of banking correspondents).

In addition to moneylenders, informal finance enterprises include indigenous banks (often caste based) and pawnbrokers. In his short story 'Livelihood' in *Poisoned Bread* (2009), a collection of poems, stories and essays translated from modern Marathi Dalit literature, Bhimrao Shirwale narrates an encounter of the protagonist Kashi's husband, Dharma, with a pawnbroker.

> Kashi was hungry. Dharma was hungry. No money had come in that day. Neither from a straight job nor from a crooked one. And the two were hungry. Just, simply, hungry.
>
> Amongst these aluminum pots and pans was a brass pot.
>
> …
>
> He grabbed the brass pot with hasty hunger and ran all the way to the Marwari.
>
> …
>
> He pleaded again with Shah Bhanwarilal Khiwarchand. The Marwari said with great generosity, "Look brother, you know I don't like any crooked business. But since you are in need … I'll take this pot on my own responsibility. But you'll have to pay four annas interest on the money. And you'll have to pay off the interest first. See if it suits you."
>
> Interest and principal and such mathematical words meant nothing to Dharma. He was beyond them…. His mental faculties were concentrated in

that single point within him, his stomach. He took twenty-five rupees at four annas a rupee monthly interest from Shah Bhanwarilal Khiwarchand and ran to his hut.

Twenty-five rupees was equal to five days of life....

And then, for the first time in a month, Dharma had a decent sum of money on him. ...

He went to Shah Bhanwarilal Khiwarchand to get his brass pot, but the man asked to see the receipt. Dharma had no receipt. The pot had been pawned against government rules. There was no receipt for such rules.... the Marwari refused to part with the pot. (pp. 198–200)

In the above story, notice that the primary reason for borrowing money from a pawnbroker is unemployment. And caste matters too. Also notice the exorbitant interest rate; how much does the interest rate amount to per annum (16 annas equal 1 rupee)?

Since informal finance enterprises provide credit without much collateral, the rates of interest charged vary between 20 and 30 per cent per annum as opposed to the 10–15 per cent per annum from formal sources (Pradhan 2013). However, do remember that an understanding of financial flows must be viewed in the light of production (recall Figure 2.2). This excerpt from Sarah Joseph's *Gift of Green* (2011) provides an indication of the close connection between credit, production and debt.

It was Kumaran who had advanced Komban the money to take Kunjimathu's paddy field on lease to farm prawns. Earlier, lured by the rumour that fish-farming the northern paddy fields yielded astronomical profits, Komban had invested in prawn farming in several places ... but had incurred terrible losses. The income from prawn farming did not suffice even to pay the EMIs on the loans he had taken at crushing rates of interest. To defray his debts, he'd had to sell even his house. (p. 171)

Moreover, in rural India, the moneylender is often *also* a landlord *and* a seller of seeds—this nexus of power is encapsulated in the idea of 'interlinked markets' put forth by Krishna Bharadwaj (for a detailed discussion, see Section 6.4). The following excerpt from Joseph's *Gift of Green* (2011) is quite telling on this matter.

Seeing Kaaliappan, who stood upright like the trunk of a teak tree, the landlord said: "Yes, I have the seeds. I shall give them to you, but there is a condition.

You have to work in my paddy field for a year. Reinforce the ridges, trap water and cultivate paddy." (p. 160)

In this way, both financial and commodity flows in the economy are significantly influenced by the extant power relations in the processes of production. As an exercise, contemplate on the familiar structures of power in your neighbourhood and describe the routes through which it might influence economic decisions and outcomes.

Financial regulators

The responsibility of regulating these myriad financial institutions rests with agencies such as the RBI, Securities and Exchange Board of India (SEBI), Insurance Regulatory and Development Authority (IRDA) and National Housing Bank (NHB). SEBI is the principal regulator of the capital market. IRDA regulates insurance and re-insurance companies. NHB regulates the housing financial institutions, a constituent of NBFCs.

In addition to serving as the banker to our commercial banks, the RBI is also entrusted with the maintenance of stable (moderate) inflation and a stable currency while keeping in mind the objective of economic growth. It is in the capacity as a banker to our banks that the RBI plays the important role of the 'lender of last resort'. That is, when a solvent bank faces a temporary liquidity crunch and no other financial institution is willing to lend to it, the RBI will provide it with liquidity/credit. As a regulator of India's financial system, the RBI maintains the public's confidence in the system and protects the interests (no pun intended) of the depositors. Let me now share an interesting piece of economic history without further comment: RBI, India's central bank, was privately owned prior to it becoming a fully owned Government of India bank in 1949.

The purpose of the preceding discussion was not to provide you with an exhaustive account, but to give you an overview of the financial architecture of India.

Financial instruments

After we get a sense of the relative importance of bank deposits, insurance claims or cash in India's overall financial assets, we will be ready to discuss what money is. We can obtain this information from the 'Flow of Funds Accounts of the Indian Economy', published by the RBI (see Table 3.1).

Table 3.1 Composition of financial assets in the Indian economy

Financial instruments	As a % of total financial assets
Currency	2.41
Deposits	19.07
Debt securities	9.89
Loans and borrowing	24.06
Equity	11.42
Investment fund (shares/units)	1.47
Life insurance and annuity entitlement	4.85

Source: 'Flow of Funds Accounts of the Indian Economy: 2015–16', *RBI Bulletin*, August 2017, Statement 7.2.

Notes: The data pertains to 2014–15. The value of total financial assets is INR 61,166 billion. Financial assets are represented as 'uses' or 'uses of funds' in FoF. The total does not add up to 100 because the table does not include *all* the financial instruments.

The most striking observation from this table is the low acquisition of currency and the high acquisition of non-currency among the overall financial assets. Also, note that, in terms of the acquisition of financial assets, equity is not as preferred as bank deposits. It should now be evident that currency alone does not constitute money flows. However, it would be helpful for you to talk to some of your neighbours and find out what proportion of their 'money' is kept in the form of currency and other financial instruments. So, then, what is money?

3.3 What is money

Money is a financial obligation (an IOU, short for 'I Owe You') which is widely accepted as a means of payment and a store of value. However, money has been in existence long before coins and currency notes. Items such as shells, cattle, tobacco and iron were once considered an acceptable medium of exchange, as John Kenneth Galbraith reminds us in his 1987 book *A History of Economics: The Past as the Present* (p. 14). Given that we use various financial instruments to park our savings and for raising funds, any meaningful definition of money must clearly state why some of them are money and the others are not.

All the instruments listed in Table 3.1 cannot be characterised as money because not all of them are (universally) acceptable means of payment. For instance, to pay the food bill at a restaurant in Guntur (a city in Andhra Pradesh popular for its chilli production), I can use cash or a debit/credit card but I cannot transfer a portion of my investment fund shares or life insurance policies to the restaurant's cashier in exchange for the food I consumed; it is the same with debt and equity securities too. But why not? This is because cash/currency and bank deposits (which underlie both debit and credit cards) are extremely *liquid* vis-à-vis investment fund shares, life insurance policies, debt securities and equity securities. While all the financial instruments listed in Table 3.1 are stores of value, not all of them are widely accepted as means of payment. Although all of them store value, are their purchasing powers the same, say, after one year? What factors do you think will have an influence on their respective purchasing powers?

When economists and the RBI use the term 'money', they are usually referring to the stock of currency in circulation, demand deposits with the banks and savings deposits of post office savings banks, all of which are highly liquid in nature. Together, they constitute the monetary aggregate M2. M3 (or broad money) is arrived at through a summation of M2 and the time deposits with the banking system. Note that M2 is more liquid than M3. The volumes of monetary aggregates are published by the RBI at regular intervals. The RBI has been compiling and disseminating monetary statistics from July 1935. From the RBI website, find out the constituents of M1 or narrow money.

It follows from the preceding discussion that liquidity is an important characteristic of money. Currency is the most liquid form of money in India; but strictly speaking, for many transactions above a certain amount, bank deposits are preferred. These deposits can be converted into cash/currency on demand and can be directly used for payment (via the facility of debit cards). The liquidity of the financial instrument is a matter of degree which is dependent on how widely accepted it is as a means of payment in markets, and the speed and economy with which it can be converted into money. The instruments listed in Table 3.1 have been arranged from left to right in an increasing order of liquidity in Figure 3.2.

Figure 3.2   Degree of liquidity of select financial instruments in India

Life Insurance	Debt Securities	Investment Fund	Equity	Bank Deposits	Currency

In India we have a well-developed ('thick') market for equity and mutual funds, but the corporate bond market is very 'thin' and, therefore, debt services are relatively less liquid than equities. Since 'life insurance and annuity entitlement' have restrictions on liquidation, they are not easily convertible into means of payment (the conversion can take time and one might incur a penalty for premature withdrawal).

This chapter started with a discussion of financial institutions that mediate between those with surplus funds and those with deficit funds through various financial instruments. As noted previously, funds may be required for purposes of investment or consumption. The financial institutions increase their profits by developing and issuing 'novel' financial instruments or products. Look up and describe the different kinds of such 'innovative' financial products that were widely bought and sold prior to the 2008 Global Financial Crisis.

Until now, we have not discussed the basis on which firms choose to park their surplus funds in equity instead of depositing it in a bank. The counterpart to this question when firms require funds is: what factors go into the decision of firms to raise funds through the issuance of debt securities over that of issuing equity or by borrowing from the bank? The two key factors are risk and return. If you are a depositor of funds, as a household or a firm, you would like to be assured that the amount you deposit will grow, and that at the end of your deposit period, you will obtain both your principal (the original deposit) and the interest intact. Here, the rate of return is entirely captured by the rate of interest. In the case of financial instruments like equity shares, returns include dividends received and the appreciation in the share price. The rate of return on financial instruments varies depending on the risk and the time to maturity. For instance, government securities are considered to be much safer or less risky when compared to corporate securities issued by private companies because governments are much less likely to go bankrupt than private companies. Since the risk is less for government securities, the return is also less. The idea underlying this is that those who undertake risks must be compensated; hence, financial products that are risky offer higher returns than less risky ones. And the longer the maturity period, the higher the risk and, therefore, the return. The difference in expected returns between a financial product and the risk-free government security is known as the risk premium. In sum, in an economy with multiple financial instruments, there exist multiple interest rates (or yields). (Currently, the term 'yield' is often used to represent the rate of return on financial products. The origin of the term, however, is from agricultural harvest or yields. Try to trace the transmission routes of the term 'yield' from agriculture to finance.)

In the previous chapter (as well as the previous section), it was mentioned that governments (centre, state and local) also borrow funds to meet their investment needs—whether for building roads, schools or hospitals. Besides borrowing from its citizens and the RoW, the government can also borrow from the RBI. The central government as well as all the state governments are expected to maintain a minimum balance with the RBI; for the states, the balance depends on their planned income and expenditure (as outlined in their budgets) as well as the volume of their economic activity. The figure (3.1) representing the financial architecture of India shows that one route through which a government can obtain funds is by issuing government securities (G-Secs) via the capital market.

To meet its various financing needs, the Government of India issues G-Secs with different yields and maturities. As noted in an earlier paragraph, it is usually the case that the longer the maturity, the higher the yield (because the risk is higher). However, as of 20 January 2020, in the case of the Government of India bonds, no steep difference was visible between the G-Secs maturing in 2024 and 2049. Since the yield depends on various risk factors, expectations regarding inflation and the RBI's policy rates, among others, the shape of the yield curve varies across time. Figure 3.3 depicts the yield curve of G-Secs issued by the Indian government as on 20 January 2020.

Figure 3.3 Yield curve of Government of India bonds

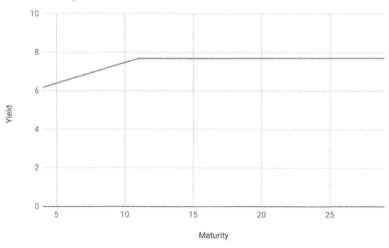

Maturity

Source: Reserve Bank of India, Press Release, 20 January 2020.

Note: The yield is in percentage terms and the maturity is measured by the number of years from the date of issue of the bond.

Since these are Government of India issued bonds, the risk of default is the lowest, and this yield curve is the benchmark 'risk-free' one. One could view the different yields of financial instruments as being built on or tied to this risk-free rate. More than 50 per cent of such central government issued securities in India are held by commercial banks and insurance companies.

While government securities are issued to meet long-term financing needs, the government also issues short-term (less than one year) instruments such as treasury bills (T-bills), commercial paper and certificates of deposit. While around 50 per cent of the T-bills are owned by commercial banks, 14 per cent is owned by mutual fund companies and 18 per cent by state governments (*RBI Bulletin February 2020*, p. 92). Although G-Secs are traded in the capital market, T-bills and other short-term instruments are traded in the money market. As of the current week, what are the yields of the 91-day, 182-day and 364-day T-bills?

As noted in the previous chapter, despite the presence of the three tiers of government, we usually treat the government as a homogenous sector. The state governments also issue securities to meet their financing needs. The majority of the ownership of state government securities is with commercial banks, insurance companies and provident funds.

After surveying the necessary characteristics of money—a universal medium of payment and a store of value—we discussed the degree of liquidity of various financial instruments, building on the nature of the Indian financial structure. Subsequently, it was highlighted that there are multiple interest rates in reality, although several economics textbooks talk as if only a single interest rate exists. This was demonstrated by taking a close look at the G-Secs that are traded in the capital market. Armed with the basic knowledge of India's financial and monetary institutional architecture, it is now time to survey the two broad theories of money.

3.4 Theories of money

As discussed earlier, money is demanded by households, firms (financial and non-financial) and the government for both consumption and investment purposes. Note that when we write 'money is demanded', we are referring to the conversion of relatively illiquid financial instruments into money—currency and bank deposits (which are highly liquid). In a sense, the demand for money is really a demand for liquid financial instruments/products. I use 'products' to highlight the fact that bank deposits, LIC, mutual fund shares and other instruments are commodities 'produced' by the financial sector.

Why do we need money? In the economics literature, the following three reasons or motives for money demand can be identified: transactionary motive, precautionary motive and speculative motive (see Keynes 1936, pp. 195–6). First, as households, we need money to purchase groceries, pay electricity bills, pay for transportation, and so on; and firms (businesses) need money to pay salaries, buy raw materials, pay electricity bills, buy/rent machinery, and so on. Second, money is needed for unexpected expenditure—a medical illness or a sudden trip to our hometown or to hire machinery and labour to meet an unexpected surge in demand. The third and final demand for money is the speculative demand for money. This refers to a speculative decision to go liquid rather than hold bonds, equities and other financial products. In other words, speculative demand refers to the demand for liquid financial products (money) relative to other illiquid ones. The speculative demand for money, therefore, depends on the difference between the interest on the savings account and the interest on bonds and other financial instruments (this difference is also termed the interest spread).

Generally, the speculative demand for money is low when the interest spread is high and vice versa. Or, simply put, if you assume that holding money earns zero interest, then we will hold money if the rate of interest on bonds is low and we will hold bonds if the rate of interest on bonds is high. Conversely, if the interest rate is high, the opportunity cost of holding money for transactions is high and, therefore, the transaction demand for money and the interest rate are also inversely related.

Putting together the aforementioned factors which influence the demand for money, it can be concluded that the demand for liquidity (money) is determined by the volume of transactions and the cost of borrowing (interest rate). For simplicity, let us assume that the demand for money is linearly related to the rate of interest. This enables us to draw a straight line which slopes downwards from left to right (see Figure 3.4). Pay close attention to how we swiftly moved from an inverse relationship to a functional relationship of a linear nature. Think about and note down the various assumptions that have to be made when we mathematically translate the idea of an inverse relationship into a precise functional form.

How is money supplied or, more accurately, created in the economy? There are two broad approaches to answer this question in the economics literature: (*a*) exogenous money and (*b*) endogenous money. As the names suggest, the first approach argues that money supply is given from *outside* the monetary production economy by the central bank, whereas the second approach argues that money is created *inside* the monetary production economy, particularly by the (private) banking sector, when responding to the economy's demand for liquidity. Before we enter into the details of these approaches, let us depict the money demand and supply functions for both the approaches.

Figure 3.4   Exogenous and endogenous money

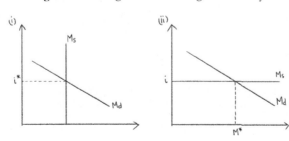

An equilibrium is reached when the demand for money and the supply of money functions intersect. To reiterate, in the first approach, the quantity of money is exogenously set by the central bank, whereas in the second approach, the quantity of money is endogenously determined at the point where the demand for money (M_d) intersects the supply of money (M_s). (More precisely, in endogenous money, it should be demand for credit and not demand for money.) In exogenous money, an upward shift in the demand for money puts upward pressure on the interest rates because the money supply is fixed. However, in endogenous money, at the set rate of interest, the supply of money adapts to the demand for money. Also, conversely, note that in the exogenous money approach, the rate of interest is determined endogenously and in the endogenous money approach, the rate of interest is exogenously set by the central bank. Unfortunately, most economics textbooks do not discuss the endogenous money approach.

In 2014, the Bank of England published a report explaining and endorsing the endogenous money approach titled 'Money Creation in the Modern Economy'. The report also laid to rest two popular misconceptions about money creation in the macroeconomy, which were widely propagated by several bestselling economics textbooks: (*a*) banks are passive intermediaries and (*b*) money is limited by deposits. Instead, it argued that banks are active profit maximisers and that money is created by lending. It is the latter argument that makes the money supply curve horizontal.

How do banks make profits? Just like other firms, banks too make profits by selling dear and buying cheap. The financial products the banks sell are deposits and loans. The interest on loans is always higher than that on deposits. To maximise profits, the banks will try to increase the spread between the lending rate and the deposit rate, and increase the volume of loans relative to deposits. That is, if there is an increased demand for money, the banks will meet that by increasing its supply of loans without needing to alter the interest rate (or the volume of deposits); this is, in fact, the insight provided by the endogenous money approach, also represented visually in the second panel in Figure 3.4. Go to the website of the State Bank of India (SBI), the largest commercial bank in India, and compare its deposit rates with the lending rates for different maturities.

Banks, also like other firms, use the principle of double-entry bookkeeping to record all their financial transactions. If the history of ideas interests you, you might appreciate the following piece of history: one of the first systematic expositions of the principle of double-entry bookkeeping took place in Venice in 1494 by an Italian mathematician, Luca Pacioli, a close friend of the famous artist Leonardo da Vinci. His 1494 book in Italian, *Summa de Arithmetica, Geometria, Proportioni et Proportionalita* (A Summary of Arithmetic, Geometry, Proportion and Proportionality), also deals with matters such as how to conduct business, business letter writing and business ethics. For further understanding, construct fictional balance sheets of a bank and a firm before and after a new loan is offered by taking the help of the 2014 Bank of England report. This accounting exercise will drive home the point that money is not created out of pre-existing bank deposits.

How can policy influence the multiple interest rates prevailing in the economy? Do these rates impact the volume of aggregate savings? Do these rates have a role to play in controlling inflation? Do these rates influence the inflow of funds from foreign countries? The third and fourth questions will be tackled in Sections 8.3 and 3.5, respectively. The RBI sets the 'Policy Repo Rate' (henceforth, repo rate), and the changes to it are transmitted to the interest rates prevailing in the economy (see Figure 3.5). At regular intervals, the RBI meets to decide the repo rate; the RBI's Monetary Policy Committee (MPC), which is responsible for setting this crucial rate, is required to meet at least four times a year. Therefore, this repo rate is an important economic policy lever. But pause here and think about how these policy rates might impact the informal lending rates in India.

Once you learn how the change in policy interest rate influences the residents within the financial architecture, you will have gained a sound foundation to understand contemporary monetary policy decisions. Also, this complements our discussion of the endogenous money approach where the policy interest rate is set by the central bank and not the quantity of money.

Figure 3.5 captures the important channels that link monetary policy (the setting of the policy interest rate) with the volume of savings and borrowings in the macroeconomy. In our simplified version of the monetary transmission mechanism, the nodal institutions responsible for transmission are the commercial banks and the money market participants. The latter contribute to the transmission through their expectations, primarily about the future course of interest rates, inflation and bond prices. These expectations, in turn, influence current bond prices and yields. Given the policy interest rate, commercial banks set the lending rate such that it maximises profits. Both these routes or channels take time and, consequently, the impact of monetary policy

Figure 3.5 Monetary transmission mechanism

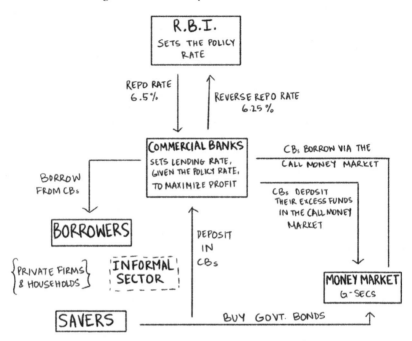

Source: My adaptation of Fig. 11.14 in the 'Credit, Banks and Money' unit in CORE, p. 32.

Note: The repo and reverse repo rates are as of 14 September 2018.

on the macroeconomic variables of credit (or borrowing) and saving occurs with a time lag. In addition to the interest rate and expectations channels, there exist the credit channel, asset price channel and exchange rate channel. However, the relative efficacy of each of these channels requires further study.

Some of the obstacles to a smooth monetary transmission are fixed lending rates of commercial banks and underdeveloped money markets. If these issues are addressed, that is, the nodal machinery is well oiled, so to speak, then a change in the RBI's repo rate will smoothly transmit to all financial instruments in the Indian economy. Commercial banks are at the forefront of this transmission mechanism; for instance, if the RBI reduces the repo rate by 25 basis points (one basis point is one-hundredth of a percentage point), the commercial banks should pass this on to the households and firms by proportionately reducing their lending rates. Since banks need to make profits, they will reduce the deposit rates proportionately. If the transmission is smooth, a higher policy interest rate will also affect G-Secs proportionately, such that the entire yield curve shifts upwards (Figure 3.3). That is, the RBI's repo rate serves as an anchor for all the other interest rates in the macroeconomy. The direction and strength of the transmission between the RBI's repo rate and informal lending rates are not very clear, and this warrants further work, especially through longitudinal surveys.

This brings us to the last point before moving on to discuss the interaction between the inflow of foreign savings and interest rates in the Indian economy in the next section. Although households and private firms were placed within a single analytical box in Figure 3.5, their decisions to borrow arise from fundamentally different reasons. While the borrowing decisions of households are often derived from consumption needs—to pay for a two-wheeler, car, wedding, plot of land or an apartment—those of the firms arise from their plans to expand productive capacity and/or increase the utilisation of existing productive capacity. The firms' investment plans depend on their expectations regarding future sales, interest rates, competition, research and development (R&D), and so on. For example, if a firm expects competition to intensify in the future, it may decide to expand productive capacity today by borrowing more (even if there has been an increase in the interest rate). To conclude, interest rate is only one among the several factors that influence the borrowing decisions of firms and households.

3.5 Money in the open economy

So far, in this chapter, we have discussed the money flows, or, more accurately, financial flows or the flow of funds, which happen within the political boundaries of India. The accurate term is 'financial flows' because the preceding discussion on monetary transmission mechanism, as well as the financial architecture of India, was not restricted to only the flow of money—currency and bank deposits—but it also included the flows of other financial instruments such as equities and government securities. However, for purposes of consistency, we shall now use 'money flows' and 'financial flows' interchangeably, and 'money' shall refer to all financial instruments, possessing various degrees of liquidity. It is now time to examine the structure of money flows between India and the RoW. The volume and intensity of money flows and commodity flows depend on the degree of India's openness with the RoW. To obtain a reasonable idea of India's degree of openness, find out the nature and degree of controls India imposes on the inflow and outflow of commodities, money and labour.

Within India, the financial instruments are issued in rupee terms, whether it is the SBI's SENSEX Mutual Fund or the 91-day T-bill. However, when the residents of India choose to park their surplus funds by purchasing the shares of a company listed in the United States Dow Jones stock market, they need to buy it using US dollars (USD) and not Indian rupees (INR) because the shares are issued in dollar terms. Similarly, when an Indian company wishes to purchase a piece of equipment from Germany, the Indian importer must pay the German company in Euros, or perhaps the payment can be made in USD because of its wide acceptability as a means of payment across the world. Given the latter example, is it right to say that, in the world economy, the USD possesses more 'moneyness' than the INR?

To obtain USD, the Indian importer has to exchange INR for USD. But how do we know how many INRs have to be given in exchange for 1 USD? Just like how share prices are determined in the stock market, there is a market for foreign exchange ('forex' in short). The demand for forex depends, among other factors, on the extent of commodity flows, investor/speculator expectations about future exchange rates and the RBI's forex requirements to keep exchange rates stable, lest they destabilise import and export operations. Table 3.2 gives us the foreign exchange rates of the INR as on 21 September 2018 (5 p.m.).

Table 3.2 India's forex rates

US Dollar (USD)	72.2
British Pound (GBP)	95.2665
Euro (EUR)	84.979
UAE Dirham (AED)	19.7073
Singapore Dollar (SGD)	52.8666

Source: XE Currency Charts.

Note: The rates are as of 5 p.m. on 21 September 2018.

Table 3.2 tells us that an Indian importer has to give 72.2 INR to obtain 1 USD if the transaction was happening on 21 September 2018. And that fewer INRs were required to obtain 1 AED.

If an American can obtain a higher rate of return by buying the shares of an Indian company listed in the Bombay Stock Exchange (BSE) than by parking her surplus funds in America or elsewhere, it would be financially 'attractive' for her to park her funds in the Indian capital market (it is only 'attractive' because she faces risk from exchange rate variations which influences her returns in USD terms). This thought experiment was carried out to underscore the fact that the domestic interest rates and the foreign exchange rates are connected. This implies that the setting of the policy rate of interest by the RBI (that is, monetary policy) has an impact on exchange rates, and, consequently, the volume of inflows and outflows of money and commodities. Hence, both international finance as well as trade are affected by monetary policy.

Besides monetary policy, what other levers exist to influence the international financial and commodity flows? The government can directly control these flows by imposing restrictions such as capital controls (to regulate and limit the inflow of foreign funds and outflow of domestic funds), price controls (by imposing taxes on imports and/or by providing subsidies on exports) and quantity controls (by imposing a 'quota' for imports of commodities and/or regulating the international mobility of labour).

Now, suppose that the RBI increases the policy rate of interest in order to attract foreign finance. But its effects will be felt throughout the Indian economy via the monetary transmission mechanism (see Figure 3.5). It is the duty of the policymakers to study all the anticipated effects when adjusting the policy lever and before rolling out a new policy. An increase in the interest rates will make the Indian lenders better off vis-à-vis borrowers if the interest rates

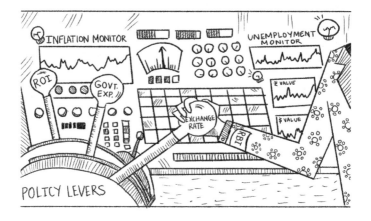

are on a floating and not fixed basis. And it will also make the international investors/lenders better off. What about the effect on government borrowing or debt? It will not affect the interest component on the existing stock of debt because G-Secs are financial instruments with a fixed interest rate. But the newly issued G-Secs will be affected as the servicing of debt will become costlier. In the foreign exchange market, an increase in India's interest rates leads to a higher demand for the INR relative to other currencies, ceteris paribus—thus resulting in an appreciation of the INR. That is, fewer INR need to be exchanged to obtain 1 USD or EUR or GBP. When the INR appreciates, we say that the rupee is getting stronger.

What happens to the quantity of money in the economy when the interest rate increases? Take the aid of Figure 3.4 (ii) to answer this question. One more possible effect of an interest rate increase is the following: if *all* the businesses/firms pass on the increased cost of borrowing in the form of increased prices (that is, the aggregate price level increases), then our exports also become more expensive, and, consequently, their demand falls, resulting in a decrease in the demand for the INR, ceteris paribus. This leads to a depreciation—a weakening—of the INR. The impact of exchange rate (and interest rate) changes on output and employment levels will be discussed in the next chapter. It is now evident that exchange rate variations have multiple effects within the economy, and depending on the direction of the change, exporters, importers, creditors and debtors are differently affected. To compute the firm-level effects, more information is required, such as the relative proportion of exports and imports to the total output of the firm, and the volume of debt and credit in its balance sheet.

Since interest rates also influence exchange rates, monetary policy needs to keep track of international financial and commodity flows as well. A few paragraphs earlier, it was pointed out that the RBI requires foreign exchange in order to influence the exchange rates of INR. It does this by the strategic buying and selling of foreign currencies in the foreign exchange market. To get a better sense of monetary policy, the typical line items in the RBI's balance sheet—the annual record of its assets and liabilities—are given in Figure 3.6; consult the latest annual report of the RBI and fill up the empty cells in the figure.

Figure 3.6   RBI's balance sheet: an overview

LIABILITIES		ASSETS	
DEPOSITS		GOLD COIN & BULLION	
• GOVERNMENT		INVESTMENTS	
• BANKS		• FOREIGN SECURITIES	
OTHER LIABILITIES & PROVISIONS		• DOMESTIC SECURITIES	
NOTES ISSUED		LOANS & ADVANCES	
		• GOVERNMENT	
		• BANKS	

RBI's loans to the commercial banks (CBs) are an asset, while the deposits of the commercial banks at the RBI are a liability. The government bonds, foreign exchange and gold held by the RBI are assets. The loans and advances made to the central and state governments are also assets because they 'belong' to the RBI. The deposits of the government with the RBI are a liability because they do not belong to the RBI. But how are 'notes issued' or 'currency with the public' RBI's liability? As an exercise, advance arguments for and against the claim that 'currency with the public' is actually a problematic piece of accounting.

When foreign finance flows into India, our forex reserves or the foreign currency assets increase. These flows could be purely speculative and short term, to exploit the higher rates of return in the Indian financial market, and/or for purposes of adding to the productive capacity in India. The short-term financial inflows are driven by foreign institutional investors (FIIs). The financial flows that add to India's productive capacity are termed foreign direct investment (FDI) (FDI will be discussed in Section 4.3).

It is now time to conclude this section, but only after briefly describing the accounting framework that is used to capture all the inward and outward financial flows. These transactions are captured in the 'Capital Account'. In a similar way, the inflow and outflow of commodities (goods and services), remittances and foreign aid are summarised in the 'Current Account' (see Figure 4.2). The current account and capital account together make up the 'Balance of Payments' of a country. Like the previous exercise, fill in the empty columns in Figure 3.7 by searching for the appropriate values on the RBI's website.

Figure 3.7   Capital account

	INFLOW	OUTFLOW
FDI		
FII		
COMMERCIAL BORROWINGS		
NRI DEPOSITS		

If the total outflows are greater than the total inflows, we say that the capital account is in deficit, and if the total inflows are greater than the total outflows, it is in surplus. For the Indian economy as a whole, a capital account surplus might seem desirable, but it is not quite, because it entails a build-up of Indian liabilities to foreigners. Moreover, it is important to understand the source(s) of the capital account surplus because if it is mainly due to a large volume of inflows by FIIs, we know that they are extremely short term in nature and, hence, we cannot depend on them for our long-term economic needs such as the full employment of labour or technological growth. On the other hand, FDI is relatively more stable, and thus *more* reliable than FIIs.

3.6 Conclusion

This chapter began with a description of the financial architecture of India (commercial banks, capital market and moneylenders being the important players) and highlighted the presence of regulators such as the RBI, SEBI and IRDA. Subsequently, we discussed their active role in financial intermediation because they earn profits by lending dear and accepting deposits cheap. Following this, we discussed the meaning and role of money and the interest rate. In line with the recent developments in monetary economics, we introduced the endogenous money approach alongside the conventional exogenous money approach. This was followed by a brief discussion of the channels through which monetary policy influences other interest rates, as well as borrowing and lending decisions in the economy. Finally, we looked at the financial flows between India and the RoW; here, we discussed how exchange rates are determined and its links with monetary policy. Moreover, we also discussed, in brief, the nature of FIIs and FDI and their impact on the Indian economy via the RBI's balance sheet and India's capital account. And now, we shall move on to discuss the determination of aggregate income and employment in the next chapter.

Most textbooks position this chapter after the one on the theory of output and employment; do you think that the positioning matters in the way you understand macroeconomics?

Suggestions for further reading

It is strongly recommended that you read the 2014 Bank of England article 'Money Creation in the Modern Economy' cited in the chapter in its entirety; it is available for free download on the Bank of England website. For more advanced treatments of money and interest rates, consult the following: the book chapter 'The Theory of Interest Rates' by John Smithin in *A Handbook of Alternative Monetary Economics,* edited by Philip Arestis and Malcolm Sawyer in 2016 (Cheltenham: Edward Elgar) and Massimo Pivetti's 1991 book *An Essay on Money and Distribution* (New York: Palgrave Macmillan). You can complement these readings with the chapter 'The Social Device of Money' from Amit Bhaduri's 1986 textbook *Macroeconomics: The Dynamics of Commodity Production* (Hampshire: Macmillan). In case you wish to even further your understanding of money and interest rates, consult Tony Aspromourgos's 2007 article 'Interest as an Artefact of Self-validating Central Bank Beliefs' in the journal *Metroeconomica* (2007, vol. 58, no. 4, pp. 514–35). To understand money in the open economy with specific reference to India, look at the chapter 'Managing Finance in Emerging Economies: The Case of India' from Sunanda Sen's 2014 book *Dominant Finance and Stagnant Economies* (New Delhi: Oxford University Press).

4

Output and Employment Levels

4.1 Introduction

Why is the total value of all goods and services produced in 2019 in India only 170 and not, say, 250 trillion rupees? In the language of economics, 170 trillion rupees is the gross domestic product, or GDP, of India in 2019. More generally, the question we shall answer in this chapter is: what determines the level of aggregate output? And if we know how many workers are required to produce one-rupee worth of output, the knowledge of aggregate output also gives us the employment levels. This is the rationale for the title of this chapter as well as that of the following section. The knowledge of aggregate output (Y) and aggregate employment (N) allows us to estimate the output per worker (Y/N), which gives us an indication of the well-being of workers on average. If the GDP is visualised as a large *idli* (a steamed rice cake), Y/N is a rough indicator of how much of it 'belongs' to an individual worker. But as with any average, if the (wage) inequality is high or income distribution is skewed, the average will not be a very meaningful measure.

It is not enough that everyone is employed; the employment must also be secure (reliable) and well paying (gainful). You might be surprised to read that the number of unemployed people in India increased from 17.1 million in 2011 to 23.3 million in 2015 (*State of Working India* 2018, p. 37) (the nature of [un]employment in India and a prelude to thinking about macroeconomic policies to increase employment are provided in Chapter 7). The absence of India's employment context in this chapter differentiates it from the previous one, where the financial architecture of India was outlined. However, some contextual elements of the Indian macroeconomy are visible in Sections 4.3 and 4.4.

This chapter addresses the first objective of political economy as proposed by Smith (see Section 1.3): "to provide a plentiful revenue or subsistence for the people, or more properly to enable them to provide such a revenue or subsistence for themselves". How do we begin to think about the reasons for the differences in output per worker (Y/N) in India, on the one hand, and

1 Objective of political economy

To provide plentiful revenue or subsistence for the people, or more properly to enable them to provide such revenue or subsistence for themselves.

Australia or Denmark, on the other? As outlined in the first chapter, we begin with a competitive economy—an economy which is characterised by the free mobility of labour and capital—as the object of analysis. Chapter 2 engaged with three ways of conceptualising a macroeconomy: aggregate income and expenditure; inter-sectoral relations; and flow of funds across sectors. While Chapter 3 adopted the flow-of-funds approach, the present chapter eschews sectoral analysis and focuses on aggregate (or macro) analysis. But keep in mind that the economic backdrop for a macro analysis is complemented well by the second and third conceptualisations of a macroeconomy.

A disclaimer is in order before we proceed to the theories of output and employment. During my teaching of macroeconomics, I have had at least one student every year who has found the logic of macroeconomics less intuitive than that found in (marginalist) microeconomics. Our intuition is a product of the complex interaction between the knowledge we consume (via textbooks and other texts) and our individual experiences. Therefore, it is crucial to keep in mind that not all knowledge can be produced and understood on the basis of individual behaviour and experience (for related discussions, see Section 6.3).

4.2 Theories of output and employment

Much like the contending theories of money discussed in the previous chapter, there are broadly two contending theories of output and employment. The first originates from J. B. Say and was developed further by Alfred Marshall and

A. C. Pigou—and is found in a different form in the growth theory of Robert Solow (see Chapter 5). The second originates from the works of Michał Kalecki and John Maynard Keynes in the 20th century, although Kalecki's viewpoint can be traced back to ideas which are found in Karl Marx.

Writing in the 19th century, Marx recognised that a competitive economy is prone to recurrent crises, of which a central contributing factor is underconsumption. Underconsumption arises from the capitalist logic of paying workers' wages that are less in value than what they add to the process of production (see Section 2.2 for Marx's account of the circuit of capital). Owing to this, workers' consumption is insufficient to validate the output produced, leading to unsold commodities and a (temporary) crisis. In the early 20th century, Rosa Luxemburg, working in the Marxian tradition, not only argued that the demand for output in capitalist societies comes from non-capitalist societies, but also recognised the problem of aggregate demand insufficiency. As she writes in her 1913 book *The Accumulation of Capital*,

> [Marx's scheme] does indeed permit of crises but only because of a lack of proportion within production, because of a defective social control over the productive process. It precludes, however, the deep and fundamental antagonism between the capacity to consume and the capacity to produce in a capitalist society, a conflict resulting from the very accumulation of capital which periodically bursts out in crises.... (pp. 346–7)

And Kalecki arrived at his macroeconomic theory after having seriously engaged with the works of Marx and Luxemburg. Although both Kalecki (in 1933) and Keynes (in 1936) independently developed a similar theory of output and employment, in opposition to the marginalist one, we shall refer to them singularly as the Keynesian theory of output and employment. Elements of this theory have been identified in the works of classical economists such as Sismondi and Malthus; once you complete this section, as an exercise, consult their original texts, if possible, and find out which concepts in Sismondi and Malthus bear some affinities with the Keynesian theory.

Let us now list the assumptions common to the marginalist and Keynesian theories of output and employment: (*a*) the object of study is a competitive economy and (*b*) the economy operates at a given level of productive capacity. The reasons for studying a competitive economy has already been provided in Section 1.4. In a competitive economy, remember that firms are profit maximisers—who are always on the lookout for new markets and technologies as well as improved ways of operating with existing markets and technologies, which can yield them more profits. The second assumption of 'a given level of productive capacity' needs some explanation. Think of your local economy or the Indian economy. Suppose that no new coal or solar plants are constructed and no new machinery, such as water turbines or wheat threshers, are added; the capacity of that economy to produce does not undergo any change. Its productive capacity is expressed by the total number of existing plants, machinery and the state of technology. The second assumption also implies that there is no technological progress. The assumption of a given level of productive capacity is relaxed in the next chapter when we study economic growth.

In textbooks, the assumption of a given productive capacity is often referred to as a short-run situation and the long run refers to a situation where productive capacity can undergo changes. And in this manner, macroeconomics is characterised as a short-run study, while economic growth studies the long-run dynamics. However, since short run is often also used to refer to a time period that lasts less than one year, in this book, in the interest of conceptual precision, I shall qualify my use of the term 'short run'. Note that we *cannot* a priori translate the theoretical notion of the short run into a particular number of months of actual calendar time.

What characterises a macroeconomic equilibrium? Go over the discussion on equilibrium under the header 'precision in analysis' in Section 1.4 again. A macroeconomic equilibrium is one wherein planned aggregate supply and planned aggregate demand are equal. Pay attention to the fact that macroeconomic *theory* deals with 'planned' magnitudes and not 'actual' ones, as it is based on aggregate *behaviour*. That is, we are interested to know, for instance, whether the aggregate plan to supply is matched by the aggregate plan to demand exactly that volume of supply. If they exactly match, the macroeconomy is said to be in equilibrium—a state of rest as the plans (or expectations) for the economy as a whole do not warrant changes. And, here, we are not talking about actual macroeconomic outcomes that are captured by the National Accounts Statistics (NAS). 'Ex ante' and 'ex post' are another set of terms that are used to express the difference between planned and actual variables, respectively.

For a closed economy, planned aggregate demand is constituted by planned consumption, planned investment and planned government expenditure. By drawing on the discussion in Section 2.4 on characterising the economy as a web of flows, we can rewrite the equilibrium condition as one wherein planned injections (investment, government expenditure and exports) into the circular flow equals planned leakages (saving, taxes and imports) from the circular flow. And in a two-sector economy with only households and firms, this translates into planned savings equalling planned investment.

Note that the *actual* aggregate supply and aggregate demand are always necessarily equal because it (that is, actual aggregate supply = actual aggregate demand) is an accounting identity; you can verify this by looking up any volume of NAS for the Indian economy. An accounting identity refers to an equality that is true by definition. In the context of national accounts, the following is true by definition: aggregate product = aggregate income = aggregate expenditure. A theory provides us with a causal explanation of events. No causation is implicit or explicit in an accounting identity. However, as Section 6.5 will make clear, economic theories do have a role in the kind of data that is collected. Think about whether accounting principles are actually independent of any theory.

It will presently be seen that in the marginalist theory, the direction of causation runs from planned saving to planned investment or from aggregate supply to aggregate demand, whereas in the Keynesian theory the direction of causation runs from planned investment to planned saving or from aggregate demand to aggregate supply.

Marginalist theory of output and employment

Since the theory of output and employment developed by Say, Marshall and Pigou takes recourse to the marginal productivity theory of distribution—the dominant approach to understanding income distribution—we call it the marginalist theory of output and employment. Other textbooks refer to this theory as the classical theory of output and employment; in this textbook, we do not entertain this extremely popular usage because it can confuse the reader into thinking that the classical economists such as Smith, Ricardo and Malthus possessed such a theory.

Smith, Ricardo and Malthus did not possess anything resembling the marginal productivity theory of distribution; for them, wages were exogenously determined by social and political factors and not endogenously via the labour supply and demand functions. That is, classical economics left open one of its doors for history to enter. Consequently, it has been able to easily incorporate historical struggles, which strived to raise wages in general, and in particular for the equality of pay between men and women, in its account of wage determination.

The marginalist theory of output and employment posits that it is planned aggregate supply that determines planned aggregate demand; in a two-sector economy with only households and firms, this translates into planned saving determining planned investment via variations in a sufficiently sensitive interest rate. Moreover, in the labour market, the labour demand adapts to the labour supply via variations in a sufficiently sensitive wage rate—thus resulting in a full employment equilibrium. The equilibrium wage rate is one that clears the labour market, that is, all those who are willing to work at the prevailing (equilibrium) wage rate find employment.

By putting the aforementioned propositions together, it can be stated that the marginalist theory posits that the full employment level of planned saving determines planned investment. Or, more generally, that, under competitive conditions, the macroeconomy tends to a full-employment equilibrium. Or, according to Say's Law, supply always creates its own demand.

When planned saving exceeds planned investment, the rate of interest falls until planned investment has increased to such a point at which planned saving and planned investment are equal. This is so because saving and investment are both conceptualised as a volume of funds. When the demand for funds (investment) exceeds the supply of funds (saving), like in marginalist microeconomics, the rate of interest increases *until* planned investment matches planned saving. Thus, the responsibility or burden of equilibrating planned saving and investment lies with the interest rate. Try to contrast this idea of the interest rate with the multiple interest rates found in Chapter 3.

Marginalist versus Keynesian approaches

According to the Keynesian theory of output and employment, it is planned aggregate demand that determines planned aggregate supply, and this is the essence of the principle of effective demand. As noted earlier, in a two-sector economy, this translates into planned investment determining planned savings via variations in aggregate income. And in the labour market, there exists no tendency towards the full employment of labour. In fact, Keynes argues that the full-employment equilibrium found in marginalist theory is a 'fluke' and a 'special case', with the general case being that of unemployment. Hence the title of his 1936 classic: *The General Theory of Employment, Interest and Money*. Moreover, since unemployment equilibrium is the general state of affairs, Keynes wrote that the marginalist theory of output and employment "represents the way in which we should like our economy to behave; but to assume that it does so is to assume our difficulties away" (Keynes 1936, p. 8). Therefore, we jettison the marginalist theory and employ the Keynesian theory in the determination of aggregate output and employment.

Before we plunge into a detailed exposition of the Keynesian theory of output and employment, let us summarise the differences between the marginalist and Keynesian theories of output and employment in a tabular form (Table 4.1).

Table 4.1 Marginalist and Keynesian theories of output and employment

	Marginalist Theory	*Keynesian Theory*
The explanandum	Aggregate output and employment	Aggregate output and employment
Key economists	Say, Marshall, Pigou	Keynes, Kalecki
The explanans	Supply creates its own demand	Aggregate demand determines aggregate output
Key conclusion	Tendency to full employment	No tendency to full employment
Key policy implication	Government intervention to be minimised	Government needs to intervene to raise output and employment levels

The *explanandum* refers to that which is being described or explained and the *explanans* refers to the principle or the mechanism which does the explanation. Both explanandum and explanans are Latin words used in the discussion of what constitutes a scientific explanation; these terms are not commonly used in economics textbooks.

What determines or explains the current level of aggregate output? The explanans offered by the marginalist theory is based on Say's law, which, in this context, entails that aggregate supply determines aggregate output, and the explanans offered by the Keynesian theory is that aggregate demand determines aggregate output (sometimes also known as the 'principle of effective demand'). Note that while the explanandum in both marginalist and Keynesian theories are the same, the explanans are different, and, in a way, opposite to the other. In addition, the key conclusions as well as the policy implications are contrasting too. Another key difference not provided in the table is the manner in which the aggregate magnitudes are arrived at. Marginalist theory views them as an aggregation of individual behaviour (much like the industry demand curve being constructed from an aggregation of individual demand curves in marginalist microeconomics), whereas Keynesian theory does not view aggregate behaviour as a summation of individual behaviour. Indeed, these two theories are truly contending in nature.

Keynesian theory of output and employment

In what follows, the Keynesian theory of output and employment is explained with the assistance of simple graphs in a two-dimensional plane. We assign the values of aggregate supply (or aggregate output) to the x-axis and those of aggregate demand to the y-axis.

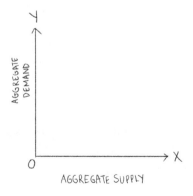

First, let us represent the macroeconomic equilibrium—aggregate demand equals aggregate supply (AD = AS)—in the graph. While discussing theory, remember that we are at all times referring to planned magnitudes. In a state of macroeconomic equilibrium, when aggregate demand is INR 158 trillion, aggregate supply must be INR 158 trillion. Or, when aggregate demand is INR 596 trillion, aggregate supply must be INR 596 trillion. By drawing a 45-degree line, we obtain a straight line that connects all the points at which aggregate demand equals aggregate supply.

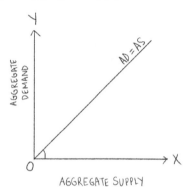

All the points on the AD = AS line are points of macroeconomic equilibrium. Let us now think about how to draw the AD line. In a two-sector economy, planned aggregate demand is made up of planned aggregate consumption and planned aggregate investment. As Keynes writes, aggregate demand "can be derived only from present consumption or from present provision for future consumption" (Keynes 1936, p. 104). That is, it is through current investment that an economy provides for future consumption.

Does aggregate consumption have a systematic connection with aggregate income? The Keynesian theory postulates a systematic relationship between the two, which can be expressed in a functional form. In a two-sector economy with households and firms, if aggregate income (Y) increases by say INR 50 trillion, how much of it will translate into an increase in aggregate consumption (C)? To put it differently, if aggregate income increases by one unit, by how much does planned aggregate consumption increase? The Keynesian theory makes the following two reasonable assumptions. If Y increases by INR 50 trillion, C will not increase by INR 50 trillion; that is, the entire increase in aggregate income will not be devoted to aggregate consumption. And if Y increases by INR 50 trillion, C will increase by at least some positive amount;

that is, the entire increase in aggregate income will not be devoted to aggregate saving. In the following graphs, it is assumed that out of the aggregate income, a constant proportion is devoted to aggregate consumption. As Y increases, C also increases, but at a constant rate.

How is planned aggregate investment (I) related to planned aggregate income (Y)? If firms expect aggregate income to rise, it can lead to an increase in planned aggregate investment because their expectation implies that aggregate demand will expand, and firms will be able to increase the volume of profits by increasing the aggregate supply. The macroeconomic concept which represents the change in aggregate investment in response to a change in aggregate income (or GDP) is the 'accelerator'. However, in this chapter, for pedagogic simplicity, we shall assume that planned aggregate investment is independent of income and, therefore, determined exogenously (contrast this with the determinants of borrowing for investment in Section 3.4). And a positive level of aggregate investment is assumed; that is, I is represented graphically as a straight line parallel to the x-axis.

When C and I are aggregated, we arrive at the AD line with the value of its intercept given by the value of I. What determines the slope of the AD line? It is given by the value of the (constant) proportion of aggregate income that is devoted to aggregate consumption. The AD line shows that planned aggregate demand increases as planned aggregate income increases owing to the positive relationship between Y and C.

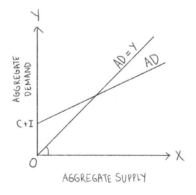

As noted earlier, under the assumption of a given level of productive capacity, investment refers to an increase in the rate of utilisation of the existing productive capacity. Remember that this is a competitive economy, and it is the profit-maximising firms that undertake investment—increase in the rate of capacity utilisation—in this two-sector economy; this increase in the utilisation of capacity generates additional aggregate output. In a four-sector economy, investment can be undertaken by the government or by foreign firms (as foreign direct investment [FDI], which will be dealt with in the next section). Moreover, recollect that the Keynesian theory assumes the presence of both unemployed labour and capital. In the following graph, the level of output corresponding to the full employment of labour is given as Y^F. The full employment level of output or simply the full-employment equilibrium (Y^F) is the level of aggregate output at which all the workers who are willing to work at the prevailing wage rate find employment and capacity is fully utilised.

The equilibrium level of aggregate output (Y^*) can be discerned by dropping a perpendicular at the intersection of planned aggregate demand and planned aggregate supply and reading the value from that point on the x-axis. It is assumed that planned aggregate supply is identically equal to the value of aggregate output supplied. (For a simple algebraic illustration, see Section 6.2.)

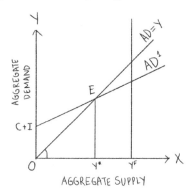

One of the properties of an equilibrium position is its ability to serve as a state of rest. A desirable property of an equilibrium is its stability. What ensures that the economy tends to rest at Y^*? If the economy is at any point to the right of Y^*, planned aggregate output is greater than planned aggregate demand, and at any point to the left of Y^*, planned aggregate demand is greater than planned aggregate output. When planned aggregate output exceeds planned aggregate demand ($Y > AD$), it results in a glut in the market with unsold commodities and this will induce firms to cut back on their output. This process of cutting back output will take place until point Y^* is reached, where planned aggregate output and aggregate demand coincide and there is no reason for the firms to revise or modify any production plans. And when planned aggregate demand exceeds planned aggregate output (AD > Y), firms will keep increasing their output since there is unmet demand in the economy—until point Y^* is reached. Thus, it is primarily through variations in the firms' production levels that the economy moves towards an equilibrium position. Note that these variations are of output levels exclusively; changes in commodity prices are not required as there is underutilised capacity—of both labour and capital—and firms can increase production without altering prices. It may be said that in this two-sector economy, private investment is central in charioting the macroeconomy to its final destination of rest—that of equilibrium.

The Keynesian multiplier

Now, let us suppose that the Government of India plans to spend INR 1,000 trillion, that is, planned government expenditure (G) equals INR 1,000 trillion. This increases the planned aggregate demand, which is the sum of planned consumption expenditure, planned investment and planned government expenditure, by INR 1,000 trillion. This is shown by the upward parallel shift of the AD line. Notice that an increase in G only leads to an increase in the intercept of the AD line and does not affect its slope. It is so because G is not related to Y in any systematic manner unlike C, which bears a systematic relation with Y.

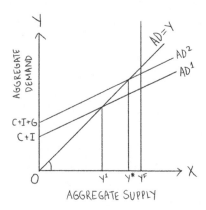

An increase in G results in an increase in the equilibrium level of output—from Y^1 to Y^*. Why does the equilibrium level of output increase? It increases because at Y^1 the AD is greater than Y (owing to the entry of G) and, therefore, the profit-maximising firms will keep increasing output until the aggregate output reaches Y^*, at which point $Y = AD$.

As economists, we are interested in knowing the extent of the increase in Y brought about by an increase in G (INR 1,000 trillion in this case). The macroeconomic concept which expresses the change in aggregate output caused by a change in any of the elements of aggregate demand is the 'multiplier'. More specifically, we are interested in knowing whether the increase in Y is greater than the INR 1,000 trillion injection. And if so, by how much? Why does the output multiply? Think of Figure 2.2, which underscores the structural interdependence in the macroeconomy via commodity and money flows. Given this structural interdependence, any injection into the economy has multiplicative effects on aggregate output. The precise value of the government expenditure multiplier can be obtained by dividing the change in aggregate output (ΔY) by the change in government expenditure (ΔG), ceteris paribus. Suppose now that the value of the government expenditure multiplier ($\Delta Y/\Delta G$) is greater than the consumption expenditure multiplier ($\Delta Y/\Delta C$) and further suppose that your aim is to increase employment. Would you devote additional resources to G or to C? And besides increasing employment, what are the other socioeconomic purposes of consumption and government expenditure?

Underlying the concept of the multiplier is the meso or structural approach to economics. In Figure 2.2, focus on the flows between the government and the non-financial sector. The expenditure of the government on the goods and services of the non-financial sector provides the non-financial sector with an income, in addition to that arising from the expenditure of the household sector. However, the additional government expenditure is not a one-off flow because it generates additional income that can generate additional employment, which further leads to additional income and additional expenditure by the household sector, so on and so forth. The value of the multiplier captures all the direct and indirect effects on aggregate output. And to understand what is happening within the black box of the non-financial sector in Figure 2.2, look at Table 2.1, which gives us an idea of the interrelationship within the non-financial sector in terms of the structural interdependence between the primary, secondary and tertiary sectors. Additional incomes are also generated within the non-financial sector. Thus, in macroeconomics, the understanding that expenditure generates income is pivotal.

Autonomous and induced elements of aggregate demand

Now, let me introduce you to the conceptual distinction between *autonomous* and *induced* elements of aggregate demand. It is pertinent not only in theory but also in policy (see Section 7.3, where it is employed to suggest macroeconomic solutions for the problem of unemployment). Let us now briefly discuss the meaning of autonomous consumption and autonomous investment. Autonomous consumption refers to variations in consumption expenditure independent of current aggregate income. A positive variation in consumption expenditure may be caused by a decrease in saving (assuming a positive propensity to save), by an increase in dissaving (briefly discussed in Section 3.2) or by selling assets (and thereby reducing wealth). Induced consumption refers to the variations in consumption expenditure that are dependent on current aggregate income. It refers to the amount of consumption expenditure that is induced or brought about by a change in current aggregate income. Similarly, autonomous investment refers to investment expenditure, such as research and development (R&D) for the economy as a whole, which is independent of current aggregate income, whereas induced investment refers to the volume of investment that is induced or brought about by variations in current aggregate income. For other determinants of private investment, revisit the final paragraph of Section 3.4. Given this discussion of autonomous and induced expenditures, would you classify government expenditure as autonomous or induced with respect to current levels of aggregate income?

The applicability to India

How applicable is the Keynesian apparatus to the Indian economy? In 1952, V. K. R. V. Rao tackled this question in his two articles, 'Investment, Income and the Multiplier in an Under-developed Economy' and 'Full-employment and Economic Development', published in the *Indian Economic Review*. And in 1954, A. K. Dasgupta in his 'Keynesian Economics and Underdeveloped Countries', published in the *Economic Weekly*, also engaged with the applicability of Keynesian economics to the Indian economy. These articles highlight the underdeveloped nature of Indian economy, in particular, the extensive informal sector, where wages are not determined as in developed countries, and the presence of significant self-employment (an outline of the key contextual characteristics of the Indian economy is provided in Sections 6.4,

7.2 and 8.2). As a consequence, Rao and Dasgupta find limited applicability of the Keynesian idea to the whole of the Indian economy because its nature is different from that of a developed economy, such as the United Kingdom or the United States of America (USA).

While the stance towards Keynesian economics adopted in this text is more favourable than that, it has been and will be emphasised that caution is required when translating *any* theory into practical policy. It is indeed true that the Keynesian adjustment from aggregate supply to aggregate output will not be smooth because of severe supply-side constraints characterising the Indian economy. Indeed, even today, India is characterised by inadequate physical and social infrastructure, plus a labour market that discriminates by caste and gender. However, it shall be seen in Chapters 7 and 8 that the Keynesian policy suggestion of government expenditure to increase output and employment levels is beneficial to the Indian economy because of its ability to directly and indirectly improve supply-side issues.

Let me now summarise this section. According to the marginalist theory of output and employment, aggregate output is determined by aggregate supply and there is a tendency towards the full employment of labour. According to the Keynesian theory of output and employment, aggregate output is determined by aggregate demand—the sum of autonomous and induced demands; in this theory, there is no tendency to the full employment of labour. More precisely, it is the autonomous elements of aggregate demand that play the focal role in determining aggregate output. In the next section, we extend the Keynesian theory to the four-sector case by incorporating the rest of the world (RoW) as an additional sector.

4.3 Open economy macrodynamics

Thus far, we have not used the prefix of 'domestic' to aggregate output levels, but with the incorporation of the RoW as a sector, it has to be used to distinguish the aggregate output of, say, India from that of the RoW. In this section, we shall provide answers to the following questions: How do exports and imports affect domestic aggregate output levels? How do countries finance their imports? How do fluctuations in exchange rates (discussed in Section 3.5) affect domestic aggregate output levels?

Once again, recall Figure 2.2, which presented the structure of commodity flows and money flows in the macroeconomy, where the RoW was omitted for visual ease. Can you redraw the diagram with the RoW as an additional sector based on the following information? The household sector provides labour to the RoW sector (migrant labour) in return for income (remittances, if they are transferred to their relatives in India). From Chapter 3, you know that the funds of the foreign institutional investors (FIIs) connect India's financial sector with that of the RoW and that foreign direct investment (FDI) is one important flow between India's non-financial sector and the RoW. The government imposes taxes on and provides subsidies to the RoW, although they go by different names (such as tariff, custom duty, anti-dumping duty, quota, relaxing of FDI norms and long-term capital gains tax, which are imposed to regulate the inflow of goods, finance and investment). Note that from India's standpoint, the RoW is a single homogenous sector, but do not forget that it comprises the household, government, financial and non-financial sectors.

Although we have briefly discussed the determinants of consumption and investment early on in this chapter, we have not yet discussed the rationale for imports and exports. If India is self-sufficient in terms of its domestic production of consumption goods (say, fruits, chocolates, mobile phones) and investment goods (say, chemicals, fuel, machinery), the need for imports would arise only if foreign goods are cheaper than Indian goods. However, India does not produce all that is necessary for domestic needs—both consumption and investment—and, therefore, imports are essential. Table 4.2 gives you the list of India's top five imports.

Table 4.2 India's top five imports

Commodities	As a percentage of the value of total imports
Mineral fuels	33
Pearls and precious metals	12
Electrical machinery and equipment	10
Nuclear reactors	8
Organic chemicals	4

Source: Export Import Data Bank (Import :: Commodity-wise), Department of Commerce, Ministry of Commerce and Industry.

Notes: The values are rounded off to the nearest percentage. The data pertains to the commodities sorted at the 2-digit level for 2019–20; the data is provisional.

Except for pearls and precious metals, all the other commodities can be easily classified as investment goods. However, a part of mineral fuels or oil imports does end up as a consumption good too. Our need to import intermediate capital goods arises from the inter-industry structure of the Indian economy. The empirical question to address, in this context, is the following: how many units of imported goods are required to produce one unit of (domestic) output in the manufacturing sector? We also import intermediate capital goods to produce exports. Find out how much of our imported pearls and precious metals are used for domestic consumption and how much are earmarked for export purposes.

We export our goods and services to the RoW to exploit larger markets and to obtain better prices (which, as you know from Chapter 3, depends on the exchange rate). Table 4.3 provides you with the top five export destinations for India.

Table 4.3 India's top five export destinations

Country	As a percentage of the value of total exports
USA	16
UAE	9
China	5
Hong Kong	4
Singapore	3

Source: Export Import Data Bank (Export :: Country-wise), Department of Commerce, Ministry of Commerce and Industry.

Note: The figures are for 2018–19.

Why these countries and not others? One reason is the size of the export market (USA, for example) and the other is a consequence of bilateral trade agreements, which aim to increase the volume of exports (United Arab Emirates, for example). In the theoretical discussion that follows, we shall assume the free mobility of labour and capital (investment goods or intermediate goods) across countries. However, in reality, this is not the case. Countries get into agreements with other countries to increase the benefits from trade; this could take the form of a reduction of trade barriers, creation of a free trade area or introduction of a common market. Trade barriers need not only assume the form of tariffs or quotas; they can also be in the form of imposing rules on packaging, standardisation and safety measures. The aforementioned economic agreements depend more on geopolitical dynamics than on pure economics. Often, India sends its best mangoes and spices to the RoW and you would also have come across goods labelled 'export quality' in India; discuss and debate with a friend on the economic merits and demerits of sending the best-quality products to the RoW.

Let us now apply the Keynesian theory to an open economy. The previous section had noted that one of the ways of expressing the equilibrium condition was as an equality between planned injections to and planned leakages from the circular money flow. And that this is analytically equivalent to the condition of planned aggregate demand equalling planned aggregate supply (and for a two-sector economy, planned investment equalling planned saving). For instance, the government expenditure is an injection into the circular money flow, whereas taxation is a leakage from the circular money flow. Are exports a leakage or an injection?

In an open economy setting as well, the macroeconomic equilibrium for the domestic economy is one wherein planned aggregate demand equals planned aggregate supply, except that now planned aggregate demand includes the demand from the RoW. The AD line for a four-sector economy comprises the consumption demand (C), investment demand (I), government expenditure (G) and foreign demand. Foreign demand is the difference between RoW's demand for Indian goods and services and India's demand for RoW's goods and services. That is, foreign demand equals net exports (NX), which is the difference between exports (X) and imports (M).

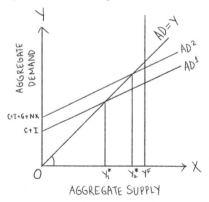

The volume of exports depends on the aggregate income of the RoW and is sensitive to changes in the exchange rate. Here too, it is assumed that Indian firms will be able to supply the foreign demand without needing to adjust prices. While India's imports are sensitive to the exchange rate, the volume of imports also depends on the domestic level of aggregate income/output. However, once again, for pedagogic simplicity, in our illustration, we have assumed that imports are entirely autonomous, that is, independent of domestic aggregate income/output. And so, the addition of a positive volume of net exports shifts the AD_1 line parallelly upwards to the AD_2 line, where the difference in the intercept of AD_1 and AD_2 lines equals the magnitude of net exports.

The macroeconomic equilibrium in this four-sector economy is at Y_2^*. Now, let us suppose that imports increase (ΔM), ceteris paribus, on account of the government deciding to import solar panels. What do you think will happen to the equilibrium output?

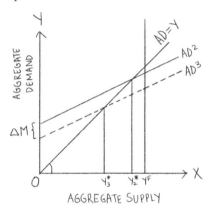

The AD_2 line shifts parallelly downwards to AD_3, as the y-intercept reduces by ΔM. When imports increase, ceteris paribus, foreign demand reduces (because the volume of the leakage increases) and equilibrium output reduces to Y_3^*, in line with the reduction of the aggregate demand. The change in equilibrium output $(Y_2^* - Y_3^*)$ is greater than ΔM because of the multiplier mechanism. Try to describe the multiplier mechanism in words as it would happen in the Indian economy, keeping Figure 2.2 as the backdrop. Now, think of what will happen to the equilibrium output when exports (X) increase, ceteris paribus?

An important—and perhaps the most important—principle in understanding open economy macrodynamics is the fact that all the open economies in the world behave as one giant closed economy. In the language of game theory, this amounts to saying that the payoffs from macroeconomic flows—commodity and money—within the world economy as a whole is akin to that of a zero-sum game; that is, one economy's loss is necessarily another economy's gain. It is such a principle that prompted Joan Robinson to term policies which attempt to maximise the gains from international trade as 'beggar-my-neighbour' policies (p. 122; read the full essay 'The New Mercantilism', published in her 1974 book). And, as Keynes writes in the last chapter of *The General Theory*, "if nations can learn to provide themselves with full employment by their domestic policy ... there would no longer be a pressing motive why one country need force its wares on another or repulse the offerings of its neighbor ..." (p. 382). In Section 1.2, we briefly introduced the key principle of mercantilism. What similarities do you find between contemporary trade policies and mercantilism?

The aforementioned principle, as you might have already noticed, is one that arises from accounting; one country's exports are another country's imports and, therefore, all countries cannot have their exports exceed their imports simultaneously. This principle is necessarily true so long as we do not trade with outer space. In a way, it can also be viewed as an economic law—an outcome that is independent of whether the individual economies are competitive, informal, dependent on the services sector or possess large foreign exchange reserves.

This principle will become clearer through a simple illustration of multilateral trade—trade between three or more countries. Suppose that India exports INR 100 trillion worth of mangoes to Australia and that this is the only trade between them, and further suppose that the total value of India's imports from the RoW (excluding Australia) is INR 800 trillion and the total value of Australia's exports to the RoW (excluding India) is INR 1,000 trillion. Figure 4.1 provides the balance of trade (BoT) for India, Australia and the RoW. BoT expresses the value of exports over imports, or net exports, over a specified period of time. In the figure, we treat the RoW as another distinct economy that comprises all the countries of the world except India and Australia.

While both India and the RoW have a negative trade balance, Australia has a positive trade balance because of its exports exceeding its imports. If you add up the trade balances of India, Australia and the RoW, you obtain zero. This simple illustration reinforces our key principle which postulates that all the countries in the world cannot simultaneously be running a (balance of) trade surplus.

Figure 4.1 Balance of trade: India, Australia and the RoW

India

Exports (to Australia)	INR 100
Imports (from the RoW)	INR 800
BoT	–INR 700

Australia

Exports (to the RoW)	INR 1,000
Imports (from India)	INR 100
BoT	INR 900

The RoW

Exports (to India)	INR 800
Imports (from Australia)	INR 1,000
BoT	–INR 200

The current account, as noted in the previous chapter, is a summary of transactions between, say, India and the RoW. It includes money inflows and outflows between India and the RoW, which arise from commodity outflows and inflows, that is, exports and imports of goods and services. It also includes money flows that have no corresponding commodity flows, but they relate to income receivable or payable for the temporary use of labour, financial resources or natural resources. From the RBI's website, look up the relevant data and populate the empty cells in Figure 4.2.

Figure 4.2 Current account

	Money Inflows	Money Outflows	Net Money Inflows
	(Credit)	(Debit)	(Credit minus Debit)
1. Trade in Goods			
2. Trade in Services			
3. Primary Income			
4. Secondary Income			

Services include communication, insurance, computer software, transportation, and so on. Primary income refers to income that arises from the temporary use of labour, financial resources or natural resources, and secondary income refers to the transfers of income between the residents and the non-residents (remittances by migrant workers is a prime example of secondary income). That is, primary income includes the compensation of employees and (foreign) direct investment, and secondary income includes workers' remittances, which are essentially current transfers between resident and non-resident households.

Exports by India generate a money inflow and are therefore treated as a credit transaction, whereas imports generate a money outflow and are therefore treated as a debit transaction. If the total money outflows are greater than the total money inflows, we can say that the current account is in deficit and if the total inflows are greater than the total outflows, then the current account is in surplus.

While remittances are usually viewed in a favourable light within macroeconomic discussions, it is important to pay attention to some of the causes for migration to foreign countries. As Sultan tellingly explains to Suresh in 'Homeland', a short story by Skybaaba (2016),

> The entire community [Muslims] is in the same situation as my family. No one chooses to leave, Suresh. There is no joy in leaving behind your loved ones—your wife, your children, your parents and siblings and friends. It is especially hard to leave the land of your birth and cross the seven seas to go to a strange, foreign land. In my community, often the entire household depends on the earnings of just one person. There are sisters to be married off, aged and infirm parents to be taken care of, and younger brothers like me who cannot find any decent employment. There are so many problems a family faces! Can't you understand these things? Do Muslims own agricultural land? Do they have traditional occupations? Do they have reservations? How long do you want us to stick to petty roadside businesses? We eat when we can earn, or else we go hungry. (pp. 61–2)

As an exercise, go through articles on migration and identify the reasons individuals and families provide for migrating to foreign countries. Also, note that not every migrant is able to eventually settle down in the host country owing to factors like educational attainment and religion. As Sultan contemplates, in response to Suresh's wish to settle down in the USA,

> We go there [countries like the UAE] in search of a livelihood, but our hard-earned money comes back to this country, doesn't it? Whereas you gain your degrees here, but prefer to settle down in countries like America. We, who have no worthwhile education, work as labourers and bring in valuable exchange

for our homeland. And no matter how long we work abroad, we always return
... to our homeland. (p. 63)

In 2019, after obtaining emigration clearances, 334,000 workers emigrated
from India, according to the 2019–20 annual report of the Ministry of External
Affairs (MEA) (p. 315). Go to that report and identify the top three destination
countries of Indian workers. The finding will reinforce the point made in the
above extract.

With a current account surplus (CAS), the volume of money inflow into
India is greater than the money outflow. If the CAS is mainly driven by exports,
the firms that are engaged in export transactions benefit. On the other hand,
if it is mainly because of the inflow of remittances by Indians working abroad,
their households benefit. Thus, in the first case, the exporters gain relative to
the importers and in the second case, the households with a worker in the RoW
gain relative to households who do not have a worker in the RoW, both ceteris
paribus. However, if other things do not remain the same and real wages in
India are growing at a faster rate than real wages in the RoW, our inference
from the second case may not be correct. Which groups in India stand to
relatively benefit when there is a current account deficit (CAD)?

Owing to the double-entry system of accounting, the surplus in the capital
account must be matched by an equivalent deficit in the current account. To
put it the other way around, for an economy to import more than it exports
(that is, $M - X > 0$), the volume of financial inflows must exceed that of
outflows by the volume of the 'excess' imports. If you are keen on obtaining
a more detailed understanding of both current and capital accounts for the
Indian economy, especially in terms of the sources of data and the accounting
procedures, consult the RBI's *Balance of Payments Manual for India* (2010).

Is there a deeper economic connection between a country's capital and
current accounts? The current account captures the net income, which accrues
from an engagement with the RoW, while the capital account captures the
net financial flows (which reflect in the financial assets and liabilities of the
domestic economy). In Chapter 3, we saw how a capital account surplus is not
really desirable for the macroeconomy. Let us revisit that issue. A capital account
surplus is good insofar as it improves the country's net borrowing position
vis-à-vis the RoW. But is being a net borrower a bad economic outcome? It
depends. It is conditional on the nature of the capital account surplus, that is,
whether the surplus is a consequence of FDI, which contributes to the creation

of productive capacity, or (temporary) financial inflows which only seek out a good rate of return. If our primary objective is to increase aggregate activity levels, a net inflow of FDI and commercial borrowings is desirable. However, if our primary objective is to only amass foreign exchange, a capital account surplus arising from net financial inflows is desirable.

The favouring of surplus balances in international trade or in government accounts appears to arise from the (flawed) logic that what is good for an individual is also good for the macroeconomy. Just earlier, it was pointed out why there is no a priori reason to favour a CAS. Instead, the decisions to influence the items in the current account ought to depend on India's *long-term* socio-economic priorities, and they are significantly influenced by the level of existing technological and natural resources. For instance, if India lacks the requisite volume of minerals and necessary machinery to manufacture solar panels for the Indian populace, until we are able to produce them domestically, importing them is essential.

This section will be complete after we discuss the impact of the exchange rate on aggregate output levels. In Section 3.5, we briefly discussed exchange rates and how they are connected to domestic interest rates. India does not let the global demand and supply of rupee *fully* determine its exchange rate; through a strategic buying and selling of foreign currencies in the foreign exchange market, the RBI partly influences and controls the exchange rate. What happens to our exchange rate when the RBI raises the policy rate of interest?

When the INR depreciates, it favours the exporters because exports become cheaper (in terms of USD). However, the depreciation of the INR discourages imports because to purchase the same quantity of imports, the importers now need to part with more INR to obtain the same amount of USD (to pay for the imports). That is, the imports become costlier. Therefore, we can say that, in general, a currency depreciation encourages exporters and discourages importers and an appreciation encourages importers and discourages exporters, ceteris paribus (that is, no changes in relative prices, technology, unchanged interdependence of exports and imports within firms, and so on).

When exports increase relative to imports, ceteris paribus, aggregate output and employment levels in the Indian economy increase. On the other hand, when imports increase relative to exports, ceteris paribus, aggregate output and employment in the Indian economy decreases. In both these situations, what do you think happens to the aggregate output and employment levels in the RoW?

4.4 Conclusion

This chapter adopted a macro approach to understand the determinants of aggregate output and employment levels, the first of the two objectives Smith assigned to political economy. In Section 4.2, the key arguments found in the marginalist and Keynesian theories of output and employment were outlined, and the latter was favoured over the former for its conceptual strength and explanatory prowess. In the marginalist theory, the free operation of market forces generates full employment of labour, whereas Keynesian theory demonstrates that there is no tendency to full employment of labour. Section 4.3 discussed macrodynamics in the open economy, drawing upon Section 3.5. Here, we outlined the role the exchange rate plays in determining the output and employment levels in the Indian economy. The role of geopolitics in international trade was mentioned after a succinct discussion about the current account and the nature of India's commodity imports and export destinations.

Two important qualifications are in order. First, in countries like India, which face supply-side constraints such as inadequate physical infrastructure, rough supply chains in agriculture and high social costs from labour migration, the adjustment of aggregate supply to aggregate demand can be slow and costly. Second, we assume that the demand and supply of labour are sensitive to changes in wages—that is, we assume the presence of wage-labour and not slave-labour or other such forms. In India, as has been noted in the previous chapters, caste-labour occupies a central presence and, therefore, the adjustment of employment we expect to see based on the theory might not happen in reality.

In the short, poignant story, 'Thakur's Well' (1932) by Premchand, Gangi, who is not allowed to draw water from the well due to her Dalit identity, overhears the following conversation between two women who are *allowed* to draw water from Thakur's well.

> If we aren't slaves, then what are we? Don't you get your food and clothes from them? Somehow or the other you also manage to get ten or five rupees. In what ways are slaves any different? (p. 4)

While the above extract is indicative of labour immobility arising from extreme poverty, Gangi's immobility is owing to her being Dalit. Therefore, a comprehensive understanding of the nature of the employment in India warrants a scrutiny of the networks and cultural privileges enjoyed by the dominant castes in securing well-paying jobs, both in private and government sectors (Section 7.2 contains a short indirect discussion on this issue).

Suggestions for further reading

A concise and accessible account of the Keynesian vis-à-vis the marginalist theory of output and employment is found in Tony Aspromourgos's 2009 article 'John Maynard Keynes and the Preservation of Liberal Capitalism', published in the journal *Australian Quarterly* (vol. 81, no. 4, pp. 17–24). For longer accounts of Keynes's theory and policy proposals, consult these books, both published in 2009, and written in the aftermath of the 2008 Global Financial Crisis: Peter Clarke's *Keynes: The Rise, Fall, and Return of the 20th Century's Most Influential Economist* (London: Bloomsbury) and Robert Skidelsky's *Keynes: The Return of the Master* (New York: Public Affairs). To obtain a critical perspective on the role of FDI in India, look at my 2016 article 'The Foreign Hand Isn't Enough' in the newspaper *The Hindu* (8 September, p. 9). A concise and critical account of the different approaches found in contemporary marginalist macroeconomics, at an intermediate level, is available in Chapter 7 (especially pp. 146–59) of Alessandro Roncaglia's 2019 book *The Age of Fragmentation: A History of Contemporary Economic Thought* (Cambridge: Cambridge University Press). A good follow-up to this chapter is the 1983 book *Keynes's Economics and the Theory of Value and Distribution*, edited by John Eatwell and Murray Milgate (New York: Oxford University Press); if this book is difficult to access, you might be happy to learn that 7 out of the 15 chapters were earlier published as articles in the *Cambridge Journal of Economics*.

5

Economic Growth

5.1 Introduction

At the very beginning of this book (Section 1.1), some of the motivating factors behind our decision to study economics were listed. One of them was the question: how to improve the per capita availability of goods and services? In other words, how does aggregate output per worker (Y/N) grow over time? The rate of growth of Y/N is an indicator of the health of an economy. For instance, if the Indian economy is growing at a good pace, it means that, on average, the income per person is also witnessing a good growth. However, owing to the effect of extreme values on averages, we can never be certain whether the growth is primarily driven by a tiny group of chief executive officers (CEOs) whose incomes grew substantially or owing to an increase in the agricultural incomes for a vast number of rural workers. And nor can we ascertain whether the agricultural sector as a whole is growing. To learn about the nature of growth (or in the language of statistics, the distribution of growth), we need to adopt a meso approach—this is what we do in Section 5.3. Given these considerations, treat the growth rate of an economy (growth of gross domestic product, or GDP) as you would treat the blurb of a book—as a reasonable guide to the story, but unable to provide the complete picture.

The previous chapter provided the determinants of output and employment *levels* in both closed and open economy settings. To continue with the analogy of the *idli*, while the last chapter examined the determinants of its size, the present chapter looks at the growth in its size over time. 'Economic growth' is the study of the evolution of the size of output or output per worker over time. Contemplate whether the determinants of output levels and output growth are necessarily the same; or would you expect the determinants of growth to be different from those of output levels?

This chapter relaxes a key assumption made in the previous chapter, that of given productive capacity. A study of economic growth warrants a study of the growth of productive capacity. What is the role of technological progress in economic growth? How much of aggregate investment is devoted to technological innovations that aid the speedy expansion of productive capacity? At the same time, growth in productive capacity (aggregate supply) by itself is not sufficient for economic growth; it requires growth in aggregate demand too. In this context, investment plays a dual role: it is a component of current aggregate demand and it also adds to the productive capacity. To put it more simply, investment contributes to *both* aggregate demand and aggregate supply.

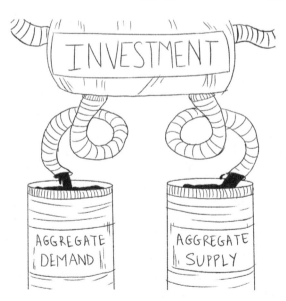

With these introductory observations, we can move on to discuss the two broad theories of economic growth found in the economics literature.

5.2 Theories of economic growth

Much like our discussion of the two broad theories of output and employment, the theories of economic growth (or growth theories, in short) can also be classified into two broad categories—supply-side and demand-led theories. There exists another connection with the discussion in Section 4.2; while the supply-side growth theories are founded upon the marginalist theory of output, the demand-led growth theories take their foundations from the Keynesian theory of output. To put it very crudely, supply-side growth theories extend the (short-run) logic of the marginalist theory of output to the long run and demand-led growth theories extend the (short-run) logic of the Keynesian theory of output to the long run. Recall that the short run refers to the state of affairs when productive capacity is given, and the long run refers to the state of affairs when productive capacity changes or evolves. And also recall that, in the previous chapter, under the short-run condition of given productive capacity, investment implied an increase in the utilisation of existing productive capacity.

Supply-side growth theories

The main workhorse of the supply-side growth theories is the aggregate production function, which expresses a functional relationship between inputs—labour (L), capital (K) and technology (A)—and output (Y), usually written as $Y = A f(L, K)$. It is assumed that the aggregate production function exhibits constant returns to scale (CRS) and diminishing returns to the following factors of production: labour and capital. That is, the first assumption tells us that if the factor inputs are multiplied by a factor of, say, two, the output will also double. The second assumption implies that the addition to total output decreases as the doses of capital are increased (while holding the labour input fixed) and that the addition to total output decreases as the doses of labour are increased (when the capital input is held constant). That is, labour and capital are characterised by diminishing marginal products. Think about how (un)realistic these two assumptions are. Now, suppose that you assume increasing returns to scale (IRS) and constant returns to a factor; trace their implications separately for an aggregate production function.

A very specific theory of functional income distribution—the theory which explains how much each social class or factor of production ought to receive in return for their contribution to the economy—is embedded in the marginalist aggregate production function. Supply-side growth theories adopt the marginal productivity theory of income distribution, which states that under conditions of perfect competition, equilibrium wage equals the marginal product of labour and equilibrium rate of profit equals the marginal product of capital. Moreover, at the equilibrium wage, there is full employment of labour.

Supply-side growth theories are inspired by the marginalist theory of exchange (wherein the factor endowments are given). This has significant conceptual (and therefore practical) implications because the idea of scarcity is built into the theoretical edifice of supply-side growth theories, and, consequently, an exogenous growth in technology (A) and primary inputs (notably, labour) are what generate economic growth. Another concept which accentuates the 'scarcity' in these theories is the assumption of diminishing returns to capital. For, as more and more capital is accumulated, the addition to the total output diminishes. This is perhaps the key reason why in the Solow growth model (1956), the foundational model within the supply-side growth theories, a growth in capital (assumed equivalent to saving) cannot *permanently* influence the growth rate of the economy.

The Solow growth model and other supply-side growth models extensively employ the aggregate production function of the Cobb-Douglas variety that exhibit diminishing returns to capital and constant returns to scale. Moreover, in the Solow growth model, given its marginalist foundations, unsurprisingly, there is full employment of labour at the steady state 'equilibrium'—a conception wherein capital and labour are growing at the same constant rate. Furthermore, since there is only one commodity in the Solow growth model, all saving is automatically invested. This implies that it does not need to address the important question of how decentralised decisions to save and invest are coordinated in a monetary production economy. Think about whether and how aggregate demand deficiency plays a role in the Solow model.

Let us now take a brief look at the intellectual context in which Robert Solow developed his growth model. Roy Harrod (1939) had extended the Keynesian theory of output to the long run. In particular, Harrod highlighted the difficulty of a competitive economy to achieve stable growth with full employment. Solow, by utilising the marginalist paradigm (especially, the theories of value, income distribution and output), and, in particular, the assumption of well-behaved and continuous substitutability between labour and capital, arrived at a conclusion opposite to that of Harrod: in the long run, a competitive economy can achieve stable growth with full employment. And thus, the pessimism of Harrod's growth model was replaced by the optimism of Solow's growth model.

The initial supply-side growth models treated technology as exogenous to the model, that is, the model did not explain the determinants of technological progress. Later models, starting from the work of Paul Romer (1986; also see his 1994 article on the origins of endogenous growth models), endogenised technology or ideas (A), leading to a class of models termed 'endogenous growth models'. In these models, A is determined by factors within the model. While A positively influences economic growth, perpetual growth still is not possible because of the counteracting force of diminishing returns to capital. But note that both the exogenous and endogenous growth models in the supply-side tradition rely on the marginalist theory of output. And, more importantly, in these models, the possibility of aggregate demand deficiency is ruled out.

The optimism of supply-side growth theories, it must be recognised, is a consequence of their marginalist foundations. The policy stance prescribed by these theories is, therefore, one of significant non-intervention by the government, or more specifically, the deregulation of labour and other markets. In addition, the policy implication from these theories is that a small government keeps the economy competitive and thereby generates stable growth with full employment. The endogenous growth model of Romer highlighted that A (or ideas) generates positive externalities, which the market mechanism is unable to price correctly and, therefore, ideas are underproduced in the market. Romer's main policy suggestions are the following: subsidies for research and development, and a market for patents. The latter aims to create an additional market—that of ideas, as it were—in order to internalise the externality.

Demand-led growth theories

Demand-led growth theories eschew such a functional one-way relationship running from the inputs or factors of production to aggregate output. Instead, they employ the conceptual tools of (*a*) structural interdependence, (*b*) autonomous elements of aggregate demand (discussed in Section 4.2) and/ or the (*c*) supermultiplier (which integrates the concepts of the accelerator and the multiplier discussed in the previous chapter).

Structural interdependence makes it impossible to visualise production as a one-way relationship between the factors of production and aggregate output because, to paraphrase the title of Sraffa's 1960 book, commodities are produced by means of commodities. To put it differently, parts of the output (Y) must also be found among the inputs; this is the circular view of production found in the classical economists as opposed to a linear view of production visible in the marginalist economists. This view of production underlies the classical theory of value and (income) distribution. Furthermore, no unidirectional causation is suggested between technological progress and economic growth; rather the link between technological progress, aggregate demand and economic growth is contingent on several factors and, therefore, the relationship is not amenable to any a priori quantitative formulation. Depending on the context, technological progress may have positive or negative effects on economic growth. For instance, in a labour-rich economy, the benefits from introducing labour-saving technology may be partly offset or even more than offset by the reduction in aggregate demand (due to the reduced aggregate income as a consequence of labour unemployment). Owing to their understanding of growth, stemming from classical economics, demand-led growth theories call for a greater engagement with history because of the important role played by contextual factors. In other words, growth is path dependent.

While there are several models within demand-led growth theories, here we focus on one class of models which originate from the pioneering work of Pierangelo Garegnani (1978; 1979), wherein he provided a synthesis of the classical theory of value and distribution and the Keynesian theory of output. Important contributions to this class of demand-led growth theories came from the works of Franklin Serrano (1995), Antonella Palumbo and Attilio Trezzini (2003) and, much more recently, Matthew Smith (2012).

According to Serrano and others, economic growth is determined by growth of the autonomous elements of aggregate demand. These autonomous elements could be autonomous consumption, autonomous investment, government expenditure or exports. Both government expenditure and exports are treated as autonomous elements of aggregate demand because they are independent of the current levels of (domestic) aggregate output. Moreover, according to this set of growth theories, owing to their Keynesian core, growth is not necessarily associated with the full employment of labour. Therefore, demand-led growth models envisage a crucial role for government expenditure in achieving economic growth and the full employment of labour.

In Smith's 2012 demand-led growth model, economic growth (g^Y_t) is primarily driven by the growth of autonomous demand (g^D_t), that is, government expenditure, autonomous consumption, autonomous investment and net exports (recall the discussion on autonomous and induced elements of aggregate demand in Section 4.2); t refers to the current time period and t-1 to the previous time period.

$$g^Y_t = g^D_t + \Delta m_t \, (D_t/D_{t-1})$$

Δm_t refers to the change in the supermultiplier. John Hicks, a pioneer of marginalist macroeconomics, had originally introduced this concept to link autonomous demand to equilibrium output via changes in induced expenditure. In Smith's demand-led growth model, variations in the utilisation of capacity allow the adjustment of aggregate supply to aggregate demand. D refers to autonomous demand and it is assumed to be non-capacity creating.

Demand-led growth theories, following Sraffa's restatement of the classical theory of value and distribution, treat income distribution as an outcome of past and present politics *and* policy. More precisely, Sraffa demonstrated in his 1960 book that if the size and composition of output, technology and wages are known (and given), the relative prices of commodities and the rate of profit can be uniquely determined. Since one distributive variable (the wage) is treated as given, this value theory is known as 'value through exogenous distribution'; this label is taken from Krishna Bharadwaj's title of her much-acclaimed review of Sraffa's book published in the *Economic Weekly* (1963). The past and present politics *and* policy include workers' movements, women's rights movements, trade union actions, collective bargaining, wage policy and monetary policy. It is important to keep in mind that monetary policy also has an impact on income distribution via its impact on the rate of profit (and consequently, on wages).

Within the demand-led growth theories, there is no 'scarcity' because they are built upon a theory of production wherein capital goods can be produced in line with their demand; after all, capital is nothing but produced means of production. It is realistically assumed that labour supply is not a binding constraint on growth owing to the presence of unemployment, underemployment and the acknowledgement that labour supply can be increased via an appropriate migration policy. It is also important to note that the classical theory of value and distribution adopts a surplus approach. That is, after the necessary expenditure is deducted from the aggregate output so as to ensure that the economic system reproduces itself, the amount that is left over is the social surplus—to be utilised as the society wishes.

In order to help you clearly and compactly see the differences between supply-side and demand-led growth theories, a tabular summary respectively outlining the key principle, policy implication and assumptions is provided in Table 5.1.

Table 5.1   Demand-led and supply-side growth theories: a table of differences

	Demand-led growth theories	*Supply-side growth theories*
Central principle	• A growth in autonomous elements of aggregate demand generates growth	• A growth in labour and technology generates growth
Policy implication	• Active and systematic government intervention in order to attain full employment of labour	• Leave markets alone, that is, minimize government intervention in order to attain full employment of labour
Key assumptions	• Classical theory of value and distribution ◆ Circular view of production ◆ Exogenous distribution ◆ Surplus approach • Keynesian theory of output ◆ Planned saving adapts to planned investment via variations in aggregate output	• Marginalist theory of value and distribution ◆ Linear view of production ◆ Endogenous distribution ◆ Scarcity approach • Marginalist theory of output ◆ Planned investment adapts to planned saving via variations in the rate of interest

Since this is an introductory book on macroeconomics, detailed discussions of the Solow/Romer and the Serrano/Smith growth models are not undertaken. However, for those interested in the mechanics of these models, I would recommend reading the original articles in which their ideas are presented, because some of the caveats found in those articles are missing in many of their subsequent representations in textbooks (including the one you are currently reading).

The further implications for macroeconomic policy in the Indian context will be dealt with in greater detail in later chapters (especially, Chapters 7 and 8). In Section 7.3, a brief critical discussion of the Mahalanobis growth model (which formed the basis of India's Second Five-Year Plan) will be carried out.

An exercise is now in order: read the book *An Uncertain Glory: India and Its Contradictions* (2013) by Jean Drèze and Amartya Sen, and ascertain whether the growth theory underlying their work is supply-side or demand-led in nature.

Classical growth theories

A common refrain from students when I introduce the Solow model in class is: were there no theories of growth before? The conventional approach has been to take Harrod or Solow as the pioneers of growth theory. It is, therefore, interesting to read Solow's own admission on this matter from his Nobel lecture in 1987: "Growth theory did not begin with my articles of 1956 and 1957, and it certainly did not end there. Maybe it began with *The Wealth of Nations*; and probably even Adam Smith had predecessors." In rare instances, Smith or Ricardo may be discussed briefly as mere historical figures who attempted to provide a growth theory. As a matter of fact, there are modern attempts to formalise and model their ideas of economic growth. One such notable attempt is Walter Eltis's *The Classical Theory of Economic Growth* (1984), which presents the growth theories of Quesnay, Smith, Ricardo, Malthus and Marx, with extensive commentaries based on excerpts from their texts as well as simple algebraic modelling. Thus, the answer to the students' question is very much in the affirmative.

In the following paragraphs, I provide a very brief overview of the growth accounts found in Smith, Ricardo and Marx. And at the very outset, I must point out that their growth frameworks are still relevant and can aid us in understanding contemporary economic growth.

In *An Inquiry into the Nature and Causes of Wealth of Nations* (1776), Smith identifies the following determinants of economic growth: net investment, technological progress ('division of labour') and, indirectly, the growth of aggregate demand (via the 'extent of the market'). The 'extent of the market' imposes a constraint on the 'division of labour' and the increase in the 'division of labour' facilitates the widening of the 'extent of the market'. The mechanism is as follows. The increase in aggregate supply brought about by technological progress needs to be validated by an equivalent aggregate demand; and to some extent, the same increase in aggregate supply generates additional incomes, which widen the 'extent of the market'. Net investment (that is, gross investment minus depreciation) implies additions to productive capacity and/or increase in capacity utilisation, both of which increase levels of production and, therefore, aggregate supply. Technological progress causes economic growth in Smith, provided there is adequate aggregate demand. Although, in Smith's writing, more attention is paid to the consequences of an improvement in the 'division of labour' relative to the constraints imposed by the 'extent of the market'.

Ricardo's and Marx's views on economic growth are found in their *Principles of Political Economy* (1817) and the three volumes of *Capital* (1867, 1885, 1894), respectively. But note that the second and third volumes of *Capital* were published only after Marx's death and they contain significant interventions by their respective editors. These texts of Smith, Ricardo and Marx are classics, and reading them from cover to cover gives the reader a comprehensive account of their entire economics—with macro, meso and micro approaches dealing with economic growth, population dynamics, social classes and their consumption behaviour, wage and profit determination, monetary issues and rich contextual discussions on the nature and progress of technology. In a way, even reading one of these texts in toto is akin to doing a crash course in economics.

Ricardo, like Smith, sees net investment as central to economic growth. However, he does not emphasise the constraining role of the 'extent of the market' in economic growth as much as Smith does, and he underscores the diminishing returns characterising land and agricultural production. Unless there is technological progress, diminishing returns to land can lead to economic decline and stagnation. In a way, this can perhaps be viewed as an early recognition of the ecological constraints on economic growth. Ricardo also understood that progress in technology almost always displaces labour and is, therefore, not beneficial to everyone.

The political economy of Marx provides us with the reasons as to why a capitalist economy is prone to frequent crisis, that is, non-steady growth. This is in complete contrast to the supply-side growth theories that, ironically, try to ascertain the (equilibrium) conditions for the steady-state growth of a competitive economy (this is a *peculiar* theoretical formulation in which all the relevant variables are growing at the same rate). Marx locates the sources of crises in primarily two macroeconomic factors: (*a*) the disproportionality between sectors in the economy and (*b*) underconsumption. The latter suggests that the aggregate consumption level is less than what is necessary to validate the aggregate supply; this is a consequence of the depressed wages of the workers. The former refers to a situation wherein the input needs of some sectors are not being accurately met by the output of other sectors (or the converse) and, as a consequence, the aggregate output contracts; the precise nature of this structural interdependence can be captured by an input–output framework (see Table 2.1).

It is possible to view the growth theories of Smith, Ricardo and Marx as being more aligned to the demand-led growth theories except for one important difference. The classical growth theories lack an account of equilibration of planned saving and investment. However, this is different from the marginalist theory of output wherein planned investment adapts to (full-employment) planned saving via variations in a sufficiently sensitive rate of interest. It must be clear to some of you by now that the natural home for the classical theories of economic growth is the demand-led growth theory framework. Or, to be chronologically consistent, some classes of demand-led growth theories take inspiration from the classical theories of growth.

5.3 The nature of economic growth in India

Understanding the nature of economic growth of any economy is, or ought to be, a contextual exercise. Here, in examining the nature of India's economic growth, I am adopting the demand-led growth theory framework, which also draws on and sits amicably with the growth theories of Smith, Ricardo and Marx, insofar as they highlight the importance of contextual factors vis-à-vis the supply-side approaches to economic growth. The following extract from Tony Aspromourgos's chapter 'Sraffa's System in Relation to Currents in Unorthodox Economics' from the third and final volume of *Sraffa and the Reconstruction of Economic Theory* (2013) provides additional inspiration for the present exercise.

... is not discontinuous growth exactly our experience of actual growth with cyclical characteristics? In any case, these kinds of dynamics—with particular sectors' autonomous demand growth only temporarily driving growth, but all the sectors together perhaps enabling something like continuous growth— amount to a 'messy' sort of growth theory. But if sustained growth of effective demand in decentralised economies is a messy and contingent business in reality, then it is not necessarily to be regretted that the *theory* of the process is messy as well. (p. 28, emphasis in original)

We, therefore, follow a macro as well as a meso approach in this section. While it is possible to look at several aspects of India's growth, I shall focus on the following:

1. economic growth and its connection to historical inequalities,
2. growth of agricultural, manufacturing and service sectors,
3. the link between economic growth and employment creation,
4. the connection between rate of profit and rate of economic growth, and
5. the impact of economic growth on our ecology.

Economic growth and unequal land ownership

Any exercise that attempts to understand the nature of growth should pay attention to the initial conditions. A good analogy to convey the significance of the initial conditions would be the idea of compound interest. How much do the initial sums of INR 1,000 and INR 1,400 translate into after five years if both earn an interest of 6 per cent compounded monthly? INR 1,349 and INR 1,888. Notice that the initial difference between the sums was only INR 400, but after the compounding, there is a difference of INR 539. One of the underlying reasons for economic growth (compounding) is the inter-sectoral and intra-sectoral linkages which produce multiplier effects (recall the discussion of the multiplier in Section 4.2). In both supply-side and demand-led growth theories, the initial level of aggregate output is not a determinant of the rate of growth of aggregate output. However, understanding the nature of economic growth warrants a study of the initial conditions.

The Indian economy's initial condition is a complex web of colonialism, caste system, patriarchy, unequal land ownership, rain-dependent agriculture, availability of minerals and natural resources, and so on. Since the majority of Indians are engaged in the agricultural sector, let us take a look at the ownership of land; it is an important marker of social and economic status and a source of financial security. The connection between land and its owner need not be purely an economic one as the following excerpt from Kesava Reddy's *Moogavani Pillanagrovi: Ballad of Ontillu* (2013), a Telugu novella, shows.

> "But I am no longer a farmer myself," he [the protagonist] said to himself, "my land has been snatched from me, the way a chick was snatched from a mother's hen by a hawk." ... He had lost his land. All the connections that had joined him to the earth were broken. Now he had nothing to do with anyone in the village. He could never show his face again anywhere. (pp. 26, 28)

According to the 2013 All-India Debt and Investment Survey (AIDIS) carried out by the National Sample Survey Organisation (NSSO), the share of land in the total value of assets in rural India is 72.60 per cent and in urban India, it is 46.95 per cent (NSS 70th Round, p. 14, Statement 3.3). This statistic underscores the fact that land occupies an important place in the asset composition of Indians, particularly of those living in rural areas.

Table 5.2   Distribution of land holdings in India

Category of holdings	Percentage of households (%)	Percentage of land owned (%)	Average area owned per household (ha)
Marginal	75.42	29.75	0.234
Small	10.00	23.54	1.394
Semi-medium	5.01	22.07	2.606
Medium	1.93	18.83	5.782
Large	0.24	5.81	14.447

Source: NSS 70th Round, *Key Indicators of Land and Livestock Holdings in India* p. 10.

Notes: The data is for 2012–13; 'ha' denotes hectares. Marginal refers to landholdings whose area is more than 0.002 hectares but less than or equal to 1 hectare; small to landholdings whose area is more than 1 hectare but less than or equal to 2 hectares; semi-medium to landholdings whose area is more than 2 hectares but less than or equal to 4 hectares; medium to landholdings whose area is more than 4 hectares but less than or equal to 10 hectares; and large to landholdings whose area is more than 10 hectares (p. 8). The 'percentage of households' column does not add up to 100 because I have excluded the percentage of landless (7.41%) from the table.

The inequality of land ownership in India is evident from Table 5.2: 75.42 per cent of households own between 0.002 and 1 hectare of land, whereas 0.24

per cent of households own more than 10 hectares of land. Also notice the wide disparity in the average area of land owned by Indian households—it varies from significantly less than 1 hectare to more than 14 hectares. The purpose of Table 5.2 is not to draw direct conclusions from it, but to indicate the presence of inequality of land ownership in India. It highlights the unequal initial conditions for Indians, which have consequences on their ability to participate and partake in the process of economic growth. As questioned in Section 1.4, why is the ownership of land so unequal? Can economic growth in the present adequately compensate for past inequalities? The answers to these questions will need recourse to the study of other social science subjects, in addition to economics. While the answers to these questions are beyond the scope of this introductory text, it should be noted that the question of economic growth cannot ignore other historical inequalities, particularly those arising from the entrenched social orders of caste and gender.

The vexed question of land ownership in India is narrated with sardonic wit in the following passage excerpted from Shrilal Shukla's *Raag Darbari* (1968).

> Outside the village, there was a wide, open plain which was gradually becoming barren. Now, not even grass grew on it. It looked like ideal land to give away to Vinoba Bhave's Bhoodan Movement. And indeed it had been. Two years earlier, this land had been donated for the betterment of the landless as part of the Bhoodan Movement. Then it had been taken back as a gift by the village council. Then the village council had gifted it to the pradhan. The pradhan had gifted it first to his friends and relations and, on a straight cash-sale basis, disposed of the remaining part to some of the poor and landless. Afterwards it turned out that the plots which had been distributed to the poor and landless were not part of this land, but in fact, fell within the boundaries of someone's farm. Litigation started over this, it was still continuing, and was expected to continue for some time. (p. 149)

To obtain a sense of the difficulty in identifying individual owners of land in India, find out the state of land records in your town or village through oral interviews. Also, find out how much of the land is owned by the government.

Sectoral economic growth

Now, let us understand economic growth by adopting a meso approach and examine the growth rates of the agricultural, manufacturing and service sectors. More than the GDP growth rate—which is anyway only *an* indicator for the growth of the economy as a whole or the macroeconomy—what matters *more* to the economic well-being of individuals is the growth of the sector to which they belong. For instance, a construction worker's economic well-being is much more connected to the growth rate of the 'industry' sector (of which construction is a part) than to the GDP. More specifically, we can assess their well-being, on average, by looking at the rate of growth of the construction industry. Hence, to have a more disaggregated understanding of the growth process, we look at the sectoral growth rates. But, of course, the growth of the sector need not always translate into an improvement in their well-being.

Table 5.3   India's sectoral growth rates

Sector	2014–15	2016–17
Agriculture, forestry, fishing	**−0.2**	**4.9**
Industry	**7.5**	**5.6**
i. Manufacturing	8.3	7.9
ii. Construction	4.7	1.7
Services	**9.7**	**7.7**
i. Trade	9.0	7.8
ii. Financial, real estate	11.1	5.7
iii. Public administration	8.1	11.3
GDP_{MP}	**7.5**	**7.1**

Source: *Economic Survey 2017–18*, vol. 2, p. 3.

From Table 5.3, two sets of questions can be posed: (*a*) Is there a relationship between agricultural growth and manufacturing growth? Is there a link between agricultural growth and construction growth? Is there some relation between manufacturing growth and growth in finance? (*b*) Should the financial sector have a high growth rate? Should public administration grow slowly? Should agriculture grow more relative to manufacturing?

Recall the discussion from Section 2.4 wherein the economy was conceptualised as a web of flows crisscrossing from one sector to another. Also, particularly, recall Table 2.1—an input–output account of the Indian economy for the year 2007–8. It was clear that a shock to or stagnation of the agricultural sector has adverse effects on the other two sectors. From Table 5.3, it may be inferred that it is the negative growth in agriculture and allied sectors that facilitated (via distress migration) a high growth in the construction sector in 2014–15. And in 2016–17, when agricultural growth picked up, the growth in the construction sector dampened. Of course, a part of the reason for the dampening of construction sector growth could be deficient aggregate demand. As an exercise, make a note of government policies that you think will improve agricultural and manufacturing growth rates.

Do you think the growth of the finance sector positively influences the growth of the other sectors? An answer to this requires us to recognise the nature of the interconnection between financial firms and other participants in the macroeconomy (illustrated in Figures 2.2 and 3.1). While the marginalist approach views the financial sector as an essential sector on par with manufacturing, the demand-led growth approach, drawing on the classical economists and Keynes, views the finance sector as a subordinate sector from the point of view of the macroeconomy (owing to its inability to directly create productive capacity). And in opposition to the marginalist economists who claimed that 'finance' does not affect the level of goods and services produced in the economy as a whole, Keynes argued that it does.

One of the arguments advanced by Aldo Barba and Giancarlo de Vivo (2012), two economists working in the tradition of classical economics, is that the households' need for finance arises from their low wages and uncertain employment. Households borrow because of inadequate incomes (see the sub-section 'Are Indian jobs well paying?' in Section 7.2). Additionally, they argue that unlike, for instance, agriculture, manufacturing, education and health, finance does not contribute to the productive capacity of an economy. More generally, it may be stated that the financial sector grows when the non-financial sectors are not doing well (or when the non-financial sectors are doing extremely well and are exuberant in their future expectations about the course of the macroeconomy).

Another question to think about is: what does a high growth of public administration reflect? For instance, we need to ascertain whether this is a consequence of a growth in government jobs or that of value added to public administration as a consequence of outsourcing their traditional jobs to private policy consultancies. Unless we examine sectoral (and sub-sectoral) growth rates, we cannot obtain a *complete* picture of the nature of economic growth.

Economic growth and employment generation

As mentioned early on in this chapter (Section 5.1), we are interested in economic growth because it provides a rough indication of the growth in availability of goods and services. However, for growth to actually manifest in the well-being of individuals, this growth must create well-paying jobs, increase wages for existing jobs and/or reduce the working hours. In India, where underemployment and unemployment are omnipresent, we need economic growth to urgently provide us with increased and better jobs. Table 5.4 is a summary of the combined growth rates of GDP and employment from 1986 to 2015.

Table 5.4   GDP growth and employment growth in India

	1986–93	1993–99	1999–2004	2004–09	2009–11	2011–15
GDP growth (%)	5.6	6.8	5.7	8.7	7.4	6.8
Employment growth (%)	2.4	1.0	2.8	0.1	1.4	0.6

Source: *SWI* 2018, p. 40, Fig. 2.1(a).

It provides us with an unequivocal insight: India's economic growth has not resulted in employment growth in general, and it has been particularly bad since 2004. This is another compelling reason to adopt the demand-led growth approach to understand India's growth experience because its conceptual structure is extremely open to different historical contexts and therefore also in incorporating contingencies or shocks. Is it the case that the benefits from growth are translated into increased wages for the majority of Indians? Unfortunately, the answer is not in the affirmative. This undesirable possibility was explicitly recognised in the second chapter of India's Second Five-Year Plan (1956–61) document created by the Planning Commission, a body under the Central Government (the Planning Commission was dissolved in 2014).

> Economic development has in the past often been associated with growing inequalities of income and wealth. The gains of development accrue in the early stages to a small class of businessmen and manufacturers, whereas the immediate impact of the application of new techniques in agriculture and in traditional industry has often meant growing unemployment or under-employment among large numbers of people. In course of time this trend gets corrected partly through the development of countervailing power of trade unions and partly through state action undertaken in response to the growth of democratic ideas.

In particular, note the emphasis on the positive role of workers' unions and planned government action. As K. N. Raj rightly notes in the first of the three lectures he delivered at the National Bank of Egypt in Cairo, later published as 'Employment Aspects of Planning in Under-developed Economies' (1957), "an approach to the problems of growth in such economies [like India], which does not take into account the employment aspects, and does not pose the issues involved in alternative courses with reference to their implications in terms of employment, is too divorced from the realities to be of any practical value" (p. 2). Should not the government we elect place employment generation (with fair wages and decent working conditions) as the central economic priority?

In a country like India, which suffers from severe supply-side constraints (in terms of the reach and accessibility of physical infrastructure), the government cannot focus only on increasing public expenditure with a view to reviving aggregate demand. It also has to focus on easing supply-side constraints directly by expanding physical infrastructure or indirectly by giving incentives to the private sector or through public–private (not private–public) partnerships. Indeed, alongside investing in physical infrastructure, the government should also significantly invest in social infrastructure, particularly in the areas of education, health and the natural environment. And such systemic economic deficiencies point to the need for systematic economic planning.

On the rates of profit and economic growth

Let us now examine the implications of the profit rate exceeding the growth rate. Thomas Piketty and his *Capital in the 21st Century* (2014) deserve praise for bringing this issue into the centre of contemporary public debate. Using a variety of data sources, he demonstrated that for advanced countries, the rate of return on capital (r) has exceeded the growth rate of the economy (g): $r > g$. A similar exercise was carried out for India by Rishabh Kumar, and its summary is provided in Table 5.5.

Table 5.5   Real growth of national wealth and income in India

Period	Real growth of national wealth (%)	Real growth of national income (%)
1950–1981	3.91	3.83
1981–2012	6.91	6.04

Source: Kumar 2019, p. 15, Table 1.

Given the limitations of statistical data relating to wealth and income in India, these figures need to be interpreted with caution. Do you think wealth begets wealth? In a way, this question is related to our earlier discussion on initial conditions and the nature of economic growth. Also recall that income is a flow variable, while wealth is a stock variable. The possibility of earning income is higher when you are wealthy. Table 5.5 conveys that r has been greater than g since 1950. What does $r > g$ really mean? It indicates that the annual returns obtained by an average wealthy person are greater than the annual income earned by an average regular salaried worker. To put it differently, the growth in rental returns accruing to the (large) landowner is greater than the growth in wages accruing to those who work on the land. Such a structure of growth favours the rentiers over the workers. Again, as expressed before, is this the kind of growth we want?

Economic growth and its ecological impacts

We shall end this section after contrasting India's GDP growth with the growth of CO_2 emissions from just the power sector (see Table 5.6). This provides a good indicator of the ecological effects of economic growth if we assume that the demand for power is positively associated with economic growth.

Table 5.6 Annual growth of CO_2 emissions from India's power sector

2011	2012	2013	2014
3.17	6.58	9.2	4.44

Source: *Compendium of Environment Statistics*, 2016, p. 111, Table 4.14.8(a). I computed the growth rate from the absolute values which were provided.

Moreover, the generation of electric power produces significant pollution. The use of non-renewable resources such as coal and natural gas as input add to the environmental cost/damage.

The following passage from Aseem Shrivastava and Ashish Kothari's 2012 book *Churning the Earth: The Making of Global India* indicates some of the ecological impacts of India's recent economic growth.

> The last couple of decades have therefore seen a massive increase in new infrastructure creation, such as several thousand kilometres of roads, dozens

of ports and airports, urban infrastructure and tens of mega and large power stations. This has meant the increasing diversion of land, mostly of natural ecosystems like forests and coasts, or agricultural fields. It has also meant a spurt in extraction of necessary raw materials, like minerals.... Most of the minerals being demanded are under forested or poor rural areas, rich in biodiversity, and where communities are heavily dependent on the area's resources. (p. 125)

Like earlier, the question to ask is, what kind of economic growth do we want? Should the growth be heavily dependent on using up non-renewable energy sources *and* those activities that produce high pollution? Can we think of an economic growth that is driven by the creation of ecologically friendly infrastructure? After all, the macroeconomy is embedded in the ecological environment (Section 2.3). It is also important to recognise the wishes of the communities living in the area where new physical infrastructure like mines or roads is proposed. An instance of such a neglect of the community's wishes is brought out clearly in 'Baso-jhi', a short story by Hansda Sowvendra Shekhar in his 2015 book *The Adivasi Will Not Dance*.

> Sarjomdih, which stands above the mineral-rich core of the Indian subcontinent. Sarjomdih, outside whose southern frontiers a mine and a copper factory were established, where the Copper Town sprang up, and which was now gradually threatening to swallow all of Sarjomdih. Sarjomdih, which bore the repercussions of development, the nationalization of the mine and the factory, the opening up of two more quarries, and the confiscation of the villagers' properties for the building of roads and living quarters. Sarjomdih, whose men were given jobs as unskilled labourers in the mines and the factory in return for their fecund land. Sarjomdih, which is a standing testimony to the collapse of an agrarian Adivasi society and the dilution of Adivasi culture, the twin gifts of industrialization and progress. (pp. 114–15)

The key point to take away is that the nature or kind of economic growth we want ought to be a matter of collective choice—via politics and policy—of a decentralised nature. For a systematic account of ecological damage through policy (in)action in the Andaman and Nicobar Islands, read Pankaj Sekhsaria's *Islands in Flux: The Andaman and Nicobar Story* (2017), primarily a selection of his previously published journalistic articles.

5.4 Growth in the open economy

According to the mercantilist Mun, who was introduced in Section 1.2, encouraging exports and discouraging imports was the way for an economy to get rich. While discussing open economy macrodynamics in Section 4.3, the zero-sum nature of gains from international trade for the world economy as a whole was noted. An active pursuit of current account surpluses, that is, a net positive money inflow (in return for a net positive commodity outflow), as Robinson had rightly remarked, is indeed a policy that impoverishes the neighbouring macroeconomies.

To reiterate, the central driver of growth according to supply-side growth theories is a growth in the 'factors of production', notably technology. In sharp contrast, in demand-led growth theories, growth is determined by the growth in autonomous elements of aggregate demand; and in the context of an open economy, exports as well. While supply-side growth theories tend to prefer minimal government intervention due to their marginalist nucleus, the demand-led growth theories favour active government intervention, given their Keynesian nucleus. Another point of difference is the way in which technological progress is understood in these two contending approaches. While supply-side growth theories view technological progress as always being favourable to economic growth, in demand-led growth theories the direction and extent of the causal effect cannot be ascertained a priori, and it depends on the context.

In line with the importance ascribed by demand-led growth theories to the contextual factors in understanding economic growth, this section also follows that approach as well as the structure followed in Section 5.3. While it is possible to carry out growth-accounting exercises from the standpoint of both the approaches, in this section we follow an approach to economic growth closer in spirit to that of the classical economists who closely engaged with their respective extant contexts. The demand-led growth theorists mentioned in this chapter are also adopting a similar stance when they call for the need to undertake a macro-historical approach to understanding growth.

Any understanding of economic growth in an open economy like India requires the study of economic inequalities arising from colonialism. While land reforms are undertaken to partly remedy historical injustices within a nation/country, think of the ways in which such restitutive justice can be envisioned for the world economy as a whole. To obtain a comprehensive account of one such approach, read Andre Gunder Frank's 1966 article 'The

Development of Underdevelopment' wherein he argues that the wealthy nations have ensured the 'dependence' of the poor nations through a variety of economic and political means. As articulated in Section 5.3, initial conditions matter, and even more so in an open economy context. For a critical history of the origins of property and the means of production in capitalism, read chapter 26, entitled 'The Secret of Primitive Accumulation', in Volume I of Marx's *Capital*.

It was pointed out in Section 5.3 that more than the growth of the GDP, it is sectoral growth rates that provide a better understanding of the nature of growth. That the nature of growth depends on the extent of inter-sectoral interdependence was also highlighted. Such inter-sectoral dependence is magnified or telescoped, depending on how you perceive it, in the case of the world economy as a whole. The division of labour was explained by Smith, using the example of pin manufacturing in the very first chapter of *The Wealth of Nations*.

> One man draws out the wire, another straights it, a third cuts it, a fourth points it, a fifth grinds it at the top for receiving the head; to make the head requires two or three distinct operations; to put it on, is a peculiar business, to whiten the pins is another; it is even a trade by itself to put them into the paper; and the important business of making a pin is, in this manner, divided into about eighteen distinct operations, which, in some manufactories, are all performed by distinct hands.... (p. 15)

Now, think of the extent of the division of labour if the same pin manufacturing is spread across various countries within the world economy. The structural interdependence with respect to production' (and consumption) between various open economies is massive, as it must have been visible from the Section 4.3 discussion on open economy macrodynamics. In economics, these production networks are known as global value chains. Find out the proportion of intermediate goods (that is, neither primary agricultural goods nor final consumption goods) traded—both exports and imports—to the value of total trade by India. The answer will give an indication of the extent to which India is structurally interdependent on other countries for its production.

India's exports depend on global demand (for both capital and consumption goods), assuming a given exchange rate (see Section 4.3). Moreover, given the volume of global demand and the exchange rate, ceteris paribus, the magnitude of exports depend on relative prices—the price of Indian exports relative to, say, that of the United States (US). Given both past and present international political inequalities, the competitiveness of Indian exports depends on the extent of subsidies provided to US farmers by their government. As already noted in Section 4.3, both national and international trade agreements influence open economy dynamics. In addition, an understanding of economic growth in an open economy warrants the study of geographical conditions or, more broadly, the productive capacity of all the member countries in the world economy.

While constraints of caste, gender and language make inter-state migration of workers difficult, in the open economy context, immigration policies pose an additional constraint. Community networks based on caste and religion have played a critical role in international migration (this has been briefly alluded to in Section 4.3). In fact, given the presence of underemployment and unemployment in most countries, the full employment assumption of marginalist economics belies any empirical foundation. As an exercise, find out the caste and 'skill' compositions of Indians who have migrated for work to the United Arab Emirates and the US in the last five years. Also, go through the list of occupations welcomed by countries such as Australia and Canada, and discuss the underlying reasons for demanding such labour.

International financial flows (foreign institutional investors, or FIIs, being one such route) search for the economy that offers the highest rate of return (adjusting for risk) in order to maximise the return on their financial capital. However, international investment flows (such as foreign direct investment, or FDI) look for economies that are characterised by macroeconomic stability and stable economic growth. In reality, such a strict separation of international investment and financial flows may not be found because of the connections, owing to policies, between interest rates and economic growth. Despite this simplification, FII, as noted in Section 3.5, is more volatile than FDI and, therefore, cannot be relied upon to generate stable growth. However, insofar as FDI searches for the sector/economy offering the highest rate of profit, like any other kind of private investment, the heavy reliance on FDI is not wise from the perspective of the Keynesian theory of output and employment. Often, owing to their adherence to the marginalist principles, economists and policymakers favour the 'free' coming in and going out of financial flows. And, just like the states within India compete with each other for FDI, countries compete too, by relaxing labour laws and providing tax concessions. Given the higher volatility of FDI relative to private domestic investment, the classical–Keynesian demand-led growth theories favour domestic investment over foreign.

CARBON CREDITS

CARBON TAX

While Section 5.3 highlighted the fact that the *nature* of growth is a matter of collective choice for a closed economy, it is extremely difficult, as history has shown, even with bodies like the Intergovernmental Panel on Climate Change (IPCC), to have collective decision-making for the world economy as a whole. Even with these international decision-making organisations, apart from the geopolitical power dynamics in play, their adherence to the supply-side growth approach is problematic. Let us look at one such problematic instance. William Nordhaus had extended Solow's growth theory to ecological issues by incorporating environmental protection as an important constraint; for this, he was awarded the 2018 Nobel prize along with Romer. Nordhaus introduced energy as an additional 'factor of production' in the Solow model. As noted by the Royal Swedish Academy of Sciences (2018), Nordhaus's research suggests that "the most efficient remedy for the problems caused by the greenhouse gas emissions would be a global scheme of carbon taxes that are uniformly imposed on all countries" (p. 6). In other words, Nordhaus's strict adherence to the supply-side growth theory entails the following policy recommendation: create an international market for greenhouse gas emissions. On the contrary, demand-led growth theory acknowledges the historical and contextual nature of technological progress, ecological impacts and economic growth. No formula or model can or ought to substitute collective decision-making, although they can be used as *one* of the inputs when systematically thinking about the issue.

The preceding paragraphs have attempted to highlight the role of geopolitics as well as the importance of collective decision-making in generating economic growth in the case of open economies, much more than in closed economies. While supply-side growth theories favour market forces to bring about economic growth, demand-led growth theories envisage a significant role for both national governments and international organisations in achieving economic growth, owing to their explicit recognition of historical and contextual factors. That is, the latter set of theories endow a greater responsibility on citizens and their elected political representatives to plan and execute policies that can result in a good life for all.

5.5 Conclusion

This chapter outlined the two broad approaches—supply-side and demand-led—in understanding economic growth. The latter adopts a more contextual and historical approach than the former and, therefore, falls in the tradition of doing economics found in the classical economists Smith, Ricardo and Marx. Subsequently, by looking at select data related to the Indian economy, such as land inequality, sectoral growth rates, employment growth, growth of wealth and CO_2 growth, several connections were made between these variables and economic growth in Section 5.3. This section adopted a meso approach and posed several what-is and what-ought-to-be questions. A similar approach was followed in Section 5.4, which looked at economic growth in the context of an open economy; it highlighted the role of geopolitics and the need for collective decision-making bodies at the international level to achieve economic growth that can promote a good life for *all*.

Suggestions for further reading

In order to understand the various models within the supply-side and demand-led theories of growth, I strongly recommend Hywel G. Jones's 1976 book *An Introduction to Modern Theories of Economic Growth* (London: Nelson) because it scrutinises the assumptions of the growth models and provides historical context, both of which are lacking in more recent books. For those who wish to engage further with demand-led growth theories, the pioneering articles by Pierangelo Garegnani in the *Cambridge Journal of Economics* in 1978 (vol. 2, no. 4, pp. 335–53) and 1979 (vol. 3, no. 1, pp. 63–82) are a must-read. A related but different approach to demand-led growth theories is found in Luigi L. Pasinetti's collection of essays *Growth and Income Distribution: Essays in Economic Theory* published in 1974 (Cambridge: Cambridge University Press). And if you are a reader who is wondering how the choice of the growth theory might have an impact on policy, look at my 2015 critical commentary 'Economic Survey 2014–15: Growth Policy and Theory' published in the *Economic and Political Weekly* (vol. 50, no. 32, pp. 62–5). For a critical appraisal of the Nobel contributions of Romer and Nordhaus, read my 2019 article 'Romer and Nordhaus's Nobel Winning Contributions', also published in the *Economic and Political Weekly* (vol. 54, no. 35, pp. 10–13); it outlines the policy implications of the marginalist core in their supply-side growth theories. An advanced critical and historical treatment of the marginalist endogenous growth theories can be obtained from Heinz Kurz's 1997 article 'What Could the "New" Growth Theory Teach Smith or Ricardo?' published in *Economic Issues* (vol. 2, no. 2, pp. 1–20); the article is written in an unconventional manner—with Smith and Ricardo as if in a modern conversation about marginalist growth theories.

6

Why Economic Theory Matters

6.1 Introduction

Many textbooks of economics provide the reasons and rationale for the study of economic theory in the first chapter itself. Having already introduced you to the various macroeconomic theories—of money and interest rates, of employment and output and of economic growth—in the previous chapters, and by discussing the importance of economic theory in the present chapter, this textbook adopts a different approach. Moreover, note that this is a transition chapter, as the next two chapters deal with economic policy issues relating to unemployment and inflation, respectively. Just like some students in my economics classes, some of you might also wonder why learning economic theory is important. We have already remarked on the nature of theorising in Section 1.4 and the structure of a theory in Section 4.2. This chapter provides four substantive reasons for a close and critical study of economic theory (and their attendant models).

6.2 The need for discipline

Economic facts surround us, be it the price we pay for a ride in the autorickshaw, the value of our shopping expenses at the local vegetable market, the number of hours we spend at work, the number of hours of household work or the number of people who look for jobs daily. How do we decide which prices and quantities to focus on? Is it possible to process facts unaided? Or do we require some sort of a disciplining device akin to a sieve to sift through facts or a lens to magnify select facts? It is in such situations that theory plays an important role—by informing its student which of the key economic aspects to focus their attention upon. Often, these aspects are not directly observable, and will need to be measured or computed by the process of estimation or imputation. For instance, aggregate output (Y) is not directly observable, but, as we have noted in Chapters 4 and 5, it provides a useful indicator of the activity levels in an economy. Similarly, although we are able to see that people purchase food items, consumer durables and transportation, the relevant macroeconomic variable is aggregate consumption (C)—a directly non-observable variable. Indeed, the appropriate aphorism that captures the power/ability of theory to make sense of a vast amount of economic information is one that is commonly attributed to (but does not originate from) the psychologist Kurt Lewin: "There is nothing as practical as a good theory."

Section 1.4 outlined the importance of theoretical precision in relation to understanding equilibrium tendencies of the economic system and in making definitive statements. A theory can be viewed as a conceptual framework to understand phenomena. And it is the disciplining nature of a theory that aids us in making definitive statements. Very frequently, a model is constructed to impose further discipline. For example, the growth model of Solow, discussed in Chapter 5, is a particular application of supply-side growth theory.

The use of mathematics renders clarity to the model by showing the restrictions that are necessary to arrive at the equilibrium outcome. If these logically necessary conditions are too restrictive from an economic standpoint, it could be concluded that the model in question is not very useful in understanding the economy. For example, if one of the restrictions to arrive at an economic equilibrium is that the price of a commodity has to be negative, then we realise that there is some problem. And often, it is difficult to identify these restrictions without employing mathematics. But do note that depending on the nature of the economic theory, you can use calculus, linear algebra or other branches of mathematics. If a theory does not use marginal concepts such as marginal utility and marginal cost, do the models warrant the use of calculus?

Calculus is the study of change and in the context of marginalist economics, it transforms into an analysis of *potential* and not actual change (for instance, marginal product of labour refers to the addition to total output when it is supposed that one more labour input is added to the process of production, ceteris paribus). The kind of mathematics employed, therefore, depends on the nature of economic theory. For a history of economics with special attention devoted to its use of mathematics, you can read E. Roy Weintraub's 2002 book *How Economics Became a Mathematical Science.*

To illustrate the above point, let us model the Keynesian theory of output and employment (already detailed in Section 4.2) for a two-sector economy with households and firms. Households provide labour services to firms in return for wages. And most of these wages are spent on consumption needs. The firms utilise a part of their profits for investment—leading to an increase in the rate of utilisation of capacity. Recall that the productive capacity is taken as a given in the theories of output and employment. And that the equilibrium or position of rest in this macroeconomy occurs when planned aggregate output (Y) coincides with planned aggregate demand (AD). At this point, neither the households nor the firms have an incentive to revise their economic plans.

$$Y = AD$$

Planned aggregate demand can be further sub-divided into planned consumption (C) and investment expenditure (I), and, therefore, the macroeconomic equilibrium can be represented as follows.

$$Y = C + I$$

Suppose that planned investment expenditure is entirely autonomous (I_o), whereas planned consumption expenditure contains an induced element (cY) as well as an autonomous element (C_o) with respect to Y (recall the discussion on autonomous and induced elements of aggregate demand from Chapter 4).

$$I = I_o$$
$$C = C_o + cY$$

The marginal propensity to consume (MPC) out of income, c, is a parameter of the model. In a way, it represents and captures a structural feature of the macroeconomy. Or, to put it differently, it is determined by factors not included in the model. MPC tells us by how much planned consumption increases when there is a unit increase in Y. In general, the propensity to consume can be arrived at and understood in two ways: (*a*) when we divide aggregate consumption by aggregate output (C/Y), we arrive at the average propensity to consume (APC) and (*b*) when we find out by how much aggregate consumption changes when there is a unit increase in aggregate income ($\Delta C/\Delta Y$), we have arrived at the MPC. In the simple macroeconomy we have modelled, when does the MPC coincide with the APC?

Let us now solve Y = AD to arrive at the equilibrium output, at which point there is no tendency for the households and firms to alter their respective consumption and investment plans.

$$Y = C + I$$
$$Y = C_o + cY + I_o$$
$$Y - cY = C_o + I_o$$

$$Y^* = \frac{1}{1-c}(C_0 + I_0)$$

The equilibrium output in this simple two-sector macroeconomy is positively related to autonomous consumption, autonomous investment and the marginal propensity to consume. That is, an increase in autonomous consumption and investment increases equilibrium aggregate output, and an increase in MPC (which is equal to one minus the marginal propensity to save [MPS]) also increases equilibrium aggregate output. In other words, an increase in MPS has a negative impact on equilibrium aggregate output; this is because savings are a leakage from the circular flow of income. The (short-run) macroeconomic logic present in the preceding sentences is the basis on which demand-led growth theories are founded (see Section 5.2).

For the equilibrium output, Y^*, to take an economically meaningful value, certain restrictions have to be imposed on the values that the marginal propensity to consume, c, can take. What happens if c is equal to 1? Can c be less than 1? What about Y^* if c exactly equals 0? And think about and write down what it means to say that c equals 0, 1 or less than 0. Although some of you might have identified the restrictions on c from the graphs in Chapter 4, the use of linear algebra makes it more precise and explicit.

The disciplining device of a mathematical model renders explicit the assumptions as well as the consequences of altering the values of a parameter. Thus, from the equation for equilibrium aggregate output provided earlier, we are able to know, ceteris paribus, by how much Y^* increases if c increases by, say, 10 per cent. With an increase in the inter-relationships among the variables and parameters, even the consequence of a change in one of them on the equilibrium output becomes more complex to trace without having recourse to a mathematical model.

Most importantly, since policymakers—both governments and monetary authorities—frequently employ economic models, if the variables are not well defined or are irrelevant to the context, a policy action can lead to unintended consequences. Since policies affect the livelihoods of many, they have to be undertaken with utmost caution. And once the policies are undertaken, significant attention must be devoted to critically scrutinising the underlying economic models and their theories found in those policy documents.

Finally, if a model/theory is internally inconsistent, it is extremely dangerous to use it for any kind of policymaking because it can be used to validate any policy action. If a model/theory is internally inconsistent, it means that it has lost its ability to discipline the interrelationships and to make definitive statements. In a way, with such models, 'anything goes', and such models/theories can be used in support of even contradictory policies. Such a formulation is made possible via ad hoc modifications to the assumptions or to a portion of the causal network of such models/theories. If you are interested in knowing more about modelling in economics, a good starting point is Mary S. Morgan's 2012 book *The World in the Model: How Economists Work and Think*.

6.3 Wrong theories result in bad policies

Given the existence of different contending theories in economics (briefly outlined in Section 1.2), characterising a theory as wrong depends, to an extent, on one's own standpoint. And this standpoint partly (or mostly) depends on the economics education that one has received via school and college textbooks. So far, in this textbook, two distinct approaches to understanding money, output levels and output growth have been provided. In this section, we shall critically engage with some of these theories.

The theories of money, output and economic growth, arising from the conceptual hub of marginalist economics, are based on the following four 'wrong' principles and theories: (*a*) what is true for an individual is true for the economy as a whole, (*b*) the rate of interest is a 'real' phenomenon, (*c*) planned saving determines planned investment and (*d*) the marginal productivity theory of income distribution. And because these principles are 'wrong', the application of these theories results in bad policies—bad in terms of the economic effects it has on people's lives.

Mainstream macroeconomics is built on the idea that what is true for an individual must be true for the macroeconomy as well—via a simple aggregation of individual actions. Prima facie, there is no reason to think that this approach is wrong. This approach has led economists, both past and present, to argue that saving is good not only for an individual but also for the entire economy. The logic is simply this: since it is good for an individual household to accumulate savings, it is good for other economic entities too, like the government. Is there an issue with this argument from an economics perspective? Yes, most significantly, it is illegitimate to treat the government on a similar footing as a household because of their respective constitutional standing, legal aspects, ability to borrow funds, social roles and public accountability. (As an exercise, make a note of the socio-political differences between a household and a firm.) The government, very often, performs the function of the 'provider of last resort', much like the central bank is the 'lender of last resort'. In many countries, the government pays an allowance if an individual is unable to find employment; in India, the government provides employment through the Mahatma Gandhi National Rural Employment Guarantee Act (MGNREGA), thereby underscoring the right of every individual to work. Such social functions are not performed by private households or firms. This is because the government represents a distinct entity, which can neither be understood by considering it as an extension of a rational economic individual nor as a sum of rational economic individual decisions.

As already divulged in Chapter 4, I have had students tell me that they find microeconomics to be more intuitive than macroeconomics. In a way, this is because marginalist microeconomics asks its student to place herself within the rational utility calculus, and subsequently various thought (or perhaps, more accurately, pedagogic) experiments are carried out in support of the marginalist view on how individuals function, that is, maximise utility, under various constraints. On the other hand, since macroeconomics deals with the economy as a whole, it is not possible to employ such individual thought experiments to provide a basis for macroeconomic understanding. The logic and behaviour of an economic system is different from the logic and behaviour of an individual economic agent. However, marginalist macroeconomics tries to reduce macro behaviour to micro behaviour—as clearly visible in the 'microfoundations' approach to macroeconomics (see later). Hence, the marginalist standpoint falls under methodological individualism and the Keynesian standpoint adopts methodological holism.

In 1936, Keynes demonstrated that the use of methodological individualism to understand macroeconomics—the theory of output, employment and money—is logically flawed. Let us suppose that all households decide to save more with a view to increasing aggregate (national) savings. Given current incomes, this implies that they reduce their current consumption. What happens in the macroeconomy? Owing to reduced household consumption, firms will be unable to sell their planned output, leading to a reduction in firms' incomes, which may result in a reduction in labour employed and, consequently, to a reduction in households' incomes and, therefore, of household savings. This is called the paradox of thrift because the attempt to increase aggregate savings by increasing individual savings has a paradoxical (or counter-intuitive) effect. However, recognise that this is a paradox only from the standpoint of economic theories that adopt methodological individualism. Discuss in class, using examples, how a paradox in one paradigm fails to be one in another. A paradigm can be understood as a set of foundational principles (which generates a 'standard' set of associated theories, models and methods) that provide *a* perspective of understanding the world. In this sense, marginalist economics and classical economics are two distinct paradigms. Now, let us move to the next 'wrong' principle.

The determination of the interest rate is fundamental to macroeconomics. But is the interest rate determined exogenously or endogenously? In other words, is the rate of interest *set* by monetary authorities (like the Reserve Bank of India [RBI] in India or the Federal Reserve in the United States [US]) or is it an outcome of market forces? In Section 3.4, we discussed two theories of money—exogenous and endogenous. It was pointed out there that the correct theory is that of endogenous money. However, because of the dominance of exogenous money in academic and policy circles, especially in India, people in key positions continue to believe that money is exogenous, and therefore they also believe its subsidiary principle that money is created by lending.

Underlying exogenous money is the idea that the 'real' rate of interest is determined by 'real' factors such as productivity and thrift, and not by 'monetary' factors. That is, the equilibrium 'real' rate of interest is said to depend on technology and savings. You might be wondering why this is the case. This is because exogenous money draws on marginalist economics, which treats the rate of interest as the equilibrator between the supply of capital (savings) and the demand for capital (investment); savings is positively related to the rate of interest and investment is negatively related to the rate of interest. Moreover, the propensity to save depends on the economic agents' preference for future consumption over current consumption. If the economic agents prefer future consumption over current consumption, they will save more and, ceteris paribus, the rate of interest will fall in order to equilibrate saving and investment. What is the underlying mechanism? When economic agents plan to save more, it means that planned investment is less than planned savings and the rate of interest must fall *until* the increase in planned investment it generates equals planned savings. Within the exogenous money framework, the equilibrium interest rate is fundamentally determined by the preferences (to save) of the agents under the assumption of a given technology, that is, given productivity. It is in this manner that the causation has been shown to flow from individual preferences to the saving and investment market and the consequent determination of the rate of interest—the 'microfoundations' of the interest rate, so to speak. The proponents of endogenous money, notably Thomas Tooke and Hyman Minsky, in the 19th and 20th centuries respectively, have questioned various aspects of both the premises and the working of exogenous money (for an account of endogenous money, see Section 3.4).

In terms of policy, the proponents of exogenous money suggest measures to increase bank deposits or, more generally, savings. This is because of the marginalist view that $S_{FE} = f(roi) = I$, with the causation running from full-employment planned saving (S_{FE}) to planned investment (I). An increase in savings reduces the rate of interest (roi). And the fall in the rate of interest increases investment. Moreover, marginalist economists and policymakers may argue against the lowering of the interest rate by stating that it reflects the current individual preferences and, therefore, any intervention is bad for the economy. It is bad for the economy because, according to them, the intervention creates distortions in the *natural* functioning of the macroeconomy. Such views need to be put in their proper theoretical context and warrant criticism. And indeed, the aims of learning economics are not restricted to the retrospective engagement with the underlying theory of an economic policy, but include an active engagement with theory, so as to meaningfully sculpt correct economic theories and policies.

The third 'wrong' theory is the marginalist account of saving and investment (briefly discussed in the previous paragraphs too). This theory posits that, under competitive conditions, planned investment adapts to the full-employment planned saving, via variations in a sufficiently sensitive rate of interest. Two key observations made by marginalist economics may now be stated. First, in a competitive economy, there is a tendency towards the full employment of labour. Second, the policy lever must influence planned saving because it is the causally significant variable. In the 1930s, Kalecki and Keynes had argued that there is no tendency to the full employment of labour in a competitive economy, and that it is planned investment which determines planned saving and that too via variations in aggregate output (and *not* the rate of interest). The marginalist theory of saving and investment, unfortunately, continues to remain dominant. The dominance of marginalist economics makes policymakers focus their attention on supply-side policies and neglect demand-side issues.

Since aggregate demand is made up of private consumption, private investment, government expenditure (consumption and investment) and rest of the world (RoW) expenditure (captured by the difference between exports and imports), it is important to directly target these components of aggregate demand in order to boost aggregate activity levels—both output and employment. This can be done easily and meaningfully through government expenditure. I used 'meaningfully' because government expenditure can be used to set up facilities that are important from the societal point of view—like hospitals, renewable energy plants, schools and waste treatment plants. As Smith rightly recommends in *The Wealth of Nations*, the "education of the common people requires, perhaps, in a civilized and commercial society, the attention of the publick" (p. 784).

The Keynesian theory of saving and investment does not suggest that we ignore supply-side constraints. For example, neither Kalecki nor Keynes are arguing that in the absence of food storage facilities, increased government procurement of food will automatically result in the creation of food storage facilities. This is a sectoral or, to use the term employed in this book, a meso issue. What Kalecki and Keynes provide us with is a macro framework. Just like it is illegitimate to extend the micro logic to macro issues, it is illegitimate to extend the macro logic to both meso and micro issues. While their logic might coincide in some cases, it cannot be asserted a priori.

It is the same $S_{FE} = f(roi) = I$ logic that provides the basis for austerity measures. As the word suggests, it recommends that governments be austere or frugal in their expenditure. By cutting down government expenditure, marginalist economists believe that the macroeconomy will become better off, because they consider government expenditure (particularly via borrowings) to be bad for the economy—since a rise in government borrowing raises the rate of interest, ceteris paribus, and crowds out private investment. However, here too, note that they are extending what is good for an individual—to spend within its means—to that of a fundamentally different entity, the government.

The last theory to be discussed in this section is the marginal productivity theory of income distribution. Although this is conventionally taught in microeconomics, it has significant implications for marginalist macroeconomic theories and policies. Under competitive conditions, the marginalist theory posits that, in equilibrium, wages are determined by the marginal product of labour and profit by the marginal product of capital. Hence, in the language of modelling, income distribution is fully determined endogenously via the economic forces of labour demand, labour supply, capital demand and capital supply.

Even in a competitive economy, as the classical economists like Smith, Ricardo and Marx correctly observed, wages are determined by history and culture—leading subsequent commentators to describe wages as exogenous in classical economics. Recall that the demand-led growth theories described in the previous chapter relied on 'value through exogenous distribution'. The policy implications vary significantly between the classical and marginalist theories of income distribution. For instance, since $W = MP_L$ is the equilibrium state in the marginalist theory, any intervention, such as collective bargaining or minimum wage, is expected to distort the labour market, and is therefore considered bad for the economy. However, from a classical standpoint, since wages are determined exogenously, wage bargaining and minimum wage legislations are viewed favourably as they allow for wages to be set at socially acceptable levels. For a book-length treatment of wages in classical economics, see Antonella Stirati's *The Theory of Wages in Classical Economics: A Study of Adam Smith, David Ricardo and their Contemporaries* (1994).

From the principles/theories discussed in this section, it is abundantly clear that the choice of economic theory has a significant effect on economic policies. If the theories are wrong, they cannot be used as reliable guides for policy, as they can have unintended effects. And insofar as economic policies impact the livelihoods of people, it is dangerous to employ wrong theories in the service of public policy.

6.4 Good theories recognise context

In the first chapter, we had outlined the object and level of analysis employed in this book—a macro approach to understand a competitive economy, despite not living in one. In the chapter dealing with money and interest rates, there was a substantial discussion on the financial architecture of India—the specifics of the Indian financial system—in Section 3.2, before engaging with the two theories of money. In the introduction and conclusion to the chapter on output and employment levels, the importance of acknowledging the context was highlighted (Sections 4.1 and 4.4). Aspects of the nature of India's economic growth presented in Section 5.3 also dealt with specificities of the Indian economy.

The context being referred to in this section is narrower than the givens and the non-economic systems mentioned in Figure 2.1. In this chapter, context refers to what may be understood as the (deep) structural aspects of a particular economy. Two such structural aspects of the Indian macroeconomy will be discussed in this section: (*a*) the role of agriculture and (*b*) the presence of a large informal 'sector'.

Role of agriculture

No theory can take into account all the particularities or specificities of an economy. Some factors or elements must be selected or chosen from the various specificities. K. N. Raj, in his 1990 book *Organizational Issues in Indian Agriculture*, rightly underscores the agrarian nature of the Indian economy and the need for recognising this crucial specificity when employing economic theories in policymaking.

> These are features of agrarian economies that have to be borne in mind when applying Keynesian economics (or any other kind of economic analysis) to them. How the markets are structured, which of them are the crucial ones, and how exactly they function and interact with each other, are likely to differ not only from one phase of historical evolution to another but even as between different regions in the agrarian economy. Further complications are introduced when (as is often the case) a small section of rural society dominates a number of factor and product markets *simultaneously* and these markets are linked by price as well as non-price links, since the differential positions of the participants in any particular market cannot be fitted into the conventional model of monopoly and monopsony and absorbed into the framework of general equilibrium analysis. While Keynesian economics, as also general equilibrium analysis, have some insights and clues to offer, *their uncritical use without paying adequate attention to these vital features of agrarian economies* is still unfortunately all too common today, concealing a great deal of superficiality behind a façade of theoretical elegance and sophistication. (p. 87; emphasis added; 'simultaneously' in italics in the original)

As discussed in Section 1.4, policymaking is a sophisticated practice that warrants the knowledge of theories, the available quantitative methods and equally, or perhaps more importantly, the context. It is as if there is a black box connecting theory and policy. The current section and the following one attempt to shine some light on the possible constituents of that box.

In 1898, M. G. Ranade, in his book *Essays on Indian Economics*, made a case for 'Indian economics' that was built on Indian specificities and institutional framework, as opposed to 'Western' economics. Since Ranade's book is now out of copyright and freely available online, read parts of it and assess whether the specificities Ranade highlighted are visible in contemporary India; also see if you can discern any particular theoretical standpoint in his writings.

Attempts to understand the Indian macroeconomy are incomplete without a discussion of agriculture. This is because agriculture and allied sectors provide employment to 47 per cent of Indian workers; to put this in perspective, the corresponding figure for the services sector is 30 per cent (*State of Working India* [*SWI* hereafter] 2018, p. 58). Moreover, Indian agriculture is not characterised primarily by wage labour as in developed countries like the US. To understand Indian agriculture, we need to understand how village economies function (also see the discussion under 'Object of analysis' in Section 1.4).

A village economy cannot be understood as a simple departure from the competitive macroeconomy we have discussed thus far. It requires us to understand how village space is divided and demarcated (typically on the basis of caste). The spatial inequality present in a village economy is captured very well by Kota Neelima in her depiction of a poor and indebted farmer's house in *Death of a Moneylender* (2016).

> Madhav's house … was in the middle of a series of huts in one corner of the village, quite a distance away from the better households. (p. 167)

Although it is a digression from village economies, a recognition of spatial restrictions in urban spaces is helpful to understand labour mobility. Skybaaba's short story 'Vegetarians Only' (2016) depicts the difficulties faced by a young non-Telugu, non-burqa-wearing Muslim couple to find a rented house in the big city of Hyderabad. The following happens after being rejected as tenants in a Hindu as well as a Muslim neighbourhood.

> I saw another TO LET sign nearby. I walked towards it hopefully. There was something written beneath the words TO LET. I moved closer wondering what it was. 'Vegetarians Only', it said. Oh god. This was direct speech. No need for any further information. The board simply said: Get Out! (p. 37)

Such social barriers place severe restrictions on the free mobility of labour (and therefore capital) both within and across rural and urban spaces, a crucial aspect of theories which assume a perfectly competitive economy.

It is also important to understand how labour is allocated in village economies between tilling the land, grazing cattle, tapping toddy, catching fish, weaving, carpentry, pottery, washing clothes, care work, and so on. This allocation is also significantly determined by caste, which is, to paraphrase Ambedkar, a division of labourers and not a division of labour. Another crucial factor that determines the allocation of labour, especially between household work (including caring for members of the family, both young and old) and agricultural or rural manufacturing work, is gender; the burden and responsibility of household work almost entirely falls on women. And just like with caste, there is no reason to presume that the bias against women's wage labour is absent in urban economies. Gender also plays a role in the sectoral composition of employment; for instance, in 2015, there were relatively more women working in agriculture (28.6 per cent) than in services (16.3 per cent) (*SWI* 2018, p. 124).

Just like understanding the village economy is necessary to understand Indian agriculture, so is understanding the political economy of land. The historical inequality of land ownership in India has already been briefly discussed in Section 5.3. The history of land ownership, the distinction between farmers and labourers, the regional distribution of natural resources, and the role of caste and gender in determining land ownership are all essential particulars while formulating policy. Indeed, even the concept of a village economy is too abstract: the village economy of Dibuia in Nagaland is very different from that of Neelakudy in Tamil Nadu or Koyilandy in Kerala or Chunapur in Bihar.

Another important characteristic of Indian agriculture is the interlinked markets for agricultural inputs. This is visible in the excerpt from Raj's *Organizational Issues in Indian Agriculture* provided earlier. That is, the seller of seeds also sells pesticides and lends money. This exacerbates the inequality prevalent in a village economy and, particularly, in the agricultural sector. A lengthy excerpt of the conversation between the journalist Falak and two senior workers of a textile mill from Neelima's *Death of a Moneylender* (2016) perceptively describes how profits in the textile sector are made at the expense of the farmers (pp. 137–8).

> "I could tell you a hundred methods for making sure our mill gets the best cotton at the lowest rates."
>
> ...
>
> "I just have to 'manage' the market agents. If the marketing committee official decides that the farmer's cotton is second or third grade, I get *first* grade cotton at *third* grade prices. The farmer could also bribe the right man and get a first grade certification. But the farmer usually does not even have the money to pay the transporter who gets the harvest to the market."
>
> ...

"Or I can locate traders who lend seeds, fertilizers, pesticides and farm implements to the farmers after pledging their produce. I could support the trader and make sure I get the produce at a much lower rate, usually at the government's minimum support price. It is set as a benchmark to make sure the prices do not fall lower, but we know how to use it otherwise."

Falak thoughtfully asked, "Don't the farmers complain against you?"

The two men exchanged smirks. "Farmers cannot complain. They are at the bottom of the rung. They cannot complain against market agents because they have to meet them at the time of every harvest."

…

"How about moneylenders?" he asked.

"The farmers need to be on the best of terms with the moneylender for the sake of emergencies, and even if the interest rate is 36 per cent per annum. They can't protest against the banks either, even if they give less than the stipulated crop loan per acre."

The above conversation highlights the unequal economic conditions due to interlinked markets prevalent in the village economy, particularly in the agricultural sector.

This brief overview of Indian agriculture will be completed after providing you with a sketch of the nature and extent of uncertainty in agriculture. Besides the uncertain arrival, departure and volume of rains, the farmer also faces uncertain sale prices and harvest quantities. However, the Indian farmer is certain about: debt repayments, the lack of storage facilities, and the collusion between moneylenders, sellers of seeds, pesticide dealers and marketing agents. When all these uncertainties and certainties are taken together, the extreme precarity of the Indian farmer is an inescapable fact.

The presence of informality

The other key characteristic of the Indian macroeconomy is the significant presence of informal employment. According to the National Commission on Enterprises in the Unorganised Sector (NCEUS), informal workers refer to those "working in the unorganised sector or households, excluding regular workers with social security benefits, and the workers in the formal sector without any employment and social security benefits provided by the employers". Based on this definition, as per the 2018 *SWI* report, over 80 per cent of the Indian workforce is in informal employment (p. 94). Self-employment (a component of informal employment) occupies a prominent position in Indian employment. As the term suggests, the self-employed workers "operate a farm or non-farm business on their own, whether by themselves or with paid or unpaid workers" (*SWI* 2018, p. 93). In fact, the category of wage labour, which is *the* typical category used in economic theory, accounts for only 20 per cent of the Indian workforce (*SWI* 2018, p. 93), and this 20 per cent constitutes both regular salaried workers and contract workers. Therefore, the application of *any* economic theory in policymaking must be preceded by an understanding of informal employment.

As some of you might already know, most of the workforce in agriculture is informal. This has led some economists, following the work of Arthur Lewis (1954), to characterise economies, such as India, which have a substantial non-capitalist sector (for instance, Indian agriculture) alongside a growing capitalist sector (for instance, parts of India's services sector) as dual economies. Another notable economist who contributed to the literature on non-capitalist economies is A. V. Chayanov, a Russian agricultural economist; those interested in this line of thinking should consult Chayanov's 1924 essay 'On the Theory of Non-capitalist Economic Systems' and his 1925 book *Peasant Farm Organisation*. But remember that both the concepts of 'dual economy' as in Lewis and 'peasant economy' as in Chayanov are simplifications—just like the 'village economy' we discussed earlier. As an exercise, read Ambedkar's 1918 article 'Small Holdings in India and Their Remedies', published in the *Journal of the Indian Economic Society*, and identify the key arguments regarding the economics of agriculture.

What do agricultural workers do during the lean season? Unlike the job of a government clerk or a doctor, agricultural work is seasonal. After agriculture, it is the construction sector that provides the most employment to rural workers (*SWI* 2018, p. 62). The construction sector employs around 50 million workers—this is as much as the entire manufacturing sector! Looking at aggregate output and employment like we did in Chapter 4 alone will not suffice in the formulation of economic policies for India because of the specific characteristics unique to it. Owing to the seasonal nature of agricultural work in rural areas (or village economies) and, therefore, seasonal construction work in urban and semi-urban areas, looking at migration patterns will aid us in making better sense of the multiple jobs being done by a rural worker over the span of, say, a year.

While discussing the financial architecture of India in Section 3.2, the predominance of informal sources of finance like moneylending were stated. And consequently, it was noted that the presence of informal finance has an impact on the working of the monetary transmission mechanism (see Figure 3.6). Acknowledging, understanding and incorporating informal finance is, therefore, essential to frame good monetary policy in India (more discussion is forthcoming in Chapter 8). To further your understanding, evaluate the models used in the various Five-Year Plans of India by assessing the degrees to which they have incorporated the informal sector; for this purpose, you may consult the mathematical models presented in the appendix to the 2009 book *Macro-Modelling for the Eleventh Five Year Plan of India*, edited by Kirit S. Parikh for the erstwhile Planning Commission. We will end this section on the interregnum between theory and policy after a brief discussion on black money in India, which also serves as a preamble to the next section on good theories and the demand for data.

The black economy is made up of black incomes and black money; while the latter is a stock variable, the former is a flow variable. According to the economists Arun Kumar (1999) and Saumen Chattopadhyay (2018), the black economy constitutes around 60 per cent of India's gross domestic product (GDP). And, as they rightly point out, it is incorrect to view the black economy as a parallel economy because black and white money are simultaneously generated by the very same processes of production. However, this has significant consequences for the Indian macroeconomy because black investment is a leakage from the circular flow of income and has a negative effect on output and employment levels. Thus, those who are interested in understanding the Indian economy must possess at least a rudimentary knowledge of the black economy and its attendant features such as the emergence of tax havens, the logic of transfer pricing, illegal activities like smuggling and illicit global capital outflows.

In sum, the black box between theory and policy ought to be filled with rich institutional details of the kind listed in this section. A theory that can accommodate such details without much difficulty can be of better service in policymaking and, therefore, is one that is good.

6.5 Good theories and the demand for data

Economically relevant data does not present itself automatically. They need to be collected via the regular government machinery and/or through surveys by the government, private research organisations or individual researchers. Irrespective of who collects the data, the 'which data?' question depends on the particular research question or, in the case of the government, on the relevant ministry. Our tax data is with the Ministry of Income Tax. And the collection of agricultural statistics is done by the Ministry of Agriculture and Farmers Welfare.

Often, with research organisations and individual researchers, the 'which data?' question depends on the theoretical framework directly or indirectly underpinning their research (and survey). Let me use an anecdote to illustrate the point. After listening to Werner Heisenberg's talk on quantum mechanics in 1926, Albert Einstein presciently told him, "Whether you can observe a thing or not depends on the theory which you use. It is the theory which decides what can be observed" (p. 40); this conversation was reported by Heisenberg in his contribution to the collection of autobiographical essays by physicists published in a 1989 volume titled *From a Life of Physics*. In other words, a good theory can drive the quest for better policies by demanding more relevant data. Of course, the conceptual clarity and coherence provided by good theories must necessarily be supplemented with contextual information.

Although the measurement of GDP is now commonplace, there are still debates on what ought to be included and excluded in it, and rightly so (recall, as noted in Section 2.2, the demand for time-use surveys to obtain an estimate of women's unpaid labour). The following passage from Richard Stone's 1951 monograph *The Role of Measurement in Economics* highlights the role of theory in empirical measurement.

These empirical constructs are well illustrated by the example of the income of an individual or a nation. No amount of searching in primary records, that is the originating entries, actual or imputed, in the books of a firm or individual, will enable us to detect the income that has been made. To ascertain income, it is necessary to set up a theory from which income is derived as a concept by postulation and then associate this concept with a certain set of primary facts. To be sure the theory must take into account possible primary facts if it is to be of any practical use since if it does not the theoretical concept of income will be left hanging in the air, with no empirical correlate. But some theory is necessary since without it income does not reveal itself in the simple way as do the individuals and pieces of equipment which are largely responsible for generating it. (p. 9)

Similarly, in the next few paragraphs, it will be argued that, given the Indian realities, we need better empirical measures for the Indian macroeconomy.

In Section 3.3, we posed the question 'What is money?' The answer given by the RBI is that money refers to the stock of currency in circulation, demand deposits with banks and savings deposits with post office banks. However, now that you have learnt about the presence of informal money in the previous section (Section 6.4), how can a definition of money for the Indian macroeconomy not include informal money?

And although an explanation for the presence of unemployment in a competitive economy was provided in Section 4.2, you now know about the extent of informal employment in India from the previous section (Section 6.4). Given this context, should we not demand more detailed rates of unemployment specific to the nature of employment—self-employed, contract, regular salaried—which will be published at more frequent intervals?

Table 2.1 captured the inter-sectoral relations of the Indian economy. Such a meso approach to understanding an economy, as pointed out already, is especially found in the theories of Quesnay, Marx and Sraffa, and in the applied work of Leontief. The macro approach to understanding an economy gives rise to concepts such as aggregate output and employment. While the wide acceptance of the macro approach has led to the generation of frequent GDP data, the relative neglect of the meso approach, particularly in India, has meant a decline in the demand for inter-sectoral data and, consequently, its supply. Moreover, as Stone writes in *The Role of Measurement in Economics* (1951), "it is necessary to collect information which will reflect theoretical variables defined in advance, rather than to rely on the manipulation of existing statistics collected for a narrower administrative purpose" (p. 83). In sum, insofar as good theories provide us with relevant concepts and accommodate relevant aspects of the economic context, it pushes us to demand for and/or collect appropriate data.

I will end this section after discussing, in brief, a problem on the other side of the spectrum—the perils of relying *only* on large volumes of data, or big data, as it is called. Note that there are some debates in economics that cannot be settled by any amount of data, big or small. For instance, what determines commodity prices? Or does planned saving adapt to planned investment, or is it the other way around? These conceptual debates are based on an economy where labour and capital are freely mobile, and since no economy is characterised by such free competition, the data we collect cannot be used to test such theories. One of the worrisome tendencies in mainstream economics has been the tendency to abandon pure theory and seek policy solutions solely based on data, with the aid of either econometrics and/or machine learning. As Cathy O'Neil reminds us in the penultimate paragraph of her 2016 book *Weapons of Math Destruction: How Big Data Increases Inequality and Threatens Democracy*,

> Data is not going away. Nor are computers—much less mathematics. Predictive models are, increasingly, the tools we will be relying on to run our institutions, deploy our resources, and manage our lives. But as I've tried to show throughout this book, these models are constructed not just from data but from the choices we make about which data to pay attention to—and which to leave out. (p. 218)

If I were to adapt this observation of O'Neil to our discussion, it can be stated that the choice of economic theory and its clear presentation will make the statistical sieve through which the big data is passed more transparent. Siddhartha Mukherjee, in *The Laws of Medicine: Field Notes from an Uncertain Science* (2015), also expresses a similar concern about the use of big data (and 'technological' solutions) in medicine.

> The advent of new medical technologies will not diminish bias. They will amplify it. More human arbitration and interpretation will be needed to make sense of studies—and thus more biases will be introduced. Big data is not the solution to the bias problem; it is merely a source of more subtle (or even bigger) biases. (p. 65)

In sum, we must not sacrifice the conceptual clarity provided by economic theory at the altar of big data.

6.6 Conclusion

As a transition chapter, this covered some issues in the methodological plane between theory and policy. Through the aid of simple mathematics, it was shown that a model helps us reduce the problem of unintended consequences and in assessing its relevance. Both theory and model *discipline* our understanding of the economy. Subsequently, by using some examples from marginalist economics, the negative outcomes of policies arising from wrong theories were outlined. The importance of context alongside concept (or theory) was then highlighted by focusing on agriculture and informal employment, with specific reference to the Indian economy. Finally, the connection between the demand for policy-relevant data and good theories was made; this section also expressed the need for caution while using big data for economic solutions. The next two chapters, respectively, deal with policies to attain full employment and low inflation.

Suggestions for further reading

For a clear statement of the marginalist theory of value and distribution, you can consult Tjalling Koopmans's 1957 book *Three Essays on the State of Economic Science* (New York: McGraw-Hill Book Company), especially the first essay. To obtain a fuller and deeper understanding of the Indian economic context, I particularly recommend the chapter 'Petty Production and Poverty' from G. Omkarnath's 2012 book *Economics: A Primer for India* (Hyderabad: Orient Blackswan). Both the general reader and the economics student can treat my review of Kota Neelima's 2016 book of fiction, *Death of a Moneylender*, published as 'The Fact/Fiction of Indian Agriculture' in the Foundation for Agrarian Studies (FAS) blog (2019, June 20), as an extremely short introduction to understanding agricultural economics in India. You can obtain a wealth of information on India's agrarian relations by looking at books such as the *Socio-Economic Surveys of Two Villages in Rajasthan* edited by Madhura Swaminathan and Vikas Rawal and published in 2015 (New Delhi: Tulika and FAS); FAS has published books based on similar village studies conducted in Andhra Pradesh and Karnataka. If you wish to understand the nature of the black economy in India, you can read Arun Kumar's 2017 book *Understanding the Black Economy and Black Money in India* (New Delhi: Aleph), which is written for a general audience. However, if you wish to possess only a brief understanding of the issue, you can read my 2019 review of Saumen Chattopadhyay's 2018 book *Macroeconomics of the Black Economy*, published in the *Economic and Political Weekly* (vol. 54, no. 33, pp. 47–8). For a critique of marginalist economics based on the specificities of the Indian economy, and an alternative framework significantly rooted in methodological holism, consult C. T. Kurien's 1996 book *Rethinking Economics: Reflections Based on a Study of the Indian Economy* (New Delhi: Sage Publications). For an assessment of Thomas Tooke's contributions to monetary economics, see Matthew Smith's 2017 article 'Ricardo the "Logician" versus Tooke the "Empiricist": On Their Different Substantive Contributions to Classical Economics' in the *History of Economics Review* (vol. 67, no. 1, pp. 46–58).

7

The Policy Objective of Full Employment

7.1 Introduction

In the previous chapters, we discussed the determinants of output and employment (Chapter 4), the link between economic growth and employment growth (Chapter 5) and, very briefly, the informal nature of employment in India (Chapter 6). As Adam Smith had written, the central objective of political economy is "to provide a plentiful revenue or subsistence for the people". And the pursuit of full employment is one of the ways through which all the people can secure a 'plentiful revenue'. Additionally, as already stated in Section 4.1, the employment ought to be secure (reliable) and well-paying (gainful). Together, this can contribute to a good life for all and, therefore, full employment is viewed, in this book, as an extremely desirable policy objective.

This chapter summarises the nature of employment in India by measuring its various aspects—drawing upon, primarily, the context. Recollect from the previous chapter that the 'what to measure?' question is heavily dependent on concept (used interchangeably with theory) and context. Subsequently, this chapter reiterates relevant aspects of the Keynesian approach to employment and provides broad-based macroeconomic solutions to tackle India's unemployment problem. The chapter concludes by underscoring the need for a comprehensive employment policy, which meaningfully *integrates* wages policy, growth policy, agricultural policy and education policy, in order to attain full employment as envisioned here.

7.2 The nature of employment in India

There are innumerable ways of looking at employment within the macro, meso and micro approaches. Some of the macro questions we hear take the following form. How much employment has the economy added in the past year? What is the quality of the existing state of employment in the economy as a whole? Do gender and/or caste play a role in determining the overall employment rate? The meso questions are of the following kind. How much employment does the services sector generate every year? What is the extent of distress migration from one sector to another? Do gender and/or caste influence sectoral employment? Questions from a micro approach take the following configuration. How is labour distributed within the members of the household? Does gender play a role in household allocation of labour? What are factors that push or pull individual households to migrate? What are the various kinds of jobs a household takes up during the course of a year?

Let us divide the macroeconomic issue of (un)employment into two parts— quantity and quality. While the first deals with issues such as the number of jobs created, the second looks at the working conditions as understood broadly. Given the Indian context, as outlined in Section 6.4, a holistic account of (un)employment must account for the nature of agricultural as well as informal jobs. Although we primarily engage with meso questions in this section, let us first look at some macro numbers.

Based on the data collected from household surveys, the 2015 unemployment rate was estimated at 5 per cent, which is equivalent to 23.3 million unemployed workers (*State of Working India* [*SWI* hereafter] 2018, p. 37). A complete picture of unemployment requires us to examine the labour force participation rate (LFPR) because it provides us with the percentage of the labour force— those who are working or are seeking to work—relative to the working-age population. The working-age population comprises all individuals between the ages of 16 and 64. The *SWI* 2018 estimates India's 2015 LFPR at 50.3 per cent (p. 37). Now, supposing that India's working-age population for 2015 is 92.6 million, based on the data provided in this paragraph, compute the labour force (in millions).

Where is the rest of India's working-age population, given the LFPR of 50.3 per cent? Such a low LFPR can partly be explained by the fact, noted in Section 2.2 in connection with national income accounts, that regular household work such as cooking, cleaning, helping with children's studies and caring for all members of the household, especially the elderly, is not treated as 'work'. Indeed, as Antonella Picchio sharply articulates in her 1992 book *Social Reproduction: The Political Economy of the Labour Market*, "Housework is the *production* of labour as a commodity, while waged work is the *exchange* of labour" (p. 96; emphases in the original). Picchio further observes: "Within the work of reproduction performed by women in the family, it is impossible to distinguish between material tasks and the psychological care of persons" (p. 98). Recall the discussion in Section 2.2 on the history of the measurement

139

of the gross domestic product (GDP) and the unsatisfactory resolution with respect to including women's unpaid work. To obtain a clearer picture of what is happening, compute the LFPR for India separately for men and women.

The LFPR is determined by several factors not necessarily of an economic nature. For instance, if it is the culture of a certain community to not allow women to engage in paid work after getting married, ceteris paribus, the LFPR reduces. Or, if the societal expectation among the urban middle class is that their children need to obtain a Master's degree and not work immediately after their Bachelor's degree, this may cause the LFPR to vary. Therefore, it may be stated that, in general, the LFPR significantly depends on social dynamics—which arise from the norms relating to gender, caste, class and their intersection—specific to the community or region.

The quality of employment

Let us now proceed to examine the quality of employment. Over the years, employers have increased the hiring of contract workers relative to regular workers (*SWI* 2018, p. 97). The former are workers hired by the firm indirectly through a third-party contractor and hence the term 'contract labour'. These contracts are short term or fixed term in nature. For continuous employment, the workers are dependent on the continuous renewal of their contracts. Contract workers do not receive the same quantum of benefits as regular workers do and are easily retrenched or laid off. Note that although contract workers are employed, it is neither secure nor well paying—both contributing to the precarity of such workers. Also keep in mind that precarity has not only economic effects but also psychological effects. The *India Wage Report* (2018), a publication of the International Labour Organization (ILO), had noted that the wages received by the contractual workers were either less than or equal to the statutory minimum wage (p. 86). As an exercise, go through the key features of the Contract Labour (Regulation and Abolition) Act, 1970; after this, assess whether your home state has amended this Act in the last 10 years and whether the emendations have been in the interest of the workers.

While we noted the extent of informal employment in India (around 80 per cent of the workforce or labour force) in Chapter 6, to understand its quality, let us focus on the proportion of casual workers. The 554th report of the National Sample Survey Organisation (NSSO), entitled *Employment and Unemployment Situation of India* (2014), defines a casual worker as "[a] person who was casually engaged in others' farm or non-farm enterprises (both household and non-household) and, in return, received wages according to the terms of the daily or periodic work contract" (p. 17). Casual workers do not have any long-term employment arrangements and are employed to meet short-term labour demand; they are not entitled to benefits like medical insurance and they have no job security. In Abokali Jimomi's short story 'Vili's Runaway Son' (2019), the following description of casual work, done by Vili and her husband in a small town in Nagaland, is telling of its quality.

> Both she and her husband were daily-wage workers, doing odd jobs in town people's houses; he sometimes fixing broken windows and doors, or pruning trees, and constructing pig pens and cleaning water tanks, and she collecting pig fodder and weeding vegetable gardens. (p. 150)

The above excerpt gives a glimpse of the lack of security prevalent in such odd jobs. Casual workers made up 32.8 per cent of the Indian workforce in 2015 (*SWI* 2018, p. 93).

It ought to be clear by now that focusing on the (un)employment rate alone is grossly inadequate, given the dominance of the precarious nature of employment. As noted in the first chapter of this book (Section 1.4), a principled understanding of the Indian economy requires the coming together of macro, meso and micro approaches, and, as a consequence, our focus cannot be restricted to a macro measure of India's (un)employment rate. However, this book, as it would have already been evident, does not engage with micro measures or concepts.

In 2015, while the overall unemployment rate was 5 per cent, the unemployment rate among those who possessed an undergraduate degree was 16.3 per cent and that among those with a postgraduate degree and above was 14.2 per cent (*SWI* 2018, p. 42). Such a meso outlook illustrates the details of the macro unemployment rate of 5 per cent. What reasons can you identify for the relatively high unemployment rate among the educated?

Another meso approach is to look at the unemployment rate from the perspective of various age groups. In 2015, among the youth (aged between 15 and 25), the unemployment rate was 16.5 per cent (*SWI* 2018, p. 43). Given this situation in 2015, it is perhaps unsurprising to see this age group most frequently employed in the gig economy via platforms such as those which offer taxi rides (Ola, Uber) or help deliver food from restaurants (Swiggy, Zomato). The term 'gig' is taken from musical gigs, where the musicians perform live music usually in return for a payment; here, the musician is viewed as a freelancer who is not working permanently for any firm. Owing to these workers being viewed as freelancers, they are not guaranteed a minimum quantum of work per month and, therefore, their monthly earnings are uncertain.

So far, we have looked at the quality of employment by focusing on its nature, that is, whether the workers are in contractual or casual employment. Additionally, we zoomed in on India's overall unemployment rate from the viewpoints of education and the 15–25 age group to obtain a better understanding of the structure or nature of India's unemployment. As reiterated in the beginning of this chapter, employment ought to be secure and well paying; when the preceding paragraphs are read alongside the discussion on informal employment in Section 6.4, it is clear that for most workers in India, their employment is anything but secure. Now let us briefly explore whether Indian employment is well paying (or gainful).

Are Indian jobs well paying?

In discussions relating to the Indian macroeconomy, the view that aggregate savings are inadequate is quite commonplace. To improve aggregate savings, the government has taken the mandate of financial inclusion seriously by extending banking facilities to rural India and by providing financial incentives to individual savings. For now, let us keep aside the Keynesian point about the paradox of thrift, discussed in Section 6.3, and focus on the source of the individual savings. Shrilal Shukla's description of government advertisements in *Raag Darbari* (1968) goes to the heart of the matter. Although the story is set in the late 1950s in "a fictional village typical of the Raebareli district" (p. xxiv) in Uttar Pradesh, the issues the novel engages with continue to be relevant.

> One advertisement said simply, 'Save More Money'. Most villagers had been told to save money for generations and practically everyone knew about it. The only innovation in the advertisement was that it mentioned the nation. It hinted that if you can't save for yourself, then save for the nation. The sentiment was just. Moneylenders, important officials, lawyers and doctors were all saving money for themselves, so how could small farmers object to saving for the nation? ...
>
> Where and how to deposit your money when you had it was also explained

clearly in speeches and posters, and no one raised any objection to the methods outlined. The only thing people were not told was how to get money to save, in other words, how much money they should be paid for their labour. (p. 59)

The point highlighted in the above excerpt is that the fundamental problem is inadequate wages (in connection to this, recall the Section 5.3 discussion on the growth of the financial sector). Moreover, unless such prompts for increasing savings are not accompanied by clear policies that ensure employment and just wages, the central objective of political economy, as laid out by Adam Smith, is not being addressed. In pursuing this line of thinking, the following paragraphs assess whether Indian jobs are well paying.

Table 7.1 shows the average monthly earnings of India's workers (in 2015), classified according to the nature of employment.

Table 7.1 Average monthly earnings of India's workers

	Self-employed (%)	Regular wage/ salaried (%)	Contract workers (%)	Casual labour (%)
Up to INR 5,000	41.3	18.7	38.5	59.3
INR 5,001–7,500	26.2	19.5	27.9	25.0
INR 7,501–10,000	17.4	19.0	20.3	12.0
INR 10,001–20,000	11.1	23.6	11.0	3.5
INR 20,001–50,000	3.5	17.7	2.1	0.3
INR 50,001–100,000	0.4	1.4	0.1	0
Above INR 100,000	0.1	0.2	0	0

Source: *SWI* 2018, p. 103, Table 4.2: 'Average Monthly Earnings by Employment Status, 2015–16'. The *SWI* table is based on the *Employment–Unemployment Survey 2015* conducted by the Labour Bureau, Ministry of Labour and Employment.

One striking observation from the table is that almost all the workers, irrespective of the nature of employment (salaried, self-employed, contract or casual), earned less than INR 50,000 a month. And a majority of the self-employed workers, contract workers and casual workers earned less than INR 7,500 a month. Do you consider such employment to be well paying?

Poor wages imply poor housing and difficulties in accessing other basic amenities for the workers. In the following excerpt from 'Nowhere to Turn' by Skybaaba, the state of Osman's house is vividly described.

The house, constructed during his grandparents' time, was congested. On one side, there was Osman and Sajida's bedroom. In the middle was a small verandah with a tiled roof and a small corridor, one end of which led to the outer door. At the other end, in the corner was an open toilet. A gunny sack hung like a curtain at its entrance. Next to it was a small bathroom with a shahbad stone floor, enclosed by old sarees and bedsheets for its walls. In the verandah lay a small cot, an old sewing machine in a corner, and a wooden table with beddings on it. (pp. 102–3)

The psychological effect of low and uncertain income on Osman is poignantly captured in the following longer extract from the same short story.

Sajida put her arms around Osman and fell asleep. With his head full of thoughts, Osman could not. Work at the watch shop took up his whole day. He was forced to sell things for ten rupees or less and repair clocks and watches until his eyes watered in order to keep the few customers who came by. Yet, there was no end to his worries. Money was never enough. Whatever he earned was barely enough to manage the household. How could he repay the loans? How would he get his two sisters married? There were two growing children to think of, besides. And now Sajida is pregnant again! His sisters, his mother, no one seemed happy or content. Every day he left home early and returned only after the children had gone to sleep. There was no time or money for any leisure or entertainment. He could not indulge the children in any way. Sometimes, there wasn't even small change in his pocket. How to cope with the children's education, their books, their clothes? In the midst of all these worries, now his brother-in-law was pestering him for financial support. And caught between the two, his sister was under great stress. Osman didn't know where to turn. His life seemed completely rudderless. (pp. 105–6)

While the quantity of employment can be reduced to numbers, the psychological effects of low-quality employment can perhaps be better communicated through such storytelling.

Why are Indian jobs not gainful? Is it because the output per worker is small and, therefore, the firms/employers do not have enough surplus to share with the workers? This could be the reason if output per worker or labour productivity is growing at a snail's pace. Figure 7.1 represents the growth of labour productivity and wages.

Figure 7.1   Divergence between the growth in the productivity and
remuneration of India's workers

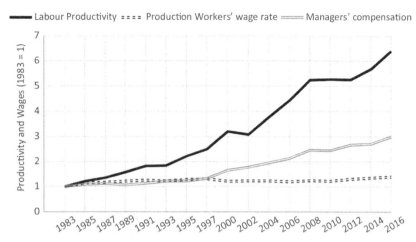

Source: *SWI* 2018, p. 105, Fig. 4.6: 'Productivity and Managerial Compensation Have
Risen Much Faster than Workers' Wages in Organised Manufacturing'. This figure has
been drawn based on the data from the Annual Survey of Industries (ASI), which uses
the National Industrial Classification (NIC) at the 2-digit level, taken from Economic
and Political Weekly Research Foundation India Time Series (EPWRFITS). The figure
expresses the magnitudes after deflating them by the appropriate price indices.

Exercise: Look at the various NIC codes (the latest being NIC-2008) since the 1962
Standard Industrial Classification (SIC), and see how they have incorporated the structural
changes in the Indian economy. The NIC is a statistical device which facilitates the creation
and maintenance of comparable estimates of all economic activities that contribute to the
national income.

This graph may surprise many of you because it goes against the common-
sense view you might have heard or read. It tells us compellingly that despite
the marked increase in labour productivity, the wages of the workers have
stagnated. Moreover, this has happened in organised manufacturing, which
provides some of the best available jobs. And at the same time, managers'
compensation has increased. Think about and discuss whether this divergence
between output per worker and wages per worker is fair or just from an
economic standpoint.

Recollect the discussion on the two theories of wage determination in
Section 6.3, especially that of the classical economists. Why do you think
that there exists such wage disparity across the different kinds of workers as

visible from Table 7.1? Also, think about the role collective bargaining has played in determining the wages, especially of regular workers. What kind of cultural and historical factors have played a role in wage determination?

Finally, it may be noted that a satisfactory understanding of the state of wages in and across India also warrants a basic knowledge of the legal infrastructure, such as the 1926 Trade Unions Act, 1947 Industrial Disputes Act, 1948 Minimum Wages Act, 1948 Factories Act, 1970 Contract Labour Act, and 1979 Inter-State Migrant Workers Act. Recently, on 8 August 2019, the Code on Wages, 2019, was passed by the central government. How does this Act compare to the older ones? Moreover, find out how a resolution is arrived at in your state when two statutory Acts cover the fixing of minimum wages for contract labour.

It is now opportune to share an important passage from Smith's *Wealth of Nations* on wage determination and the role of the government in protecting the interests of the workers.

> What are the common wages of labour, depends everywhere upon the contract usually made between those two parties, whose interests are by no means the same. The workmen desire to get as much, the masters to give as little as possible. The former are disposed to combine in order to raise, the latter in order to lower the wages of labour.
>
> … We have no acts of parliament against combining to lower the price of work; but many against combining to raise it. In all such disputes the masters can hold out much longer. A landlord, a farmer, a master manufacturer, a merchant, though they did not employ a single workman, could generally live a year or two upon the stocks which they have already acquired. Many workmen could not subsist a week, few could subsist a month, and scarce any a year without employment. In the long run the workman may be as necessary to his master as his master is to him; but the necessity is not so immediate. (pp. 83–4)

What is telling in the above extract from Smith is his recognition of the power that the employers (or 'masters') have over the workers—which could also partly explain his adoption of methodological holism.

The preceding discussion strongly indicates that employment in India— for the majority of the workforce—is neither secure nor gainful. We will end this section after undertaking other meso studies of the state of India's (un)employment situation.

Employment in India: further meso approaches

Let us first examine the unemployment rate across some of the different industries within the (organised) manufacturing sector. Between 1983 and 2015, the following industries had a relatively high rate of employment creation: apparel, plastics and footwear (*SWI* 2018, p. 76). During the same period, while the furniture industry had more than doubled employment, the following industries witnessed an absolute decline in employment: textiles, food and appliances (*SWI* 2018, pp. 76–7). This inter-industry difference in employment creation within the organised manufacturing sector could be due to the difference in industry-specific technologies. For instance, an industry which employs a production technique that requires fewer workers to produce a unit of output will generate less employment than an industry which employs a production technique that requires more workers to produce a unit of output, ceteris paribus. However, the volume of employment generated will depend on the quantum of output being produced. Hence, the industry-specific employment generation also depends on the demand for its products, whether by domestic and/or foreign firms/consumers. The focus on industries is extremely important from the perspective of policy because of industry-specific characteristics relating to both the production and consumption of its output. When labour-intensive industries like textiles show an absolute decline in employment over the years, it *is* a cause for concern. Under what situation do you think that this might not be a cause for concern?

Through extracts from stories, Chapters 1 and 2 introduced you to the role of caste and gender in economics. More specifically, Section 2.3 noted that owing to the presence of such norms, the economic logic of a competitive economy operates very differently in the Indian economy vis-à-vis that in theory. And Section 1.4 underscored the constraints imposed by caste and patriarchal norms on the mobility of labour within India. Labour immobilities due to the caste system were briefly mentioned in Section 4.4 too. The historical inequalities arising from caste and gender were alluded to while discussing unequal land ownership in Section 5.3. In Shukla's *Raag Darbari*, he narrates an instance of caste being the primary identity.

"Who are you, brother?"

Every Indian has just one easy answer to this question and that is to give promptly the name of his caste. So he said, "I'm an Aggarwal." (p. 279)

And in the following excerpt from Perumal Murugan's *Seasons of the Palm*, the description of the difficulties faced by Shorty, a Dalit boy, in doing his job evokes a grim picture.

> Shorty has to take the can [of milk] to where the Nadar caste people live. This is not easy, for he has to hold the heavy can by the cloth. On no account must he touch the can directly. Once he gets to the houses in the Nadar neighbourhood that buy milk, he sets the can down and stands away. The lady of the house opens the cloth lid, pours her share of milk into a vessel and ties up the can's mouth once more. This happens in all the houses to which Shorty goes. (p. 12)

Given the above instances in this chapter and some of the previous ones, discuss the ways in which the socio-historical institutions of caste and patriarchy might influence employment.

In *SWI* 2018, one of the ways of capturing the role of caste in employment is through an estimation of how well represented different caste groups are, relative to their share in the workforce. That is, if Scheduled Caste workers comprise 30 per cent of the workforce, but only 15 per cent of the 'professionals', the representation index is 0.5; in other words, the Scheduled Caste workers are underrepresented in the occupational category of 'professionals', who are the best-paid workers. And if the Scheduled Caste workers make up 60 per cent of 'elementary occupations' (the least-paid occupations), the representation index is 2, and we can say that the Scheduled Caste workers are overrepresented in 'elementary occupations'. Figure 7.2 demonstrates very clearly that workers from Scheduled Castes (SC) and Scheduled Tribes (ST) are overrepresented in poorly paid occupations and upper castes are overrepresented in well-paid ones.

The reasons for such unequal representation of castes across the various categories are connected to historical inequalities which restrict(ed) the access of lower castes to land, education and public amenities like water and roads. Such socio-economic restrictions imposed by the caste system go against the very core of a competitive economy—the idea of competition. And competition presupposes mobility—mobility not just of capital (produced means of production such as tractors, agricultural tools and wind turbines) but also of labour and, therefore, labourers.

Before I provide a brief description of the nature of employment for women, let me pose a few leading questions. What do you think is the share of women workers in different sectors—agriculture, manufacturing and services—of the

Figure 7.2 Caste and unequal employment in India

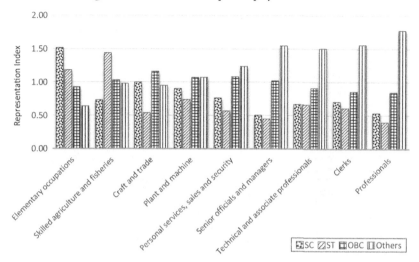

Source: *SWI* 2018, p. 133, Fig. 5.10: 'SC and ST Groups Are Over-Represented in Poorly Paid Occupations while Upper Castes Are Over-Represented in Well-Paid Ones'. This figure is computed based on data from the *Employment–Unemployment Survey 2015* published by the Labour Bureau, Ministry of Labour and Employment.

Note: SC refers to Scheduled Castes, ST to Scheduled Tribes, and OBC to Other Backward Classes.

economy? In which sector would you expect it to be the most? The factors that determine the sectoral shares of women workers are also socio-historical in nature. In particular, social stereotypes about women's roles and aspirations play an important role. In connection to this, find out whether more women go to work from rural households than urban households, and if so, why? Discuss the kind of community norms that prevent women from participating in the workforce. Does patriarchy prevent women from migrating in search of work? When women migrate, is it primarily for marriage or work? How do childbearing and the subsequent sharing of parental responsibility influence women's participation in the workforce?

Figure 7.3 shows the share of women workers in the three major sectors—agriculture, manufacturing and services—and in construction (a significant employment-generating sector within manufacturing).

Figure 7.3 Women and unequal employment in India

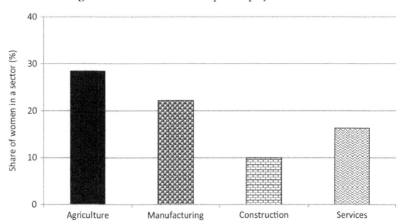

Source: SWI 2018, p. 124, Fig. 5.2: 'Share of Women in Various Sectors'. This figure is computed based on data from the *Employment–Unemployment Survey 2015* published by the Labour Bureau, Ministry of Labour and Employment.

Think about reasons why the share of women workers in agriculture is 28.6 per cent and in services only 16.3 per cent. Perhaps, one of the reasons is found in Picchio's (1992) book: that jobs in agriculture allow women to easily combine their agricultural work with housework (p. 109). Within the manufacturing sector, the share of women workers in the following three industries is the highest: textiles, apparel and tobacco. And within the services sector, the share of women workers in the following three industries is the highest: education, health and domestic services. Now, discuss with your friends about the possible factors that might explain the significant presence of women in these particular industries.

Socio-historical forces have an impact on policies relating to employment and wages. For instance, in the state of Kerala, the minimum wage in tea plantations, an industry in which there is a high concentration of women, is far lower than that in rubber tapping, an activity in which there is a high concentration of men (*India Wage Report* 2018, p. 84). As the classical economists rightly pointed out, wages are determined by social and historical forces. Therefore, *just* wages can be achieved through a combination of good politics and policy. As an exercise, find out the maternity leave benefits offered to women in your college/university.

To sum up, through a variety of sources, it has been demonstrated that the quantity and quality of employment is particularly abysmal in the case of Scheduled Castes, Scheduled Tribes and women. It is now time to move to the next section, which aims to provide you with a palette to begin thinking about macroeconomic solutions for the problem of unemployment (in India)—with a view to achieving reliable and gainful full employment.

7.3 A prelude to the solutions

This section first assembles the policy implications arising from the marginalist and Keynesian theories of output and employment and subsequently those arising from supply-side and demand-led growth theories. While some of the discussion is of reiterative nature, others are novel. The role of markets in ensuring full employment of labour and economic growth is mostly a reiteration, and the discussion on conceptual matters related to the role of the government in determining employment and economic growth, with specific focus on government borrowing (and public debt), is mostly novel. Then, this section animates the tension arising from the coming together of both concept (that is, the Keynesian approach) and context (that is, the Indian macroeconomy) through some of the contributions of P. C. Mahalanobis and V. K. R. V. Rao. Rao's name has already been introduced in relation to India's macroeconomic accounting. Mahalanobis was the chief architect of the Second Five-Year Plan of India. The section ends by advocating an anti-cyclical fiscal policy.

Theories of output and growth: policy implications

In Chapter 4, we had discussed the two approaches to the determination of output and employment (Section 4.2). While the marginalist theory posits a tendency to the full employment of labour in a competitive economy, the Keynesian theory points out that there exists no such tendency. The policy implication arising from the marginalist theory is that government intervention ought to be minimised because the markets will ensure that supply creates its own demand, in the case of both commodities (which includes capital goods as they are produced means of production) and labour. However, in a diametrically opposite vein, the Keynesian theory calls for government intervention because the markets cannot ensure aggregate demand sufficiency.

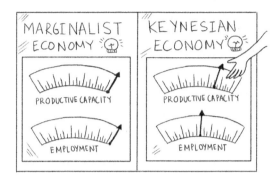

Both marginalist and Keynesian theories of output and employment take the productive capacity as given. In other words, there is no technological progress in the theoretical worlds they study. Theories of growth account for technological *progress* and provide explanations for the evolution of output over time. Chapter 5 provided two contrasting explanations of growth—supply-side and demand-led growth theories. Let me reiterate the policy conclusions emanating from these two theories discussed in Section 5.2: demand-led growth theory warrants active (and targeted) government intervention so as to influence the growth of the autonomous elements of aggregate demand, whereas supply-side growth theory, owing to its marginalist core, will be partial to policies favouring the expansion of aggregate supply via the market (mechanism). As pointed out in Sections 5.2 and 5.4, the extension of the supply-side growth framework by Paul Romer to 'ideas' and William Nordhaus to 'nature' have resulted in policy suggestions aimed at creating a market for 'ideas' (or intellectual property rights) and 'nature' (through the buying and selling of carbon credits), respectively. And owing to the reliance on the marginal productivity theory of income distribution and the $S_{FE} = f(roi) = I$ principle, supply-side growth theories also favour the loosening of labour laws and imposition of austerity measures (recall the brief discussion on austerity in Section 6.3). To read book-length historical treatments of austerity, consult Mark Blyth's *Austerity: The History of a Dangerous Idea* (2013) and Florian Schui's *Austerity: The Great Failure* (2014).

The role of the government

Both the marginalist theories of output and growth essentially presume (and demonstrate) the tendency to the full employment of labour. That is, these theories assume that the economy is a system that is operating at its full capacity. This is another way of saying that the economy is characterised by scarcity, wherein the use of one resource implies a reduction of the other as if in a zero-sum game, to use a term from game theory. As a consequence of this assumption/belief, they argue that government expenditure is bad for the economy, as it will push out or crowd out private expenditure; besides such physical crowding out, they also argue that government expenditure that is funded by borrowing (from the people in that economy) raises the interest rate and will crowd out private borrowing; this is termed as financial crowding out. Recall that the idea of financial crowding out aligns with exogenous money, and is difficult to align with endogenous money (see Section 3.4).

In the Keynesian theories of output and employment, there is no assumption of scarcity because capital—the *produced* means of production—can always be produced. Moreover, in the Keynesian theories of output and employment, the tendency of the economic system is towards the unemployment of labour because of aggregate demand insufficiency. Thus, in this conceptualisation of a competitive economy, surplus labour exists and capital is not scarce. As a consequence, additional government expenditure increases aggregate demand and raises output and employment; the increase in aggregate output is often of a higher magnitude than the initial increase in government expenditure, owing to multiplier effects arising from structural interdependence in the economy (for a discussion on the multiplier, see Section 4.2). Therefore, in the Keynesian framework, government expenditure *crowds in* private investment.

Contemporary concerns about public debt and its negative impact on the macroeconomy, it must be noted, emanate primarily from a marginalist standpoint. The view that the government should not undertake any significant investment in the economy, as we have just discussed, is also a close friend of this standpoint. The marginalists, who generally operate within the exogenous money framework, believe that rising public debt will intensify the crowding out of private investment. As discussed in Chapter 6, they expect the government to behave like a household that spends within its income. However, a government is a very different entity compared to a household (see especially Section 6.3). And, therefore, if a government borrows from its people to meaningfully spend on education, health, environment, museums or roads, it is undoubtedly good for the macroeconomy. Make a list of reasons commonly found in newspaper articles that oppose government borrowing and discuss them from the contending standpoints of marginalism and Keynesianism.

If the government borrows and does not enhance the productive capacity of the macroeconomy through additions to either physical or social infrastructure, then questions can be raised on macroeconomic grounds. However, note that these additions also include salary payments to the workers who are employed in offices of public administration. Therefore, the expenditure budget of our central government breaks down its expenditure ministry-wise, into 'capital' and 'revenue'. While capital expenditure includes the setting up of a power plant and creating ponds for irrigation, revenue expenditure includes salary payments and administrative costs. Consult the most recent Union Budget and note down the capital and revenue expenditure items for the Ministry of Agriculture and Farmers Welfare.

Since increasing government expenditure is an important—perhaps the most important—way to increase employment in any macroeconomy, a brief discussion on government borrowing follows. The government borrows because the combined revenue from direct taxes such as income tax and corporate tax and indirect taxes such as the goods and services tax (GST) falls short of planned government expenditure, which includes not only the creation of physical and social infrastructure (through various government schemes), but also the payment of salaries to various ministries' employees, subsidies (mainly for food, fertilisers, petroleum and interest) and interest payments. As economists, we need to focus on the flow of debt more than its stock in order to assess whether the debt is sustainable over a certain period of time. However, the debt stock is also important because it determines the volume of interest payments, assuming a given rate of interest; since the rate of interest influences our understanding of debt sustainability, it follows that the view of money as being exogenous or endogenous also matters. Additionally, the rate of economic growth provides an indication about the repayment capacity of the economy.

In the classic paper 'The "Burden of Debt" and the National Income' (1944), Evsey Domar, writing in the Keynesian tradition, argued against the dominant view (both then and now) that governments must refrain from borrowing to finance their expenditure. The following passage from Domar reinforces our earlier point that what matters for debt sustainability is the nature of government expenditure. Domar writes that "the term 'investment expenditures' may be misleading, because it is too closely associated with steel and concrete. If healthier people are more productive, expenditures on public health satisfy these requirements. The same holds true for expenditures on education, research, flood control, resource development and so on" (p. 820). To obtain a learned understanding of the role of the government in creating infrastructure, read Mariana Mazzucatto's 2013 book *The Entrepreneurial State: Debunking Public vs. Private Sector Myths*.

Given the theoretical superiority of the Keynesian standpoint over the marginalist one, we shall employ its policy conclusions to arrive at a solution framework for unemployment. The Keynesian principle of effective demand states that autonomous expenditures, in combination with the expenditures they induce, determine the equilibrium level of aggregate output via the multiplier process. What are these autonomous expenditures? Autonomous consumption, autonomous investment, government expenditure and exports fall under this category (for a definition of autonomous consumption and investment, see Section 4.2). Another way to increase aggregate activity levels, as mentioned briefly in Section 4.3, is through foreign direct investment (FDI).

What is common among autonomous consumption, autonomous investment, exports and FDI? They are all undertaken by individuals or firms within the private sector. The primary aim of the private sector, especially businesses or firms, is not the generation of employment but the maximisation of profit. So, when better business opportunities are found in a different sector, they shift their activities to that sector. Similarly, if better business opportunities are found in a different region/state in a country, businesses shift their operations to that region/state. And such shifting of operations happens across countries when FDI is involved. Moreover, the aim of profit maximisation of firms might warrant adopting labour-saving techniques of production. Given their central aim of profit maximisation, private investment is extremely *volatile* and FDI is even more volatile. Therefore, the pursuit of reliable and gainful employment cannot be solely vested with the private sector.

Following the Keynesian standpoint, it is strongly suggested that the autonomous expenditure by the government is a good route to achieve full employment that is both reliable and gainful. Against this backdrop, it needs to be reiterated that so long as government expenditure expands the productive capacity of the economy by investments in physical and social infrastructure, there is no grave *economic* reason to worry about the sustainability of public debt or government borrowing. In a way, the preceding paragraphs have provided an extended rationale for choosing government expenditure as a means to achieve full employment.

Concept and context: Mahalanobis and Rao

The discussions in this section so far have been conceptual and have not made any reference to the Indian context. In the following paragraphs, the concept (in this case, the Keynesian theory) and context are brought together to arrive at more specific ways of formulating policies to attain full employment in the Indian economy. In Section 4.2, the question of the applicability of the Keyensian theory of output and employment to India was raised by taking recourse to the points made by Rao (1952) and Dasgupta (1954).

Through a brief engagement with the work of P. C. Mahalanobis and V. K. R. V. Rao, the concept and context shall be brought together, and, as it will be seen, not without resistance. Mahalanobis provided the economic model for the Second Five-Year Plan of India (1956–61), which aimed at increasing aggregate output as well as reducing income and wealth inequalities. The role of the private sector in achieving *our* economic aims was neither unqualified nor apologetic (as they seem to be these days), but outcome dependent. In the second chapter titled 'Approach to the Second Five-Year Plan' of the Plan document, it was written:

> The private sector has to play its part within the framework of the comprehensive plan accepted by the community.... Private enterprise, free pricing, private management are all devices to further what are truly social ends; they can only be justified in terms of social results.

The above excerpt underscores the fact that the support for private enterprise cannot be unconditional, irrespective of whether it arises from adherence to the marginalist framework or not. For a succinct account of the intellectual and historical backdrop of the Second Five-Year Plan, read the second chapter of Sukhamoy Chakravarty's 1987 book *Development Planning: The Indian Experience*.

In the book *A History of Indian Economic Thought* (1993) written by Ajit Dasgupta, there is a discussion of the Mahalanobis model, owing to its significance for post-independence Indian economic thought and policy. The Mahalanobis model is a two-sector model with the sectors producing capital goods and consumption goods respectively. The model determines the optimal allocation of investment between these two sectors such that it maximises economic growth. Indeed, owing to the structural interdependence between the two sectors, one sector cannot grow without the growth of the other. This is because, to produce consumption goods, capital goods are required, and the workers producing capital goods require consumption goods. Besides this inter-sectoral relationship, each sector uses its own outputs as inputs. For example, the outputs of capital goods enter as inputs into the production of capital goods and the workers in the consumption goods sector consume the output of the consumption goods sector.

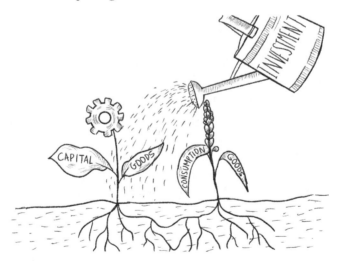

Given the poor productive capacity of the Indian economy, the Mahalanobis model focused on the supply-side factors, notably the creation of physical infrastructure. The model has been rightly criticised subsequently for ignoring the role of aggregate demand and for not assigning enough importance to social infrastructure such as education and health. K. N. Raj, an important architect of the First Five-Year Plan, expressed dissatisfaction with the Second Five-Year Plan because of the inadequate attention it accorded to the agricultural sector. And C. N. Vakil and P. R. Brahmananda criticised the Mahalanobis model for not according importance to the sectors that produce the necessaries of the workers (especially, that of food). How will you modify the Mahalanobis model by taking into account demand-led growth theories and the state of the contemporary Indian economy?

As discussed in Chapter 2, understanding the macroeconomy requires some basic knowledge of macroeconomic accounting. Among the economists mentioned in Section 2.2, let us engage briefly with a point made by V. K. R. V. Rao, who contributed substantially to India's national income accounting (NIA). Rao had concluded his 1944 article on the computation of the 'National Income of India', published in *The ANNALS of the American Academy of Political and Social Science*, by highlighting the importance of careful economic planning: "I cannot help recording the belief that Indian poverty is not inevitable and that, given a national government and the adoption of a planned economy, a substantial increase can be brought about in Indian income and considerable improvements effected in India's standard of life and conditions of real income" (p. 105). As students of macroeconomics and/or of the Indian economy, reading Rao's 1983 book *India's National Income 1950–80: An Analysis of Economic Growth and Change* would be very enriching, although it is quite difficult to access a copy.

The preceding paragraphs especially tried to highlight that good policymaking needs to take cognisance of both concept and context. Given the presence of a large informal sector, the estimation of aggregate income was, and continues to remain, difficult. Rao, with his knowledge of the Indian context, did not favour—and rightly so—a blind application of Keynesian economics to Indian economic issues (see the brief discussion on the applicability question in Section 4.2). This note of caution applies to all theoretical frameworks when employed in the service of policy.

Anti-cyclical fiscal policy

By embracing the Keynesian theory of output and employment (and demand-led growth theory), the following general approaches to policy will help attain the full employment of labour. Very broadly, the nature of our economic policy meant to combat unemployment ought to be primarily anti-cyclical in nature, supported by counter-cyclical policies; most certainly, it should not be pro-cyclical in nature.

Owing to the volatility of private investment, economies go through (often, alternating) phases of ups and downs with respect to aggregate output and employment. These phases are commonly known as business cycles. When the government increases its expenditure and reduces taxes during the down phases, it is called a counter-cyclical (fiscal) policy. That is, counter-cyclical policies are adopted to reduce the cyclical fluctuations of aggregate output. However, if the government reduces its expenditure and increases taxes during the down phases, it is termed as pro-cyclical (fiscal) policy. This might be done in order to ensure that the balance sheet of the government does not go into a deficit position. Austerity is an example of an extreme pro-cyclical policy. However, if our aim is to achieve reliable and gainful full employment, then the government should structure its planned expenditure in such a way that the ups and downs of aggregate output and employment levels are not only minimised (as in counter-cyclical policy) but also avoided (as in anti-cyclical policy). The following excerpt from Keynes's policy discussions, found in volume 27 of *The Collected Writings of John Maynard Keynes*, further clarifies the character of anti-cyclical policy.

> If two-thirds or three-quarters of total investment is carried out or can be influenced by public or semi-public bodies, a long-term programme of a stable character should be capable of reducing the potential range of fluctuation to much narrower limits than formerly, when a smaller volume of investment was under public control and when even this part tended to follow, rather than correct, fluctuations of investment in the strictly private sector of the economy.... The main task should be to prevent large fluctuations by a stable long-term programme. If this is successful it should not be too difficult to offset small fluctuations by expediting or retarding some items in this long-term programme. (Moggridge 1980, p. 322)

And, this kind of an anti-cyclical (fiscal) policy calls for *thoughtful* economic planning.

An effective anti-cyclical policy, which also seeks to provide reliable and gainful full employment, cannot be confined to just an employment policy. It is advisable to formulate an integrated economic plan which cuts across, for instance, India's employment policy, growth policy, agricultural policy, industrial policy, wage policy, education policy and ecological policy.

When it comes to any economic policy (with specific schemes), it cannot but be integrated, because the policy affects the macroeconomic variables by influencing the economic decisions of households and firms.

The extent of the influence depends on the context. The following is a sample of contextual questions. Are the economic units primarily located in the formal or informal sector? Are the households and firms mostly engaged in the agricultural or services sector? Do they mostly reside in rural or urban India? What is the extent of inter-state, intra-state and foreign migration of workers? For example, if the government constructs a road in a rural area by employing workers directly through a contractor or indirectly through an unemployment scheme such as the Mahatma Gandhi National Rural Employment Guarantee Act (MGNREGA), is it not a good government scheme? The answer is: it depends. Some of the factors the answer depends on are: whether the workers are paid market wages or minimum wages, for how many days they get work and how the land for constructing the road was purchased by the government. Now, discuss the following scenario by identifying the relevant considerations: if a road construction project requires the felling of 100 trees, is it still a good government scheme?

Given that India's productive capacity—particularly with respect to physical infrastructure and essential social infrastructure such as health and education—is woefully inadequate, the government ought to directly invest in these sectors. This will not only provide reliable and gainful employment, but will also enhance the productive capacity. Similarly, government investment is required to create physical infrastructure such as irrigation and storage facilities for agriculture. Moreover, the government should create green (physical) infrastructure in both cities and villages. The following excerpt from M. M. Vinodini's short story 'The Parable of the Lost Daughter' (2013) describes the expectations of a Dalit Christian household from education.

> Suvarthavani had always occupied a special place in that house. She was intelligent and very good at her studies. She was good looking too. Although they lived in a small village near Guntur, Krupamma and Paladasu decided that they would help her study as much as she wanted to. They wanted her to be happy and respected, and they believed that education alone helped a person achieve these. (pp. 166–7)

Currently, good education is not available to all. Therefore, the setting up of a good government school will not only have multiplier effects on local incomes and employment, but also act as an important pathway for households to command social respect.

This chapter has eschewed very specific policy suggestions for achieving full employment because the route to achieving it is highly contextual. For instance, the people of Kerala might prefer government investment in ecologically friendly or green services, whereas the people of Bihar might prefer green manufacturing. While both create jobs, it is likely that for the same amount of investment, green manufacturing will create more jobs than green services. Moreover, recall that, by government expenditure, we are referring not only to the central government but also to the state and local governments. As an exercise, based on the guides to attain full employment of labour mentioned in this chapter, draft an economic policy for your state keeping in mind your local context; you can modify existing government schemes and also come up with new schemes.

To conclude, the policy objective of full employment of labour requires careful planning and investment by the government (at all levels). This policy aim cannot be entirely, or even mostly, left to the private sector.

7.4 Conclusion

This chapter outlined the nature of unemployment in the Indian economy by focusing on its quantity and quality. Section 7.2 highlighted the significant proportion of contract workers in total employment, the rise of casualisation of the workforce, and the unequal nature of employment with respect to caste and gender. By restating the conceptual framework of the Keynesian theory of output and employment and the demand-led growth theory, it was argued that the policy objective of full employment requires primarily an anti-cyclical fiscal policy that is well integrated across the diverse domains/ministries of labour, wages, environment, agriculture, education and manufacturing.

Suggestions for further reading

Amit Bhaduri's 2005 book *Development with Dignity: A Case for Full Employment* (New Delhi: National Book Trust) continues to remain an important text for both the general reader and the economics student. For a comprehensive account of Keynes's policy proposals based on a careful reading of *The General Theory* and his policy documents of the 1940s, read Tony Aspromourgos's 2012 article 'Keynes's *General Theory* after 75 Years: Chapter 24 and the Character of "Keynesian" Policy' in the journal *Economic Record* (vol. 88, no. s1, pp. 149–57). To obtain a deeper understanding of the power dynamics between the government and the private sector, with respect to the employment question, read Michał Kalecki's sharply written 1943 article 'The Politics of Full Employment' in the *Political Quarterly* (vol. 14, no. 4, pp. 322–31). And for a short critical commentary, written in the same spirit as Kalecki's, on India's commitment to the Fiscal Responsibility and Budgetary Management Act of 2003, see Amit Bhaduri's 2006 article 'The Politics of "Sound Finance"' in the *Economic and Political Weekly* (vol. 41, nos 43–4, pp. 4569–71). If you wish to know more about Indian economic thought, you can consult the following books in addition to Dasgupta (1993): B. N. Ganguli's 1977 book *Indian Economic Thought: Nineteenth Century Perspectives* (New Delhi: Tata McGraw Hill) and Bhabatosh Datta's 1978 book *Indian Economic Thought: Twentieth Century Perspectives* (New Delhi: Tata McGraw-Hill). However, accessing these books can be difficult because they are out of print and can be found only in some libraries; I myself acquired access to Ganguli's and Datta's books through Azim Premji University Library's Inter-Library loan from the libraries of the Institute for Studies in Industrial Development (ISID) and Jawaharlal Nehru University (JNU), respectively, both in New Delhi. These readings may be complemented by J. Krishnamurty's short introduction to his edited book *Towards Development Economics: Indian Contributions 1900–1945* published in 2009 (New Delhi: Oxford University Press).

8

The Policy Objective of Low Inflation

8.1 Introduction

When the prices of essential commodities like *dal* (pulses) and onions increase, it makes headlines in newspapers. It is similar with fuel (petrol and diesel) prices too. If we have at our disposal the knowledge regarding the determinants of these prices, then we can formulate policies aimed at reducing the prices. In the preceding chapters, we discussed the macro determinants of aggregate output (Section 4.2), the nature of India's financial architecture (Section 3.2) and the significant presence of informality in the Indian economy (Section 6.4). It will presently be seen (in Section 8.2) that a brief understanding of the aforementioned empowers our attempt to understand the nature of inflation.

This chapter introduces you to the nature of inflation—the rise in aggregate price level over a sustained period of time—by measuring its various aspects *and* posing several questions for you to ponder over. The measurement of aggregate price level requires the aid of the statistical device of index numbers, which is an average of a special kind. After outlining the problem of high inflation, the chapter provides a range of broad macroeconomic solutions relevant to the Indian context. Before we get into the details of inflation, note that the primary objective of the Reserve Bank of India (RBI), as mentioned on its website, is "to maintain price stability while keeping in mind the objective of growth".

To reiterate, the primary aim of economics, following Smith, is to ensure "a plentiful revenue or subsistence for the people". This warrants not only reliable and gainful full employment, but also that the purchasing power of wages witnesses an improvement in line with the evolution of people's social needs. Or, at the very least, the purchasing power of wages ought to remain steady. This chapter focuses on commodity flows and money flows, both of which influence commodity prices. It takes Keynes's assumption of a 'monetary production economy' seriously to arrive at an understanding of inflation. The chapter concludes by arguing that the policies to combat inflation warrant the joint forces of fiscal and monetary policies.

8.2 The nature of inflation in India

Inflation, as noted in the introductory section, is the persistent rise in the aggregate price level (P) over a period of time. While the growth of aggregate output (Y), say, 9 per cent, is considered favourable to the economy, a 9 per cent growth in P is not. Furthermore, is an inflation rate of 1 per cent desirable over 5 per cent?

Since the ex post or actual Y and P are both (weighted) averages, a rise in them does not necessarily imply that *all* sectors are witnessing an increase in the value added or prices, respectively (Section 2.5 had pointed this out in the context of P). In the language of statistics, we need to examine not only the average but also the distribution. This is another reason why this textbook adopts a meso approach alongside the central macro approach. Looking at *only* the average can be misleading and therefore can result in bad economic policies. In Section 4.1, it was pointed out that the output per worker may be viewed as an average; in Section 5.3, economic growth was viewed from the perspective of the sectoral growth of agriculture, manufacturing and services to underscore the fact that a meso approach contributes greatly to our understanding. Finally, recall the difference between theoretical and statistical/ empirical measurements as astutely pointed out by Sraffa (Section 1.4). And, while the gross domestic product (GDP) is essentially a statistical average, its theoretical counterpart, the aggregate output (Y), is not a statistical average. Although the macro theoretical conception of aggregate output is often taught using the analogy of an average, strictly speaking, it should only be treated as a pedagogic or rhetorical tool.

A brief digression on the link between theory and empirics with respect to Y and P is warranted. Although we conceive of Y as the aggregate of all commodities (both goods and services) produced in an economy, since they are heterogeneous in nature, any aggregation requires the prior knowledge of their respective prices. In theory, it is as if Y exists independently of the individual commodity prices. However, in empirics, it is not so. Similarly, in theory, P is conceived as an entity that is an expression of the aggregate price level or the price level for the economy as a whole, which is independent of individual commodities as well as aggregate output. Keynes, as quoted in Section 2.5, regarded the aggregate or general price level as being characterised by an "element of vagueness", thus making it "very unsatisfactory for the purposes of a causal analysis". Moreover, the empirical calculation of P warrants the knowledge of the quantities produced of individual commodities. Therefore, the empirical measurement of both Y and P requires the assistance of index numbers. If you are interested in economic statistics, look up how the indices of agricultural and industrial production are constructed in India; pay special attention to the methods employed in the aggregation of agricultural and industrial output, and the assignment of weights.

The general price level for India is estimated using the following price indices—wholesale price index (WPI) and consumer price index (CPI). The responsibility of publishing the WPI is with the Ministry of Commerce and Industry (more specifically, the Office of the Economic Advisor [OEA]) and that of the CPI is with the Ministry of Statistics and Programme Implementation (more specifically, the Central Statistics Office). Besides these, the Labour Bureau, under the Ministry of Labour and Employment, publishes the following price indices for the purpose of determining minimum wages: CPI for industrial workers (CPI-IW), CPI for agricultural labourers (CPI-AL) and CPI for rural labourers (CPI-RL).

While the construction of the CPI (with base year 2012) utilises price quotations from 268,351 village markets and 2,818,001 urban markets, the construction of the WPI (with base year 2011–12) uses only 8,331 price quotations, as it focuses on transactions that take place at the first point of bulk sale. The OEA captures the latter information via online reporting and field visits. Before we look at the WPI values between 2014–15 and 2018–19, let us spend a little more space and time understanding the creation of the WPI. Some of the price quotations relating to agricultural commodities are supplied by the Revenue and Civil Supplies staff, and those relating to non-agricultural commodities by the Indian Chambers of Commerce and Industry. To understand more about the different government agencies involved and the data chain, look at pages 344–7 of M. R. Saluja's *Measuring India: The Nation's Statistical System* (2017).

While the WPI was published every week since 1947, it has been converted to a monthly series from 2012. The current base year for the WPI is 2011–12, and the index is calculated using the Laspeyres formula. In 1864, Étienne Laspeyres proposed an index that takes as its weights the proportion of commodities purchased relative to the total commodities purchased during the base year; exactly a decade later, in 1874, Hermann Paasche proposed an index that takes as its weights the proportion of commodities purchased relative to the total commodities purchased during the current year. If the Laspeyres formula is used, then the WPI is computed based on the relative proportion of commodities purchased during 2011–12 acting as the weights; this may be mathematically expressed as $\Sigma P_1 Q_0 / \Sigma P_0 Q_0$. Here, Q represents the commodities, P their prices, and the subscripts 0 and 1 the base and current years, respectively. An index number transforms a heterogenous set of magnitudes, whether prices or quantities, into a single magnitude that has no unit of measurement. More will be said about the Paasche formulation towards the end of this section.

How is the base year decided? The following excerpt from an article published in the RBI's October 2010 monthly bulletin provides some guidelines for choosing a base year and therefore it also provides guidance on when the base year ought to be revised.

> In determining the base year for any index number, a set of well-known criteria is followed. These include: (a) the base year should be a normal year, i.e., a stable year in respect of economic activities like production, trade, etc.; (b) it should not suffer from business cycles; (c) availability of reliable price data for the selected year; (c) the base year should be as recent a year as possible so that by the time revised series of items and their prices are released, it should not have outlived its utility; and (d) the base year for other closely related economic indicators should not be widely off the mark. Again, it is acknowledged that it would be desirable to choose a base year that is not out of date or out of tune with the universe that it is designed to present. (p. 2073)

In a way, a revision of the base year and/or the weights indicates a change in the *structure* of the macroeconomy. But note that there exists no mathematical formula for deciding that the macroeconomy has undergone a structural change. Moreover, while the assessment is based on quantitative and qualitative facts, the final settlement is a matter of human, not machine, judgement. To obtain a good historical account of the WPI numbers in India, read pages 361–70 of Saluja's 2017 book *Measuring India*. As an exercise, look up the document 'Frequently Asked Questions on Revision of Wholesale Price Index' published by the OEA on 12 May 2017, and identify the number of times the base year for the WPI has been revised; discuss whether these base year revisions have truly captured the structural changes in the Indian economy.

The weights for primary articles, fuel and power, and manufactured products used in the construction of the WPI with 2011–12 as the base year are provided in Figure 8.1.

Figure 8.1   Weights in India's WPI

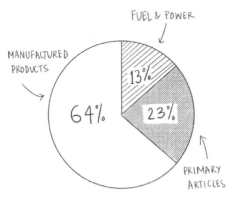

Source: Release of New Series of Wholesale Price Index, 12 May 2017, Frequently Asked Questions on Revision of Wholesale Price Index (Base: 2011–12=100), Ministry of Commerce and Industry.

Note: The values are rounded off to the nearest per cent.

The weights represent their respective contribution to the total value of commodities transacted (excluding imports) in the Indian economy during the base year 2011–12. But note that the WPI excludes services. What items constitute these empirical categories of primary articles, fuel and power, and manufactured products? Primary articles include food, vegetables, milk, meat, and non-food products such as raw rubber, raw silk and groundnut seeds; fuel and power include electricity, petrol and LPG; and manufactured products include all food products, textiles, rubber, metallic products, beverages, tobacco, pharmaceuticals and electronic products. Using the RBI's manual on determining the base year provided in the excerpt earlier, assess whether 2011–12 is a satisfactory base year. Also, discuss whether you agree with the distribution of weights in the WPI.

As a producer of commodities, I would be interested in knowing the trend of wholesale prices because of my need to both buy and sell capital goods as a producer of intermediate goods, and/or because of my need to buy capital goods as a producer of final (consumption) goods. As a trader of commodities, I would need to know the trend of wholesale prices so as to quote appropriate prices (along with a reasonable rate of profit). However, as primarily a consumer of, say, onions and sugar, the price index relevant to me is the CPI. As an exercise, find out the relative weights of commodities in the CPI and see how closely it resembles your family's distribution of monthly consumption expenditure on the same commodities. Also, what do you think it means when there is a divergence in the trends of the WPI and the CPI?

Let us now look at the annual WPI values from 2014–15 to 2018–19. Since the WPI is computed and published every month, the following values are annual averages. Table 8.1 provides the WPI for all commodities and the WPI separately for (*a*) primary articles, (*b*) fuel and power and (*c*) manufactured products.

Table 8.1   Index numbers of wholesale price in India: a trend

	2014–15	2015–16	2016–17	2017–18	2018–19
WPI (all commodities)	113.9	109.7	111.6	114.8	119.8
Primary Articles	125.1	124.6	128.9	130.6	134.2
Fuel and Power	107.7	86.5	86.3	93.3	104.0
Manufactured Products	111.2	109.2	110.7	113.7	117.9

Source: While the primary source of the data is OEA, the above data is downloaded from RBI's 'Table 37: Wholesale Price Index – Annual Average' (p. 80) found in its *Handbook of Statistics on the Indian Economy 2018–19*.

Note: The base year is 2011–12 and the wholesale prices in that period is set to 100.

Since the base year is 2011–12, a 113.9 WPI in 2014–15 means that the wholesale prices for all commodities have increased by 13.9 per cent between 2011–12 and 2014–15. Note that the WPI is a *relative* magnitude that measures the difference in wholesale prices between two points in time. In general, a price or quantity index is a ratio between two magnitudes over a period of time. However, the price of an individual commodity at a point in time, say, the price of a kilogram of onions on 5 July 2019, is not a ratio or a relative magnitude, but an absolute magnitude. Between 2014–15 and 2018–19, the WPI (for all commodities) increased by 5.18 per cent; this is arrived at by finding the difference between the WPI for the two years, then dividing it by the WPI in 2014–15, and multiplying the resultant value by 100: [(119.8 – 113.9) / 113.9] x 100. Over the same five-year period, the WPI for primary articles increased by 7.27 per cent, fuel and power decreased by 4.43 per cent, and manufactured products increased by 6.03 per cent. Think about how this meso accounting of the WPI affects you as a producer of primary articles vis-à-vis manufactured products; recall Table 2.1 when you think about this economic issue.

Prima facie, it may be argued that the wholesale sellers of primary articles (who are also buyers of manufactured products) have fared better than wholesale sellers of manufactured products (who are also buyers of primary articles) over the above five-year period, ceteris paribus. Moreover, the extent of gains depends on the degree of structural interdependence between the agricultural and the manufacturing sectors. If as a wholesale seller of primary articles, you are heavily dependent on manufactured products, your gains will be less than that of a wholesale seller of primary articles who is less dependent on manufactured products. Furthermore, since the WPI of primary articles (and manufactured products) are averages themselves, the extent of the gains also depends on the relative position of the wholesale sellers of, say, vegetables relative to meat in terms of quantities (the quantity of vegetables sold relative to the quantity of meat sold) and prices (price of 1 kilogram of vegetables relative to the price of 1 kilogram of meat) within the category of primary articles. This examination can be further magnified to assess the wholesale prices (and quantities) of, say, pumpkins and poultry.

While it makes sense to focus on the general price level at the macro level to obtain a simple measure of inflation (which is utilised in making policies), it is necessary to adopt a meso approach by examining the commodity flows and money prices across sectors, to formulate more effective policies, as it captures additional aspects of the economic context. As noted earlier, even the meso approach is an abstraction, although at a lower level than the macro approach; indeed, more information on the nature of inflation can be obtained by adopting a micro approach. A micro approach in the context of a wholesale seller of agricultural commodities would entail knowledge of the individual farmer's technological capacity, caste location, gender, the availability and access to farm infrastructure (seeds, machinery, irrigation, credit, and so on), the presence of proximate *mandi*s (markets), the frequency of such agricultural markets, the knowledge of agricultural prices in nearby areas and the such—more broadly, the specific economic and social contexts.

The inflation rate is both empirically understood and expressed as the annual increase in the WPI of all commodities. That is, in the first week of December 2020, to find out the current inflation rate, we usually compute the difference between the WPI in November 2020 and November 2019, divide it by the November 2019 WPI and multiply by 100: [($WPI_{Nov\,2020} - WPI_{Nov\,2019}$)/ $WPI_{Nov\,2019}$] x 100. Based on Table 8.1, the year-on-year (y-o-y) inflation rate between 2017–18 and 2018–19 is 4.36 per cent. Think about the merits of choosing year-on-year over month-on-month to calculate the inflation rate, and whether and how that choice matters in our understanding of inflation.

Another way to capture inflation is by charting the evolution of the ratio of GDP at current prices to GDP at constant prices over a period of time; such a ratio is called the GDP deflator. This approach eschews the notion of a representative basket of commodities as in the case of CPI and WPI. Note down the merits of the GDP deflator vis-à-vis the WPI. And, in addition to this exercise, look up India's first official housing price index launched in 2007 by the National Housing Bank (NHB), at the behest of the Ministry of Finance, and compare the rate of growth of the housing price index with that of the WPI, the CPI and the GDP deflator between 2007 and 2015. What observations can you make about the nature of inflation during this period?

Let us now take stock of the discussion so far with respect to the macro, meso and micro approaches to understanding prices by summarising it visually in Figure 8.2, before entering into a deliberation on how prices are determined.

Figure 8.2   Prices: levels of abstraction

Approach	Relevant theoretical concept
macro	General price level (P)
meso	Relative prices (P_1/P_2)
micro	Individual price (P_1)

The aim of the above classification is to highlight the degrees of abstraction that characterise the different prices in economics. The theoretical notion of the general price level (P) is at a significantly higher level of abstraction than the notion of individual prices (P_1). Think about whether the macro theoretical notions of aggregate output (Y) and the general price level (P) are at similar levels of abstraction.

Even the price of a kilogram of pumpkin (P_1) is an abstraction, for there exist many varieties of pumpkins and all the pumpkins of one variety need not be homogenous in quality. Similarly, say P_1 refers to the price of rice, but there are so many varieties of rice being produced in India and within each variety, there are different qualities (recall the discussion in Section 2.5 on quantity and quality in economic theorising). Therefore, remember that P_1 is also an abstract theoretical entity. Make a list of the varieties and prices of the most popular agricultural commodity in your region.

Price determination: two approaches

A brief discussion of how prices are determined in a competitive economy follows, because our understanding of it has a bearing on how we conceptualise the aggregate price level. Within the discipline of economics, there exist two broad approaches to explain price determination—the classical approach as revived by Sraffa, and the marginalist approach, which is commonly found in contemporary mainstream microeconomics textbooks (revisit Section 1.2 for a brief history of economics). To the question 'what determines prices?', the usual response by any mainstream economics textbook is 'demand and supply'; more accurately, equilibrium commodity price is explained by marginal utility, equilibrium wage by the marginal product of labour, and equilibrium profit by the marginal product of capital.

Without going into further details, since one of the givens (or parameters) in marginalist price theory is consumer preferences, it is termed a subjective theory. As opposed to this, the givens in Sraffa's price theory are the size and composition of output, technology, and one distributive variable (real wage or the rate of profit); hence, this is termed an objective theory. This subjective–objective classification underscores the fact that the givens in Sraffa's price theory possess objective units of measurement (quantities of inputs required, number of workers) relative to the marginalist one (utility).

The criterion is whether a commodity enters (no matter whether directly or indirectly) into the production of *all* commodities. Those that do we shall call *basic*, and those that do not, *non-basic* products.

Sraffa classifies commodities into basics and non-basics in his slim book *Production of Commodities by Means of Commodities* (1960). As Sraffa writes, "The criterion is whether a commodity enters (no matter whether directly or indirectly) into the production of *all* commodities. Those that do we shall call *basic*, and those that do not, *non-basic* products" (p. 8; emphases in the original). To reiterate, basics are those commodities which directly or indirectly go into the production of *all* commodities. Examples of basics are fuel and workers' necessaries. Non-basics include commodities like duck eggs and water purifiers. What determines the price of basics? Both the technology in use and culture, because the latter determines the constitution of workers' necessaries. As Ricardo writes in his *Principles of Political Economy and Taxation* (1817), the wages should be such that it enables the workers to consume "the quantity of food, necessaries, and conveniences [which] become essential to him from habit" (p. 93). In other words, wages are determined outside the economic model by culture and therefore the value theory of the classical economists and Sraffa has been labelled 'value through exogenous distribution' (compare this with the discussion on income distribution in Section 6.3).

The modern classical/Sraffian theory of price/value underscores the structural interdependence in the economy and argues against a cost-of-production theory of price for basics. "The price of a non-basic product," Sraffa writes in his *Production of Commodities by Means of Commodities*, "depends on the prices of its means of production, but these do not depend on it. Whereas in the case of a basic product the prices of its means of production depend on its own price no less than the latter depends on them" (p. 9). These prices, as indicated already, are an outcome of the existing technological set-up, size and composition of aggregate output, and income distribution. An important point to note here is that, owing to the exogeneity of one distributive variable in Sraffa's price theory, the conflict-ridden process of determining wages/ profits influences the determination of prices. As mentioned in Section 1.2, the conflictual nature of income distribution was highlighted by Ricardo. In contrast, in the marginalist approach, as already noted in Chapter 6, income distribution is viewed as a harmonious affair (Section 6.3 discussed the two contending theories of income distribution).

Recall the discussion on commodity flows, which was expressed quantitatively in Table 2.1. Out of the total sectoral output of the primary, secondary and tertiary sectors, 73.6 per cent, 51.8 per cent and 51.2 per cent, respectively, are consumed within the process of production. They amount to more than one-half of the total output produced by these sectors. Based on the discussion contained in the preceding paragraphs, deliberate why the knowledge of commodity flows is important for understanding inflation.

Understanding inflation: two approaches

Just like the two broad approaches to price determination that were just presented, I shall outline below two distinct approaches to understanding inflation. The reason for not including this discussion in Chapter 3 is because this book does not treat inflation as a purely monetary phenomenon (that is, as caused by an increase in the quantity of money). So far, we have seen that not only commodity flows but also income distribution has an influence on prices. Also, in a monetary production economy, changes in prices (aggregate, relative and individual) as well as expected changes in these prices impact both present and future decisions to produce and consume. Both actual and expected changes in prices also influence wage bargaining, but given that wages are exogenously determined, this can be comprehensively understood only by undertaking a systematic historical analysis of the evolution of wages (perhaps through the lenses of politics and policy).

One approach, also the one found in most introductory textbooks, views inflation as a consequence of excess money in the economy relative to aggregate output; this is often expressed by the following phrase: 'too much money chasing too few goods'. This is called the quantity theory of money (QTM), which is based on the sensible accounting idea that the value of total money used up in an economy must equal the value of total goods and services on which that money is spent. Since one unit of money, say, a two-hundred-rupee note, can change multiple hands, it is necessary to know how many times money changes hands; this is called the 'velocity of circulation' of money or V in short. Let us suppose that the stock of money circulating in the macroeconomy (in the form of currency and deposits) is M. Then M x V captures the value of total money used up or circulating in the economy as a whole. To obtain the value of goods and services for the economy as a whole, we multiply aggregate output (Y) with the aggregate price level (P). Together, we obtain MV = PY, the accounting identity which is true by definition.

Aggregate output is determined via the aggregate production function and is at the full employment level, that is, $Y = Y^F$ (see Sections 4.2 and 5.2). And V is taken as a given because it represents institutional settings such as the degrees of financial and structural interdependence in production as well as consumption. The direction of causation advanced by adherents of QTM, or monetarism, runs from M to P, given V and Y. When M exceeds Y, P has to increase in order to maintain the balance between MV and PY. When M increases, Y does not increase because of the assumption of full employment. In this approach, money is viewed only as a medium of exchange, merely a veil over the commodity flows. Therefore, M > Y expresses the idea of 'too much money chasing too few goods'. In other words, according to this theory, inflation is purely a monetary phenomenon—as a result of 'too much money'. Amongst the adherents of monetarism, Milton Friedman is the most popular.

The other approach to understanding inflation aligns itself with the Keynesian theory of output and employment and the demand-led growth theories. This approach is fundamentally based on a theory of production, whereas the QTM is based on a theory of allocation (and possesses a marginalist core). Therefore, while the latter emphasises scarcity, the former focuses on the production, distribution and consumption of surplus (recall the brief history in Section 1.2). The surplus approach to economics, as it is also called, is informed by the work of the classical economists and its modern revival by Sraffa. As noted earlier, equilibrium prices, that is, prices obtained under conditions of free competition (implying a uniform rate of profit), can vary due to changes in income distribution and in the degree of structural interdependence between sectors. Some paragraphs earlier, the idea of basics was explained. Evidently, a shock to a sector which produces basics has multiplicative effects on the economy.

If, for instance, the financial sector decides to increase its rate of profit, ceteris paribus, it will lead to an increase in the price of financial services. Otherwise, to maintain the same prices, wages have to be reduced proportionately. However, if, owing to the strong position of the workers in the financial sector, they do not find a reduction in wages admissible, the rise in the price of financial services is inevitable. In other words, the conflict over income distribution can be a source of inflation.

It is important to note that the relationship between wages and P cannot be easily reduced to a specific functional form. This is because, as we have noted before, several non-economic factors influence the determination of wages. In *An Essay on Money and Distribution* (1991), Massimo Pivetti, in the tradition of the surplus approach, clarifies this position further:

> The point is that the *responsiveness* of money wages to changes in the price level depends, as does the overall bargaining power of workers, on forces that are both economic and political-institutional in character, the weight of which greatly differs from one economy to another and for the same economy at different times. It can be said that money wage responsiveness to rises in prices is 'exogenous', in the sense that it is largely the outcome of a collective-bargaining process, which cannot be quantified *ex ante* through some statistically predictable relationship between it and the relevant economic and political-institutional factors.... (p. 35)

While the surplus approach of the classical economists and Sraffa offers a conceptual frame to study inflation, a comprehensive understanding of it warrants a historical study. In particular, such a historical study is especially necessary in the formulation of policies that aim to combat inflation.

This section, as many of you might have noticed, has taken a different approach to understanding the nature of inflation in India. Initially, it discussed India-specific aspects such as the trend for wholesale prices. This was followed by two conceptual sub-sections on understanding price determination and inflation. Such a path was undertaken to provide you with my rationale for not focusing on the growth of money supply as the explanans for inflation. The standpoint adopted here aligns itself to that of the surplus approach to economics, in the tradition of Smith, Ricardo, Marx and Sraffa.

Sources of inflation in India: agriculture and fuel

In the remaining part of this section, we are going to focus on two key historical and contemporary features of the Indian macroeconomy that have a significant influence on India's inflation: (*a*) rain-fed Indian agriculture and (*b*) India's dependence on fuel imports.

Since a large part of Indian agriculture is dependent on rain, a drought poses significant adverse consequences to the macroeconomy. Furthermore, since 51 per cent of agricultural output is used as an input in the manufacturing sector (as we know from Table 2.1), the latter is also affected. Although the agriculture sector uses only 17 per cent of its own output as input, a drought reduces their supply and therefore their incomes and their ability to repay debts (see the discussion on the nature of Indian agriculture in Section 6.4). Repeated droughts wreak economic havoc on agricultural households, lower aggregate output, and raise agricultural prices. Make a list of the number of times Indian agriculture has experienced droughts in the last two years by consulting the Indian Meteorological Department website.

Over the years, the weights assigned to primary articles in the WPI have decreased and those of manufactured products have increased (for the latest WPI weights, consult Figure 8.1). Although a significant portion of agricultural output continues to be used up in intermediate stages of production, why do you think that the weight assigned to primary articles has decreased?

In Section 4.3, open-economy macrodynamics was discussed. There, it was pointed out that India needs to import necessary capital goods like fuel. And in the preceding discussion, fuel was characterised as a basic commodity. It is, therefore, important to study the movement of international fuel prices. Rather than presenting the international price of crude oil, I am providing the index numbers of the price (or unit value) of 'petroleum and petroleum product imports', which help us better capture the role of fuel imports in India's inflation.

Table 8.2 Index numbers of India's petroleum import prices

	2014–15	2015–16	2016–17	2017–18
Petroleum & petroleum products	451	433	429	429

Source: While the primary responsibility for publishing this data lies with the Directorate General of Commercial Intelligence and Statistics (DGCI&S), the above data is downloaded from RBI's 'Table 130: Index numbers of Imports – Quantum and Unit Value' (p. 200) from its *Handbook of Statistics on the Indian Economy 2018–19*.

Note: The base year is 1999–2000, and therefore the index number for that year is 100. 'Petroleum & petroleum products' include (*a*) petroleum crude, (*b*) petroleum other than crude and (*c*) petroleum products. The value for 2018–19 was not available at the time of writing; I highlight this only because Table 8.1 contains 2018–19 WPI.

Table 8.2 indicates a fall in the price of petroleum imports. If you compare Tables 8.2 and 8.1, it is clear that fuel prices have declined. The price of imported fuel depends on not only international oil prices but also the exchange rate (recall the discussion in Section 3.5). Besides the other reasons mentioned in Section 3.5, this is another reason to 'manage' the exchange rate.

The unit value index is calculated based on the formula pioneered by Paasche. As already mentioned, it uses the current time period quantities as weights and provides us information on the difference in prices between the base year and the current year. Paasche's method to compute index numbers may be mathematically expressed as: $\Sigma P_1 Q_1 / \Sigma P_0 Q_1$. Note that an index number measures *changes* in magnitudes between two time periods or situations, but they do not and cannot provide a measure of the (absolute) *level* of the magnitude at a point in time. With Paasche's method, a new set of weights have to be computed for every period, as the quantity of petroleum imports will vary. A good book on the subject of index numbers is R. G. D. Allen's 1975 *Index Numbers in Economic Theory and Practice*. As an exercise, contemplate whether it is meaningful to compare the index numbers across different time periods and think carefully about the precise magnitudes being compared.

The nature of inflation in India, it must now be clear, is closely intertwined with the nature of Indian agriculture. This has been borne out by examining the commodity flows across and within the primary, secondary and tertiary sectors, and by identifying basic commodities. Given our significant fuel imports, the management of exchange rates becomes crucial in combating inflation. Independently of all these factors, the conflict over income distribution between workers and capitalists can also result in inflation if the increased wages/profits are transmitted in the form of higher commodity prices.

As is to be expected, the burden of inflation disproportionately falls on labourers, farmers and businesses whose incomes are low and unstable—on the producers' side. On the consumers' side, households whose employment and incomes are low and volatile and those who possess little wealth or assets are disproportionately affected. The nature of India's employment, as outlined in the previous chapter, is characterised by precarity—low and uncertain wages/employment. This precarity exacerbates the hardships of inflation. We shall now provide a template for macroeconomic policies aimed at combating high inflation.

8.3 A prelude to the solutions

Since the majority of the variation in India's aggregate price level is due to changes in the prices of domestic agricultural products and foreign fuel, the policies to combat inflation warrants the joint forces of fiscal and monetary policy. This kind of policy response emanates from our understanding of the Indian context. In addition to the context, the choice of the theoretical framework matters. That is, the conceptual framework, or in short, concept, matters. (Although a concept, a conceptual framework, and a theory are technically different, in this book they have been used interchangeably, primarily for rhetorical purposes.)

While marginalist economics operates on the assumption of scarcity (of resources) and defines itself as the science of allocation or choice, those working in the tradition of the classical economists, Sraffa and Keynes view economics as the study of production, distribution and consumption of the social surplus (recall Section 1.2). The latter tradition assumes the presence of excess capacity in production and labour unemployment as permanent features of a competitive economy—and they are also macroeconomic equilibrium outcomes. That is, there are no automatic tendencies in a competitive economy characterised by unemployment to reach full employment. As noted earlier, the quantity theory of money is closely aligned with the former tradition. Consequently, they focus only on regulating M, the money supply in the economy, to combat high inflation. Since the classical theory of prices, both in its 18th-century versions as well as in Sraffa's modern restatement, is situated within a system of production, it alerts us to the role of structural interdependence between sectors in understanding the structure of relative prices, which is essential to make sense of inflation. To put it differently, the meso approach to understanding inflation, which is adopted here, privileges fiscal policy measures to achieve low and stable inflation, given the Indian context.

The Indian economy relies on imports to meet domestic requirements of fuel (and fuel-related items), which constitutes the highest share of the total import value. And Section 8.2 had also noted the critical role agriculture plays in India's inflation story. Besides macroeconomic policies to facilitate fuel imports and to improve the agricultural sector, this section will briefly discuss the relationship between interest rates, profits and wages, so as to identify the ways in which policies influencing income distribution affect inflation.

What can policy do to influence the exchange rate such that the unit value of fuel imports reduces? In Section 3.5, it was mentioned that the RBI is able to influence exchange rates of the Indian rupee (INR) through the strategic buying and/or selling of foreign currencies in the foreign exchange market. In order to reduce the unit value of fuel imports, the RBI has to ensure that Indian importers of oil exchange fewer rupees for, say, one United States dollar (USD). If the RBI succeeds in this operation, the rupee would have appreciated (relative to the dollar). The RBI does this by selling US dollars in the foreign exchange market. But how does the RBI acquire US dollars? There are two ways: (*a*) exports and (*b*) foreign savings (assuming, for the purposes of our present argument, that they are both denominated in US dollars, a highly favoured currency). A depreciation of the rupee, as noted in Section 4.3, is favourable to exporters and, therefore, to the acquisition of US dollars. Moreover, the flow of foreign funds into India increases when the RBI raises the repo rate (recall the discussion in Section 3.5). So, while an appreciation of the rupee is favourable for fuel imports, it is unfavourable for Indian exporters. And, if the increased cost of borrowing (due to the increased policy rate) is passed on as higher prices by the Indian firms, it can fuel inflation. The key takeaway from this discussion is that tackling inflation in India requires the careful management of both the exchange rate and interest rate(s) by the RBI.

One of India's important macroeconomic targets is low and stable inflation. As a commitment to this, once every five years, in consultation with the RBI, the Government of India sets the inflation target. The inflation target is 4 per cent CPI from 5 August 2016 to 31 March 2021, with the upper and lower limits of 6 per cent and 2 per cent, respectively. From the theoretical standpoint adopted in this chapter and the Indian context, what can you say about the demerits and merits of any such inflation target?

Besides monetary policy, fiscal policy, or more accurately government policy, can help in reducing India's dependence on fuel imports by actively promoting natural gas, electricity and more green-energy options. To use the language of set theory, a branch of mathematics, fiscal policy is a subset of government policy. While fiscal policy is about altering tax rates and government expenditure, government policy also includes setting up rules for guiding individual and firm behaviour for the collective good. And monetary policy refers to the use of monetary instruments such as the repo rate (discussed in Section 3.4) to maintain price stability. The role for government policy outlined earlier strongly suggests that monetary policy and its pursuit of price stability cannot be viewed independently from our vision of ecological sustainability, and that these concerns have to be accounted for while framing these policies.

The following excerpt from the 2012 book *Churning the Earth: The Making of Global India* by Aseem Shrivastava and Ashish Kothari tellingly captures the link between macroeconomic policies and ecological issues.

> Changes in macroeconomic policies—such as interest rates, tax rates and social spending—have profound consequences for the environment and people's livelihoods, howsoever indirect. These go unnoticed since we do not have even a conceptual framework—let alone systems of national accounts—which incorporates such connections. For instance, currency devaluations lead to greater pressure on the environment, as an exporting 'developing' country necessarily gives up more of its resources in order to obtain a given amount of hard currency through international trade. Cheaper credit or tax incentives for investment usually accelerate the pace of environmental damage, especially in a context in which the state is loosening environmental regulation. When financial markets are opened up to trading in commodities and commodity futures (bargains based on expected prices), metals and other non-perishable raw materials become very attractive as items to hoard, speculate and make money on. Every time the government signs an MoU (memorandum of understanding) with a mining company, the share values of holders of equity in it rise, prompting further exploration and mining. (pp. 128–9)

Identify further such instances where you think the policies of the government and the RBI have had a detrimental impact on our ecology. Moreover, based on Figure 2.1, which expressed the macroeconomy as an embedded system within the natural environment, and the discussion on good theories and the demand for data in Section 6.5, try to generate (macroeconomic) accounting frameworks that can capture the effects of economic outcomes on our ecology. For this exercise, consult the work of the Romanian-American economist Nicholas Georgescu-Roegen, an important figure in the field of ecological economics, which is different from (marginalist) environmental economics.

Recall the Section 5.4 discussion on Nordhaus and the policy implication arising from his adoption of the supply-side growth theory. Based on his adherence to the marginalist core, particularly the $S_{FE} = f(roi) = I$ principle (discussed in Section 6.3), marginalist economists such as Nordhaus believe that society's preference for future consumption is captured by the interest rate.

This view is inconsistent with the endogenous money framework outlined in Chapter 3 and from the standpoint of demand-led growth theories. Such a belief allows marginalist economists to treat the interest rate as a price that equilibrates society's (that is, our!) preferences for the future with that of the present. Besides the problems associated with the use of subjective factors such as preferences (already mentioned in Section 8.2), the bigger problem is that the interest rate is used to determine how much of the current GDP ought to be devoted to climate change. To reiterate, the allocation of GDP for issues we consider important should never be outsourced to any such formula which is fundamentally erected on asocial and ahistorical marginalist foundations to decide the 'optimum' proportion. However, insofar as policymakers continue to rely on the interest rate to make such important socio-economic decisions, Nordhaus's work, if seen in the best light, provides an additional reason for monetary policy to incorporate ecological matters into its framework while targeting inflation.

In order to reduce extreme price volatility of food items such as vegetables and *dal*, one of the main drivers of inflation in India, the governments at the centre, state and local levels need to orchestrate an integrated region-appropriate policy. Such a policy will also improve the economic condition of India's agricultural sector. This policy must aid not just large agricultural landowners and farmers but also small landowners, small farmers and agricultural workers. It must outline a fair mechanism of seed distribution and ensure fair competition in agricultural markets so as to reduce the power of interlinked markets for agricultural inputs (this issue was discussed at some length in Section 6.4). However, we must keep in mind the limits of economic interventions in influencing the social determinants of (local) power, whether arising from the caste system, patriarchy or other oppressive institutions. As Krishna Bharadwaj observes in her 1974 book *Production Conditions in Indian Agriculture: A Study Based on Farm Management Surveys*, "The point to note is that while markets have penetrated into the rural economy in a deep and significant manner, the extent and *type* of involvement in markets of the different sections of the peasantry are not at all uniform. The character of markets reflects and to a significant extent is determined by the local patterns of power" (p. 3; emphasis in original). And these 'local patterns of power' also have an impact on the prices of agricultural commodities.

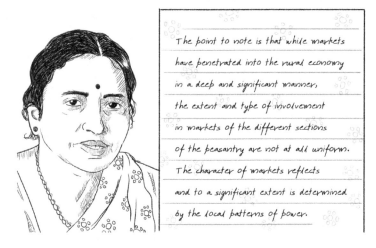

The point to note is that while markets have penetrated into the rural economy in a deep and significant manner, the extent and type of involvement in markets of the different sections of the peasantry are not at all uniform. The character of markets reflects and to a significant extent is determined by the local patterns of power.

Furthermore, initiatives must be taken to improve irrigation and storage facilities in order to reduce the reliance on rains. Agriculture in India requires a significant expansion of physical infrastructure (such as ponds, wells, cold storage, warehouses, regular electricity, road connectivity and market spaces) and social infrastructure in the form of education and training to meet the specific needs of the farmers and labourers in agriculture. The government must commit to undertaking research to improve ecologically sensitive agricultural practices. Since farmers rely mostly on informal sources of credit, the RBI should identify the nature and extent of agricultural indebtedness and work towards developing banking products to assist them. But it must be recalled that, as noted in Section 7.2, financial inclusion drives are pointless if agricultural wages are inadequate and uncertain. As an exercise, consult the First Five-Year Plan document and, keeping that as the backdrop, assess the importance accorded to agriculture in India's current economic policies.

This section can be concluded after discussing the relationship between income distribution and inflation. In the preceding section, it was argued that a sustained conflict over the distribution of income can get passed on to the buyers (of capital as well as consumer goods) in the form of higher prices. As Adam Smith articulates this conflict in his 1776 work *The Wealth of Nations*, "The workmen decide to get as much, the masters to give as little as possible. The former are disposed to combine in order to raise, the latter in order to lower the wages of labour" (p. 83; these sentences were also part of a larger extract from Smith in Chapter 7). Therefore, to both understand and combat inflation, the pricing strategies of Indian firms have to be understood. Consequently, our inflation policy has to have coordinated links with our industrial policy, competition policy, wage policy, agricultural policy, taxation policy and labour policy. Here too, the meso approach of studying the inter-industry relationship will prove beneficial in formulating a comprehensive inflation policy. In short, an inflation policy requires the joint efforts of the government as well as monetary authorities, because inflation is not a pure monetary phenomenon.

The workmen decide to get as much, the masters to give as little as possible. The former are disposed to combine in order to raise, the latter in order to lower the wages of labour.

If, as stated in Section 1.1, the RBI adopts the quantity theory of money, and, therefore, believes inflation to be caused by too much money in the Indian economy, it will try to reduce money supply by increasing the policy interest rate (under the questionable assumption that there is an inverse relationship between the rate of interest and the demand for money). Let us contemplate the consequences of an increase in the rate of interest on profits and wages. Since the cost of borrowing has increased, it reduces the profits, ceteris paribus, and if the capitalists want the profits to remain intact, they can try to reduce wages or increase the prices or some combination of the two. In other words, the impact of an increased policy interest rate on the aggregate price level cannot be determined a priori and is conceptually *not* unambiguous; the direction and magnitude of the effect depends on the nature and degree of structural interdependence between the sectors in production. Also, recall the discussion in Section 5.3, which had noted the economic and social implications of the interest rate exceeding the growth rate of the economy.

Finally, the operation of monetary policy and the transmission of the policy interest rate to the (large and varied) informal sector is unclear. Does the increase in policy interest rate cause an increase in informal lending rates? What kind of pricing strategies are followed by the informal sector enterprises? Such questions call for field research in multiple sites, given the significant diversity of the Indian macroeconomy. India's monetary policy, which aims to reduce inflation, must therefore necessarily take explicit cognisance of the varied nature of the informal sector in its formulation.

8.4 Conclusion

This chapter, like the previous one, introduced you to the theory, measurement and a broad policy template to address the issue of high inflation. While the mainstream theory of inflation focuses on the aggregate price level, this chapter argued for the importance of a meso approach, especially given the critical role of agriculture (and the informal sector, more broadly) in the Indian economy. This was complemented by a discussion of the classical ('objective') and marginalist ('subjective') theories of price determination. A very brief discussion of index numbers and the computation of the WPI in India was then carried out. From the concept (or theory) chosen and the context, it was argued that the pursuit of low inflation in India warrants the joint forces of monetary and fiscal policy. In particular, from Chapters 7 and 8, it emerges that both monetary and fiscal policy can serve as means to meet our socio-economic goals of low inflation along with quality employment and ecologically sustainable production.

Suggestions for further reading

This chapter not only pointed out the pitfalls of employing a marginalist approach in understanding inflation, but also recommended a meso approach to complement the macro understanding. To further your understanding of India's inflation issues, read Mihir Rakshit's 'Inflation in a Developing Economy: Theory and Policy', published as the seventh chapter (pp. 182–222) of his 2009 book *Macroeconomics of Post-reform India* (New Delhi: Oxford University Press). Despite Ashok Desai's adherence to the marginalist view of the role of the government, you can read parts of his 1999 book *The Price of Onions* (New Delhi: Penguin Books), especially the first chapter, 'The Dance of Prices' (pp. 1–60), where he describes the nature of price formation in the case of onion, sugar, fats (*ghee*) and cereals. For a succinct conceptual statement on the connection between monetary policy, the rate of interest and the general price level, read the 'Summary and Concluding Observations' (pp. 128–36) of Massimo Pivetti's 1991 book *An Essay on Money and Distribution* (New York: Palgrave Macmillan). An advanced treatment of inflation and unemployment in the non-marginalist tradition of the surplus approach is found in Antonella Stirati's 2001 article 'Inflation, Unemployment and Hysteresis: An Alternative View', published in the journal *Review of Political Economy* (vol. 13, no. 4, pp. 427–51).

9

Towards Good Economics

This short chapter, written in lieu of a conclusion, is also intended to serve as a prologue to your further study of economics. First, I outline the approach to macroeconomics adopted in this book by highlighting the key issues addressed in each chapter. Then, I assemble the theories endorsed in this book along with some instances of how the concept (or theory) was employed to make sense of the Indian macroeconomic context. I end by highlighting the importance of pluralism (of theory and method) in the study of economics.

9.1 *An* introduction to macroeconomics

I had strongly remarked in the preface to this book that no textbook, including this, ought to substitute for the reading and studying of classic books and articles in economics. As a consequence, this book can only, and should always, remain *an* introduction to macroeconomics. The approach followed here has been unconventional insofar as it has critically engaged with two major schools of thought found in economics. Although textbooks usually communicate a settled body of knowledge, in this book, I have adopted an 'unsettling approach', as it were. Moreover, as stated in the preface, my preference has been to adopt a problem-setting approach than a problem-solving one, as is commonplace among contemporary economics textbooks.

Chapter 1 took you through a very swift tour of the history of economic thought. A sample of key definitions of economics by Smith, Ricardo, Jevons, Marshall and Robbins was then provided, and we adopted the 'science of wealth' definition. In the epilogue to *The Science of Wealth: Adam Smith and the Framing of Political Economy* (2009), Tony Aspromourgos offers the following judgement of Smith's political economy: "The classical political economy which Smith first fashioned into a satisfying general system of inquiry or science *remains* in broad terms a sound approach to the analysis of mixed capitalistic economies, centred on the dynamics of economic development" (p. 270; emphasis added). Indeed, it is precisely this approach

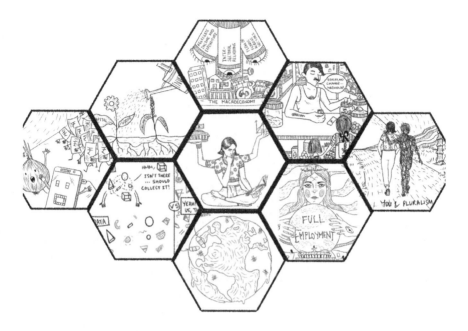

that has been adopted in this book. Subsequently, the relationship between politics and economic phenomena was highlighted. In the last section, the approach adopted in the book was made explicit: a 'macro' level analysis of a competitive economy. The chapter ended by underscoring the importance of absolute precision in theory.

Chapter 2 began with a brief history of the distinct ways of conceptualising the macroeconomy, starting from Petty: national income accounting, input–output table and flow of funds. The embeddedness of the economy within the society and the embeddedness of these two within the ecological atmosphere was highlighted next. This understanding, although elementary, is crucial especially when economists make policy suggestions. The study of monetary production economies (Keynes's term) warrants the viewing of the macroeconomy as a web of commodity and money flows; a brief discussion on Marx's circuit of capital was also carried out in relation to the web-of-flows conception. The chapter ended with two notes of caution: (*a*) the conclusions emanating from the study of a competitive production economy is to be applied to the Indian economy with great caution and (*b*) independently of (*a*), economic policies must acknowledge and incorporate the wishes of the concerned communities in terms of their vision of economic progress.

The key concepts required to understand a monetary production economy were introduced in Chapters 3 and 4. Chapter 3 began by providing an overview of the Indian financial architecture. Where do Indian households park their savings? What platforms exist for Indian private firms to borrow? What proportion of the total financial assets is in the form of equities? How prevalent is informal finance? These questions were answered by relying on the visual representations in Figure 3.1 and Table 3.1. Subsequently, the characteristics of money—a universal medium of exchange and store of value—were presented, which was accompanied by a brief discussion on the *multiple* interest rates prevalent in the Indian economy. This was followed by an account of two distinct theories of money—exogenous and endogenous money (the latter still does not figure in most textbooks). Following the endogenous money approach, it was argued that money is created by lending and not by deposits. And that banks cannot be seen as passive intermediaries, but as active profit maximisers. Through a diagrammatic representation of the economic interconnections between the Reserve Bank of India (RBI), commercial banks, private firms and households, the transmission of the RBI's policy rate to other interest rates in the economy was captured. The final section of the chapter looked at the volume and intensity of money flows between India and the rest of the world (RoW). This led to a discussion of the foreign exchange market, the exchange rate and the capital account—which captures all the inward and outward money flows (including both foreign direct investment, or FDI, and foreign institutional investors, or FII). The necessary links between managing the rate of interest and the exchange rate was briefly touched upon (this was further tackled in Section 8.3, which provided a solution framework for high inflation).

Chapter 4 was more conceptual in nature than Chapter 3; there was only a very brief discussion of the presence of caste labour in India. It began by presenting you with two contending theories of output and employment—marginalist and Keynesian. This textbook adopted the Keynesian approach to understand the factors determining aggregate output and employment, which, according to this theory, are the autonomous and induced elements of aggregate demand. Moreover, there is no tendency to the full employment of labour according to this theory. This was followed by a discussion of commodity flows and income flows between India and the RoW—which is expressed in the current account. By talking about the current and capital accounts together, the connection between international commodity and money flows was briefly engaged with. The chapter ended with some more discussion on open economy macrodynamics—the role of FDI in aggregate output levels, the link between foreign funds (money flow) and domestic investment (commodity flow), and the impact of exchange rate on aggregate output levels.

The classification of theories in Chapter 4, to reiterate, is based on differences in their conceptual characteristics and not on their chronological appearance. I want to emphasise this because mainstream macroeconomics textbooks first present the marginalist theory of output and employment under the label of classical economics and then the Keynesian theory (albeit through a marginalist lens). Unfortunately, this incorrect labelling is owing to Keynes's chronological use of classical economics in *The General Theory* (1936); Keynes labelled everyone before him as a classical economist. In fact, if you read *The General Theory*, it becomes clear that his main adversaries are Marshall and Pigou (marginalist economists, according to our definition).

While Chapters 3 and 4 discussed the aggregate levels of money, output and employment under the assumption of a given productive capacity, Chapter 5 relaxes this assumption in order to study economic growth. Here too, the chapter began with the two broad approaches to growth—supply-side and demand-led. While the former has marginalist underpinnings, the latter is Keynesian in nature. Although growth in supply-side growth models (both the exogenous and endogenous varieties) eventually arises from the growth of endowments—human capital and physical capital—the growth in physical capital accumulation alone cannot drive economic growth due to the operation of diminishing returns to factor inputs; it requires the assistance of increasing returns brought about by technological progress and/or improvements in 'human capital'. Furthermore, in this class of models, aggregate supply always creates an equivalent aggregate demand—a modern version of Say's law. On the other hand, demand-led growth models locate the source of economic growth in the growth of autonomous elements of aggregate demand (notably, government expenditure, autonomous investment, autonomous consumption and exports). To recapitulate, this is not to say that supply-side constraints of a meso nature such as poor storage facilities in agriculture or expensive logistics in manufacturing do not affect growth; of course, they do. After laying out the two contending growth theories, the chapter presented an account of the nature of economic growth in India by adopting a meso lens from a demand-led growth theory standpoint. The benefits of economic growth depend on the initial conditions; in particular, the historical inequalities with respect to land ownership were noted. Subsequently, overall gross domestic product (GDP) growth was disaggregated (Table 5.3) to get a meso understanding of the growth of agriculture, construction, finance and real estate, and public administration. It was then shown that GDP growth in India has not generated a proportionate growth in labour employment. After discussions on the implications of the rate of return exceeding the growth rate of the economy and ecologically sustainable economic growth, the next section explored similar meso questions for an open economy. The pursuit of economic growth for open economies was found to crucially depend on geopolitics and the nature of collective decision-making for the world economy as a whole.

Sometimes, a couple of the more environmentally conscious students in my class have asked me whether demand-led growth theories favour consumerism. Let me provide two compelling reasons for why it is not the case. First, the classification of supply-side and demand-led is based on the direction of causation between aggregate supply and aggregate demand. Second, as has been particularly suggested in Chapters 7 and 8, the composition of aggregate demand, notably government expenditure, can reflect our collective ecological vision. In fact, I would not be exaggerating if I state that demand-led growth theories provide much more agency for collective politics than supply-side growth theories do. Not surprisingly, the necessity of a strong *collective* political agency is intrinsic to classical economics too (unlike marginalist economics).

Chapter 6 acted as a watershed chapter between the initial ones focussed more on macroeconomic theories (albeit with adequate context) and the subsequent two chapters that dealt with the nature of unemployment and high inflation (with substantial context) and a prelude to their policy solutions. It started off by highlighting the significance of theorising in economics, as well as the positive role played by mathematics in making transparent the conceptual framework—assumptions, restrictions and equilibrium outcomes. Theorising helps discipline our thinking and allows us to be focused on the issue at hand. Through the simple modelling of the Keynesian theory of output and employment, the supporting role of mathematics was briefly outlined. Internal consistency, it was noted, is an important virtue of good models. Subsequently, the following core theories/principles of marginalist economics were critically evaluated: (*a*) methodological individualism, (*b*) exogenous money, (*c*) saving determines investment by variations in a sufficiently sensitive interest rate and (*d*) the marginal productivity theory of income distribution. Since good theories must recognise context, the next section undertook a thorough discussion of the two key defining features of the Indian economy—agriculture and the informal sector. Context, it was stated, is one of the important elements that ought to fill the black box in between theory and policy. The chapter ended by making visible some of the invisible connections between good theory and the demand for relevant data.

Chapters 7 and 8 followed the context–measurement–theory–policy approach to unemployment and high inflation. Using simple data, it was argued that any employment policy ought to acknowledge the precarious nature of employment for most Indians. The latter was reflected in the increased contractualisation and casualisation of the Indian workforce. It was also shown that Indian jobs are not very gainful—around 98 per cent of India's workers earned less than INR 50,000 a month (Table 7.1). And while the workers' wages stagnated between the years 2000 and 2016, managers' compensation witnessed a steep rise (Figure 7.1). Moreover, the nature of India's employment is such that the Scheduled Castes and Scheduled Tribes are overrepresented in poorly paid occupations, while the upper castes are overrepresented in well-paid ones (Figure 7.2). The state of women workers was also found to be similarly abysmal with respect to the quality of work/jobs. After a succinct discussion on government borrowing, the chapter brought together concept (used here interchangeably with theory) and context through the select contributions of Mahalanobis and Rao. The general policy conclusion was that the goal of full employment cannot and should not be *entirely* transferred to the private sector because its primary motive is to maximise profit and not employment. An anti-cyclical fiscal policy that is well integrated with our socio-economic priorities in the areas of agriculture, ecology, education, employment (wages included) and manufacturing was recommended.

Chapter 8 introduced you to the meaning of inflation and its measurement through the concept of a specialised average—index numbers for prices. Since the general (or aggregate) price level (P) is directly unobservable, the process of constructing a wholesale price index (WPI) was outlined, with a focus on the choice of weights and the base year. Utilising Table 8.1, it was shown that the main contributor to India's inflation is primary articles (agricultural commodities). It was then strongly suggested that our inflation policy needs to adopt the meso approach to examine and study the commodity flows and money prices across sectors. The subject of the next few paragraphs was the two contending theories of price determination—classical and marginalist theories of value and distribution. Subsequently, two theories of inflation were presented; one was based on a theory of allocation and aligned to the marginalist school, and the other based on a Keynesian understanding that is built on a theory of production, a key element of classical economics. By adopting the latter approach, the chapter focused on two sectors that produce 'basics' (a concept introduced by Sraffa): agriculture and fuel. This choice also follows from the meso approach mentioned earlier. The policies to combat inflation, it was argued, warrant a close management of the exchange rates and interest rate(s) by the RBI along with government policies to improve agricultural and green energy infrastructure (to reduce our reliance on oil imports).

The approach embraced in this textbook is one that introduces two distinct, and often contending, ways of understanding our economic surroundings, and then adopting one. A bit about this will be said in Section 9.3. Another unique aspect of this book is that while the primary subject matter is that of macroeconomics, which warrants a macro approach, to better understand the phenomena (whether unemployment or inflation), a meso approach is often necessary. The policy solutions herein, in line with the spirit of the book, are very generic in nature. As much as possible, this book provides you with a framework to think about macroeconomic problems in a holistic manner, so to speak, especially when adopting the meso approach and addressing the connections with caste and gender.

9.2 On concept and context

The preceding section has taken you through the entire book by summarising the key concepts and contexts found in these pages. It has also provided an overview of the approach, or rather approaches, found in this book. This section assembles the key concepts covered in this book and reiterates important contextual aspects of the Indian economy from a macro perspective. Even at the risk of sounding tedious, let me point out again that I have used 'concept' instead of 'theory' for pedagogic and rhetorical purposes.

Economics, in these pages, has been defined as a science of wealth, in the tradition of Smith, Ricardo and other classical economists. And the object under study, following Keynes, is a competitive monetary production economy, as opposed to the marginalist conception of a competitive exchange economy (where money is simply a veil over the commodity exchanges). The object of analysis has largely been that of a competitive macroeconomy because of the all-pervasive belief among most economists and policymakers that such an economic system is good for *all*. However, such a belief, which arises from a marginalist standpoint, has been shown to be flawed.

The *choice* of concepts (or theory) matter for measurement, in understanding the context, and in the formulation of policy. More generally, it may be stated that *theory matters*. Let me now list the theories surveyed in the previous chapters. Chapter 3 introduced you to exogenous and endogenous money; Chapter 4 to the marginalist and Keynesian theories of output and employment; Chapter 5 to supply-side and demand-led theories of economic growth; Chapter 6 to the marginalist and classical theories of income distribution (very briefly); and Chapter 8 to the marginalist and classical theories of price determination (also very briefly) as well as to the following two theories which are utilised for understanding inflation: the quantity theory of money and the one inspired by the classical/Sraffian theory of prices, which adopts a meso (or structuralist) approach.

A brief history of the aforementioned theories is to be found in the respective chapters, which can be read in conjunction with Section 1.2, which provided a brief history of economics. The conceptual standpoint adopted in this book is conspicuous; it is in the tradition of the economics of Smith, Ricardo, Marx, Keynes and Sraffa. This is another reason for placing emphasis on 'an' in the heading of the current chapter's previous section—'*An* approach to macroeconomics'.

As mentioned in the methodological section in Chapter 1 (Section 1.4), there exist many important features of the Indian economy. The choice of these features depends on what aspects are considered crucial according to the conceptual framework (or theory). Since this book's standpoint is based on a theory of production as understood by the classical economists, the degree of structural interdependence in Indian production was introduced as early as in Chapter 2. And since money cannot really be understood without understanding the context, Chapter 3 began with a discussion of the financial architecture of India. In Chapter 5, which dealt with economic growth, we explicitly engaged with the nature of economic growth in India, most notably, the inequality of land ownership and the state of our natural environment. Chapter 6 contained a thorough discussion of two key features of the Indian economy: agriculture and the informal sector (Section 6.4). The second sections of Chapters 7 and 8 engaged closely with the context; they outlined the nature of unemployment and inflation in India, respectively.

An outline of the Indian macroeconomic context based on Sections 7.2 and 8.2 ensues. Section 7.2 focused on the following issues: the extent of casualisation and contractualisation of the Indian workforce; wage inequality between self-employed, salaried, contract and casual workers; the divergence between managerial compensation and wages; the over-representation of workers from Scheduled Castes and Scheduled Tribes in poorly paid occupations; and the high proportion of women workers in agriculture vis-à-vis services. Section 8.2 complemented the nature of structural interdependence in Indian production, outlined in Table 2.1, by presenting the index numbers of wholesale prices or primary articles (mainly agricultural), fuel and power, and manufactured products. This route was followed because price changes in one sector affect prices in other sectors, depending on how structurally dependent they are. Section 8.2 also highlighted the crucial role played by agricultural prices in India's inflation and underscored India's dependence on petroleum imports as another source of inflation.

Using excerpts from Indian books of fiction, the role of caste and gender was underscored in several chapters. The aforesaid context was significantly augmented through the excerpts from fiction. These excerpts recapitulated our Section 2.3 view of the economy as being embedded in a social system and, therefore, these indirectly point at the limits of economics. Indeed, the critical observations made by M. G. Ranade, in his 1893 article 'Indian Political Economy', on the various assumptions made in both marginalist and classical economics remain acutely relevant even today.

> As these assumptions do not absolutely hold good of even the most advanced Societies, it is obvious that in Societies like ours, they are chiefly conspicuous by their absence. With us an Individual man is, to a large extent, the very antipodes of the Economical Man. The Family and the Caste are more powerful than the Individual in determining his position in life.... There is neither the desire nor the aptitude for free and unlimited Competition except within certain predetermined grooves or groups. Custom and State Regulation are far more powerful than Competition and Status more decisive in its influence than Contract.... In a Society so constituted, the tendencies assumed as axiomatic are not only inoperative, but are actually deflected from their proper direction. (p. 328)

The above excerpt from Ranade has been quoted here to further reinforce the importance of studying the social structures when learning economics and, even more so, in the formulation of economic policies.

To conclude this section, while the conceptual framework influences our selection of contexts, a contextual understanding enriches our conceptual understanding and also points out the limits of economic theory. And to do good economics, it is necessary to equip ourselves with both concept and context by *continuously* reading—the classic books (and articles) in economics, the history of economic thought, studies based on extensive fieldwork in India, government and RBI reports, books of fiction and newspapers.

9.3 Pluralism in theory and method

What determines prices? What determines wages? How are profits determined? What determines aggregate employment? Most textbooks treat economics as a discipline or subject that has settled opinions on such core issues. In reality, this is not quite the case. Research takes place continuously within the various non-marginalist conceptual frameworks, alongside the dominant and, therefore, more visible frameworks of marginalism. The dominance of an idea, concept, theory or framework does not necessarily mean that it is the best available idea, concept, theory or framework in a scientific sense. And the position adopted in this book has been that the marginalist framework is *not* well suited for understanding a competitive monetary production economy and (therefore) neither is it for the Indian macroeconomy. However, if you are a student of economics or a general reader interested in learning economics, it is my strong view that you need to engage with contending frameworks or paradigms. Our learning benefits from having to defend or oppose a conceptual framework, which necessarily calls for an in-depth understanding of the other framework(s). Consequently, the limitations and scope of a particular conceptual framework tend to become more visible. It is in line with this thinking that the book introduced you to pluralism in theory. With these considerations in mind, I think that reading Chapter 1 again will prove to be fruitful.

If you are a student of economics, you will soon study 'statistics for economists' and 'mathematics for economists'. In both these 'methods' of economics, there exist multiple concepts, theories and approaches, just like in macroeconomics and microeconomics; pay attention to the fact that these 'methods' of economics themselves both originated and are used within a social context. Moreover, a pluralistic approach to economics by itself is not sufficient when employing economics in the service of public policy; it is important to keep in mind the collective wishes of people as Xaxa's poem in Section 1.4 pointed out.

I end this book with the hope that you take pluralism as a friend, sometimes a difficult one, in your journey of learning.

Suggestion for further reading

For those who are interested in knowing more about the recent research undertaken in the classical economics tradition, an excellent starting point is Tony Aspromourgos's 2004 review article 'Sraffian Research Programmes and Unorthodox Economics', published in the *Review of Political Economy* (vol. 16, no. 2, pp. 179–206).

Data Sources

Chapter 2
Input–Output Transactions Table 2007–08, Ministry of Statistics and Programme Implementation (MOSPI), Government of India (**Table 2.1**).
http://mospi.nic.in/publication/input-output-transactions-table-2007-08, accessed 25 June 2020.

Chapter 3
'Flow of Funds Accounts of the Indian Economy: 2015–16', *RBI Bulletin August 2017*, Statement 7.2 (**Table 3.1**).
https://www.rbi.org.in/Scripts/BS_PressReleaseDisplay.aspx?prid=41345, accessed 25 June 2020.

Reserve Bank of India, Press Release, 'Government of India announces the sale of four dated securities for ₹14,000 crore', 20 January 2020 (**Figure 3.3**).
https://www.rbi.org.in/Scripts/BS_PressReleaseDisplay.aspx?prid=49200, accessed 25 June 2020.

XE Currency Charts (**Table 3.2**).
https://www.xe.com/currencycharts/?from=AED&to=INR&view=5Y, accessed 25 June 2020.

Chapter 4
Export–Import Data Bank (Import :: Commodity-wise), Department of Commerce, Ministry of Commerce and Industry (**Table 4.2**).
https://commerce-app.gov.in/eidb/icomq.asp, accessed 25 June 2020.

Export–Import Data Bank (Export :: Country-wise), Department of Commerce, Ministry of Commerce and Industry (**Table 4.3**).
https://commerce-app.gov.in/eidb/ecntq.asp, accessed 25 June 2020.

Chapter 5
Key Indicators of Land and Livestock Holdings in India, National Sample Survey (NSS) 70th Round, 2013, MOSPI, Government of India (**Table 5.2**).
http://mospi.nic.in/sites/default/files/publication_reports/KI_70_18.1_19dec14.pdf, accessed 25 June 2020.

Economic Survey 2017–18, Volume 2, Ministry of Finance, Government of India (**Table 5.3**).
http://mofapp.nic.in:8080/economicsurvey/pdf/001-027_Chapter_01_Economic_Survey_2017-18.pdf, accessed 25 June 2020.

State of Working India 2018, Centre for Sustainable Employment, Azim Premji University (**Table 5.4**).
https://cse.azimpremjiuniversity.edu.in/state-of-working-india/swi-2018/, accessed 25 June 2020.

Rishabh Kumar, 2019, 'The Evolution of Wealth–Income Ratios in India 1860–2012' (**Table 5.5**)
https://papers.ssrn.com/sol3/papers.cfm?abstract_id=3111846, accessed 25 June 2020.

Compendium of Environment Statistics 2016, MOSPI, Government of India (**Table 5.6**).
http://mospi.nic.in/publication/compendium-environment-statistics-2016, accessed 25 June 2020.

Chapter 7
State of Working India 2018, Centre for Sustainable Employment, Azim Premji University (**Table 7.1, Figures 7.1, 7.2** and **7.3**).
https://cse.azimpremjiuniversity.edu.in/state-of-working-india/swi-2018/, accessed 25 June 2020.

Chapter 8
Handbook of Statistics on Indian Economy 2018–19 (Table 37: Wholesale Price Index – Annual Average, p. 80), Reserve Bank of India (**Table 8.1**).
https://rbidocs.rbi.org.in/rdocs/Publications/PDFs/0HB2018-19A91A2988061644 70A2BCEF300A4FE334.PDF, accessed 25 June 2020.

Handbook of Statistics on Indian Economy 2018–19 (Table 130: Index Numbers of Imports – Quantum and Unit Value, p. 200), Reserve Bank of India (**Table 8.2**).
https://rbidocs.rbi.org.in/rdocs/Publications/PDFs/0HB2018-19A91A2988061644 70A2BCEF300A4FE334.PDF, accessed 25 June 2020.

Release of New Series of Wholesale Price Index, 12 May 2017, Frequently Asked Questions on Revision of Wholesale Price Index (Base: 2011–12 = 100), Ministry of Commerce and Industry, Government of India (**Figure 8.1**).
https://www.eaindustry.nic.in/uploaded_files/FAQs_on_WPI.pdf, accessed 25 June 2020.

References

When different years are provided in round and square brackets, the former refers to the year of first publication and the latter to the edition I have consulted.

Agarwal, Bina (2001), 'Disinherited Peasants, Disadvantaged Workers: A Gender Perspective on Land and Livelihood', in Alice Thorner (ed.), *Land, Labour and Rights: 10 Daniel Thorner Memorial Lectures*, New Delhi: Tulika, pp. 159–201.

Allen, R. G. D. (1975), *Index Numbers in Economic Theory and Practice*, New Brunswick: Aldine Transaction.

Ambedkar, B. R. (1918) [1979], 'Small Holdings in India and Their Remedies', *Journal of the Indian Economic Society*, vol. 1, as republished in Volume 1 of *Dr. Babasaheb Ambedkar: Writings and Speeches*, compiled by Vasant Moon, Bombay: Government of Maharashtra, available at http://drambedkarwritings.gov.in/upload/uploadfiles/files/Volume_01.pdf, accessed 25 June 2020.

——— (1936) [1979], *Annihilation of Caste*, 3rd edition (1944), in Volume 1 of *Dr. Babasaheb Ambedkar: Writings and Speeches*, compiled by Vasant Moon, Bombay: Government of Maharashtra, available at http://drambedkarwritings.gov.in/upload/uploadfiles/files/Volume_01.pdf, accessed 25 June 2020.

Aspromourgos, Tony (2009), *The Science of Wealth: Adam Smith and the Framing of Political Economy*, London: Routledge.

——— (2013), 'Sraffa's System in Relation to Some Main Currents in Unorthodox Economics', in Enrico Sergio Levrero, Antonella Palumbo and Antonella Stirati (eds), *Sraffa and the Reconstruction of Economic Theory: Volume Three, Sraffa's Legacy: Interpretations and Historical Perspectives*, Hampshire: Palgrave Macmillan.

Bank of England (2014), 'Money Creation in the Modern Economy', *Quarterly Bulletin*, no. 1, pp. 14-27, available at https://www.bankofengland.co.uk/-/media/boe/files/quarterly-bulletin/2014/money-creation-in-the-modern-economy, accessed 25 June 2020.

Barba, Aldo and Giancarlo de Vivo (2012), 'An "Unproductive Labour" View of Finance', *Cambridge Journal of Economics*, vol. 36, no. 6, pp. 1479–96.

Becker, Gary (1976), *The Economic Approach to Human Behaviour*, Chicago: The University of Chicago Press.

Bharadwaj, Krishna (1963), 'Value through Exogenous Distribution', *Economic Weekly*, 24 August, pp. 1450–64.

——— (1974), *Production Conditions in Indian Agriculture: A Study Based on Farm Management Surveys*, University of Cambridge, Department of Applied Economics, Occasional Paper 33, London: Cambridge University Press.

REFERENCES

Blyth, Mark (2013), *Austerity: The History of a Dangerous Idea*, New York: Oxford University Press.

Cantillon, Richard (1755) [2015], *Essay on the Nature of Trade in General*, translated, edited, and with an introduction by Antoin E. Murphy, Indianapolis: Liberty Fund.

Central Statistical Organisation (CSO) (2008), *National Industrial Classification 2008*, New Delhi: Ministry of Statistics and Programme Implementation, available at http://mospi.nic.in/sites/default/files/main_menu/national_industrial_classification/nic_2008_17apr09.pdf, accessed 25 June 2020.

Centre for Sustainable Employment (2018), *State of Working India 2018*, Bengaluru: Azim Premji University, available at https://cse.azimpremjiuniversity.edu.in/state-of-working-india/swi-2018/, accessed 25 June 2020.

Chakravarty, Sukhamoy (1987), *Development Planning: The Indian Experience*, New Delhi: Oxford University Press.

Chattopadhyay, Saumen (2018), *Macroeconomics of the Black Economy*, Hyderabad: Orient Blackswan.

Chayanov, A. V. (1924) [1966], 'On the Theory of Non-Capitalist Economic Systems', translated by Christel Lane, in Daniel Thorner, Basile Kerblay, R. E. F. Smith (eds), *A. V. Chayanov on The Theory of Peasant Economy*, Illinois: Richard D. Irwin (for the American Economic Association), pp. 1–28.

——— (1925) [1966], *Peasant Farm Organization*, translated by R. E. F. Smith, in Daniel Thorner, Basile Kerblay, R. E. F. Smith (eds), *A. V. Chayanov on The Theory of Peasant Economy*, Illinois: Richard D. Irwin (for the American Economic Association), pp. 29–269.

Copeland, Morris (1949), 'Social Accounting for Moneyflows', *The Accounting Review*, vol. 24, no. 3, pp. 254–64.

Curriculum Open-access Resources in Economics (CORE), 'Credit, Banks and Money', Unit 11, pp. 1–55, available at https://www.core-econ.org/wp-content/uploads/2017/09/The-Economy-beta-Unit-11.pdf, accessed 25 June 2020.

Dasgupta, A. K. (1954) [2003], 'Keynesian Economics and Underdeveloped Countries', *Economic Weekly*, 26 January, pp. 101–6, as republished in *Economic and Political Weekly*, vol. 38, no. 28, pp. 2919–22.

Dasgupta, Ajit K. (1993), *A History of Indian Economic Thought*, London: Routledge.

Demirgüç-Kunt, Asli, Leora Klapper, Dorothe Singer, Saniya Ansar and Jake Hess (2018), *The Global Findex Database 2017: Measuring Financial Inclusion and the Fintech Revolution*, Washington, DC: World Bank. doi:10.1596/978-1-4648-1259-0.

Directorate General of Employment (DGE) (2016), *National Classification of Occupations – 2015*, New Delhi: Ministry of Labour and Employment, available at https://labour.gov.in/sites/default/files/National%20Classification%20of%20Occupations_Vol%20II-B-%202015.pdf, accessed 25 June 2020.

Domar, Evsey D. (1944), 'The "Burden of Debt" and the National Income', *American Economic Review*, vol. 34, no. 4, pp. 798–827.

Drèze, Jean (2002), 'On Research and Action', *Economic and Political Weekly*, vol. 37, no. 9, pp. 817–19.

———— (2017), *Sense and Solidarity: Jholawala Economics for Everyone*, Ranikhet: Permanent Black.

Drèze, Jean and Amartya Sen (2013), *An Uncertain Glory: India and Its Contradictions*, London: Penguin.

Eltis, Walter (1984) [2000], *The Classical Theory of Economic Growth*, 2nd edition, London: Palgrave.

Feyerabend, Paul (1999), *Knowledge, Science and Relativism: Philosophical Papers*, vol. 3, edited by John Preston, Cambridge: Cambridge University Press.

Frank, Andre Gunder (1966), 'The Development of Underdevelopment', *Monthly Review*, vol. 18, no. 4, pp. 17–31.

Galbraith, John Kenneth (1987), *A History of Economics: The Past as the Present*, London: Penguin Books.

Garegnani, Pierangelo (1978), 'Notes on Consumption, Investment and Effective Demand: I', *Cambridge Journal of Economics*, vol. 2, no. 4, pp. 335–53.

———— (1979), 'Notes on Consumption, Investment and Effective Demand: II', *Cambridge Journal of Economics*, vol. 3, no. 1, pp. 63–82.

Ghosh, Amitav (2016), *The Great Derangement: Climate Change and The Unthinkable*, Gurgaon: Penguin.

Harrod, Roy (1939), 'An Essay in Dynamic Theory', *Economic Journal*, vol. 49, no. 193, pp. 14–33.

Heisenberg, Werner (1989), 'Theory, Criticism, and a Philosophy', in *From a Life of Physics*, Singapore: World Scientific, pp. 31–55.

Imayam (2012) [2015], *Pethavan (The Begetter)*, translated from the Tamil by Gita Subramanian, New Delhi: Oxford University Press.

International Labour Organization (ILO) (2018), *India Wage Report: Wage Policies for Decent Work and Inclusive Growth*, ILO Decent Work Team for South Asia and Country Office for India, available at https://www.ilo.org/wcmsp5/groups/public/---asia/---ro-bangkok/---sro-new_delhi/documents/publication/wcms_638305.pdf, accessed 25 June 2020.

Jevons, William Stanley (1871) [2013], *The Theory of Political Economy*, 4th edition (1911), Hampshire: Palgrave Macmillan.

Jimomi, Abokali (2019), 'Vili's Runaway Son', in Anungla Zoe Longkumer (ed.), *The Many That I Am: Writings from Nagaland*, New Delhi: Zubaan, pp. 150–6.

Jones, Hywel G. (1975), *An Introduction to Modern Theories of Economic Growth*, London: Nelson.

Joseph, Sarah (2011), *Gift in Green*, translated from the Malayalam by Valson Thampu, Noida: Harper Collins.

Kalecki, Michał (1933) [1971], 'Outline of a Theory of the Business Cycle', as reprinted in *Selected Essays on the Dynamics of the Capitalist Economy 1933–1970*, Cambridge: Cambridge University Press, pp. 1–14.

Keynes, John Maynard (1924) [2013], 'Alfred Marshall', in *Essays in Biography*, as vol. 10 of *The Collected Writings of John Maynard Keynes*, Cambridge: Cambridge University Press (for the Royal Economic Society), pp. 161–231.

——— (1933) [2013], 'A Monetary Theory of Production', in *The General Theory and After: Part I, Preparation*, edited by Donald Moggridge, as vol. 13 of *The Collected Writings of John Maynard Keynes*, Cambridge: Cambridge University Press (for the Royal Economic Society), pp. 408–11.

——— (1936) [2013], *The General Theory of Employment, Interest and Money*, as vol. 7 of *The Collected Writings of John Maynard Keynes*, Cambridge: Cambridge University Press (for the Royal Economic Society).

Kumar, Arun (1999), *The Black Economy in India*, New Delhi: Penguin.

Lewis, W. Arthur (1954), 'Economic Development with Unlimited Supplies of Labour', *The Manchester School*, vol. 22, no. 2, pp. 139–91.

Lutz, F. A. and D. C. Hague (eds) (1961), *The Theory of Capital: Proceedings of a Conference held by the International Economic Association*, London: Macmillan.

Luxemburg, Rosa (1913) [1951], *The Accumulation of Capital*, translated from the German by Agnes Schwarzschild, New York: Monthly Review Press.

Manto, Sadat Hasan (2008), 'Ram Khilavan', *Manto: Selected Short Stories*, translated from the Urdu by Aatish Taseer, Gurgaon: Penguin, pp. 91–101.

Marshall, Alfred (1890) [2013], *Principles of Economics*, 8th edition (1920), London: Palgrave Macmillan.

Marx, Karl (1867) [2010], *Capital: A Critical Analysis of Capitalist Production, Volume 1*, translated from the third German edition by Samuel Moore and Edward Aveling, edited by Frederick Engels, New Delhi: LeftWord Books.

——— (1885) [2010], *Capital: A Critique of Political Economy, Volume 2*, edited by Frederick Engels, New Delhi: LeftWord Books.

——— (1894) [2010], *Capital: A Critique of Political Economy, Volume 3*, edited by Frederick Engels, New Delhi: LeftWord Books.

Mazzucato, Mariana (2013) [2018], *The Entrepreneurial State: Debunking Public vs. Private Sector Myths*, Great Britain: Penguin.

Ministry of External Affairs (MEA) (2020), *Annual Report 2019–20*, 9 March, available at http://www.mea.gov.in/Uploads/PublicationDocs/32489_AR_Spread_2020_new.pdf, accessed 25 June 2020.

Moggridge, Donald (ed.) (1980) [2013], *Activities 1940–1946. Shaping the Post-War World: Employment and Commodities*, as vol. 27 in *The Collected Writings of John*

Maynard Keynes, Cambridge: Cambridge University Press (for the Royal Economic Society).

Morgan, Mary S. (2012), *The World in the Model: How Economists Work and Think*, Cambridge: Cambridge University Press.

Mukherjee, Siddhartha (2015), *The Laws of Medicine: Field Notes from an Uncertain Science*, London: Ted Books and Simon & Schuster.

Murugan, Perumal (2001) [2017], *Seasons of the Palm*, translated from the Tamil by V. Geetha, Gurgaon: Penguin.

Narayan, R. K. (1952) [2015], *The Financial Expert*, Chennai: Indian Thought Publications.

National Sample Survey Organisation (NSSO) (2005), *Household Indebtedness in India as on 30.06.2002*, All India Debt and Investment Survey (AIDIS), NSS 59th Round, January–December 2003, Report no. 501, available at http://www.mospi.gov.in/sites/default/files/publication_reports/501_final.pdf, accessed 25 June 2020.

———— (2014), *Employment and Unemployment Situation in India*, NSS 68th Round, July 2011–June 2012, Report no. 554, available at http://mospi.nic.in/sites/default/files/publication_reports/nss_report_554_31jan14.pdf, accessed 25 June 2020.

———— (2014), *Key Indicators of Debt and Investment in India*, NSS 70th Round, 2013, available at http://www.mospi.gov.in/sites/default/files/publication_reports/KI_70_18.2_19dec14.pdf, accessed 25 June 2020.

Neelima, Kota (2016), *Death of a Moneylender*, Gurgaon: Penguin.

Office of the Economic Advisor (OEA) (2017), 'Frequently Asked Questions on Revision of Wholesale Price Index', 12 May, Department of Industrial Policy and Promotion, Ministry of Commerce and Industry, available at https://www.eaindustry.nic.in/uploaded_files/FAQs_on_WPI.pdf, accessed 25 June 2020.

O'Neil, Cathy (2016), *Weapons of Math Destruction: How Big Data Increases Inequality and Threatens Democracy*, Great Britain: Penguin Books.

Pacioli, Luca (1494) [1995], 'Particularis de Computis et Scripturis', *Summa de Arithmetica, Geometria, Proportioni et Proportionalita*, a contemporary interpretation by Jeremy Cripps, Seattle: Pacioli Society, available at http://jeremycripps.com/docs/Summa.pdf, accessed 25 June 2020.

Palumbo, Antonella and Attilio Trezzini (2003), 'Growth Without Normal Capacity Utilization', *European Journal of the History of Economic Thought*, vol. 10, no. 1, pp. 109-35.

Parikh, Kirit S. (ed.) (2009), *Macro-Modelling for the Eleventh Five Year Plan of India*, New Delhi: Academic Foundation (for the Planning Commission, Government of India).

Petty, William (1690) [1899], *Political Arithmetick*, as reprinted in C. H. Hull (ed.), *The Economic Writings of Sir William Petty*, vol. I, Cambridge: Cambridge University Press.

Picchio, Antonella (1992), *Social Reproduction: The Political Economy of the Labour Market*, Cambridge: Cambridge University Press.

Piketty, Thomas (2014), *Capital in the Twenty-First Century*, translated from the French by Arthur Goldhammer, Massachusetts: Harvard University Press.

Pivetti, Massimo (1991), *An Essay on Money and Distribution*, New York: Palgrave Macmillan.

Planning Commission (1956), 'Approach to the Second Five Year Plan', *2nd Five Year Plan*, New Delhi: Government of India, available at https://niti.gov.in/planningcommission.gov.in/docs/plans/planrel/fiveyr/2nd/welcome.html, accessed 25 June 2020.

——— (1956), *2nd Five Year Plan*, New Delhi: Government of India, available at https://niti.gov.in/planningcommission.gov.in/docs/plans/planrel/fiveyr/welcome.html, accessed 25 June 2020.

Pradhan, Narayan Chandra (2013), 'Persistence of Informal Credit in Rural India: Evidence from "All-India Debt and Investment Survey" and Beyond', RBI Working Paper Series, No. 5, available at https://www.rbi.org.in/scripts/publicationsview.aspx?id=14986.

Premchand (1932) [2018], 'Thakur's Well', translated from the Hindi by M. Asaduddin, in M. Asaduddin (ed.), *Stories on Caste*, Gurgaon: Penguin, pp. 1–5.

Quesnay, François (1765) [1972], *Tableau Économique*, in Marguerite Kuczynski and Ronald Meek (eds), *Quesnay's Tableau Économique*, London: Macmillan (for the Royal Economic Society).

Raj, K. N. (1957), 'Employment Aspects of Planning in Under-developed Economies', *Fiftieth Anniversary Commemoration Lectures Series*, Cairo: National Bank of Egypt.

——— (1990), *Organizational Issues in Indian Agriculture*, Delhi: Oxford University Press.

Ranade, M. G. (1893) [2016], 'Indian Political Economy', *Journal of the Poona Sarvajanik Sabha*, vol. 15, no. 3, as republished in Bipan Chandra (ed.), *Ranade's Economic Writings*, New Delhi: Gyan Publishing House, pp. 322–49, also available at https://archive.org/details/in.ernet.dli.2015.123624/page/n9/mode/2up, accessed 25 June 2020.

——— (1898), *Essays on Indian Economics: A Collection of Essays and Speeches*, Bombay: Thacker, available at https://archive.org/details/in.ernet.dli.2015.263053/page/n5/mode/2up, accessed 25 June 2020.

Rao, Raja (1938) [1989], *Kanthapura*, New Delhi: Oxford University Press.

Rao, V. K. R. V. (1944), 'National Income of India', *The ANNALS of the American Academy of Political and Social Science*, vol. 233, no. 1, pp. 99–105.

——— (1952), 'Full Employment and Economic Development', *Indian Economic Review*, vol. 1, no. 2, pp. 43–57.

———— (1952) [2008], 'Investment, Income and the Multiplier in an Underdeveloped Economy', *Indian Economic Review*, vol. 1, no. 1, as republished in *The Indian Economic Journal*, vol. 56, no. 2, pp. 56–66.

———— (1983), *India's National Income 1950–80: An Analysis of Economic Growth and Change*, Delhi: Sage Publications.

Reddy, Kesava (1993) [2013], *Moogavani Pillanagrovi: Ballad of Ontillu*, translated from the Telugu by the author, New Delhi: Oxford University Press.

Reserve Bank of India (RBI) (2010), *Balance of Payments Manual for India*, September, available at https://rbidocs.rbi.org.in/rdocs/Publications/PDFs/IBPM221110P2. pdf, accessed 25 June 2020.

———— (2010), 'New Series of Wholesale Price Index Numbers (Base: 2004–05=100)', *RBI Monthly Bulletin*, October, pp. 2071–84, available at https://www.rbi.org.in/scripts/BS_ViewBulletin.aspx?Id=11608, accessed 25 June 2020.

———— (2020), 'No. 45 : Ownership Pattern of Central and State Governments Securities', Current Statistics, *RBI Bulletin February 2020*, p. 92, available at https://www.rbi.org.in/scripts/BS_ViewBulletin.aspx?Id=18812, accessed 25 June 2020.

Ricardo, David (1817) [1951], *On the Principles of Political Economy and Taxation*, as vol. 1 in Piero Sraffa (ed.) with the collaboration of M. H. Dobb, *The Works and Correspondence of David Ricardo*, Cambridge: Cambridge University Press.

Robbins, Lionel (1932) [1984], *An Essay on the Nature and Significance of Economic Science*, 3rd edition (1984), London: Macmillan.

Robinson, Joan (1974), *Selected Economic Writings*, Bombay: Oxford University Press (for Centre for Development Studies, Trivandrum).

Romer, Paul (1986), 'Increasing Returns and Long-run Growth', *Journal of Political Economy*, vol. 94, no. 5, pp. 1002–37.

———— (1994), 'The Origins of Endogenous Growth', *Journal of Economic Perspectives*, vol. 8, no. 1, pp. 3–22.

Saluja, M. R. (2017), *Measuring India: The Nation's Statistical System*, New Delhi: Oxford University Press.

Schui, Florian (2014), *Austerity: The Great Failure*, New Haven: Yale University Press.

Sekhsaria, Pankaj (2017), *Islands in Flux: The Andaman and Nicobar Story*, Noida: Harper Litmus.

Serrano, Franklin (1995), 'Long Period Effective Demand and the Sraffian Supermultiplier', *Contributions to Political Economy*, vol. 14, no. 1, pp. 67–90.

Shekhar, Hansda Sowvendra (2015), 'Baso-jhi', *The Adivasi Will Not Dance: Stories*, New Delhi: Speaking Tiger, pp. 112–29.

———— (2015), 'The Adivasi Will Not Dance', *The Adivasi Will Not Dance: Stories*, New Delhi: Speaking Tiger, pp. 169–89.

Shirwale, Bhimrao (2009), 'Livelihood', translated from the Marathi by Shanta Gokhale, in Arun Dangle (ed.), *Poisoned Bread: Translations from Modern Marathi Dalit Literature*, Hyderabad: Orient Blackswan, pp. 197–208.

Shrivastava, Aseem and Ashish Kothari (2012), *Churning the Earth: The Making of Global India*, New Delhi: Penguin.

Sivakami, P. (1992) [2012], *The Taming of Women*, translated from the Tamil by Pritham K. Chakravarthy, Gurgaon: Penguin.

Skybaaba (2004) [2016], 'Homeland', translated from the Telugu by R. Akhileshwari, in A. Suneetha and Uma Maheswari Bhrugubanda (eds), *Vegetarians Only: Stories of Telugu Muslims*, Hyderabad: Orient Blackswan, pp. 57–63.

——— (2016), 'Vegetarians Only', translated from the Telugu by Uma Maheswari Bhrugubanda, in A. Suneetha and Uma Maheswari Bhrugubanda (eds), *Vegetarians Only: Stories of Telugu Muslims*, Hyderabad: Orient Blackswan, pp. 33–42.

——— (2016), 'Nowhere to Turn', translated from the Telugu by Rama S. Melkote, in A. Suneetha and Uma Maheswari Bhrugubanda (eds), *Vegetarians Only: Stories of Telugu Muslims*, Hyderabad: Orient Blackswan, pp. 102–14.

Shukla, Shrilal (1968) [1992], *Raag Darbari*, translated from the Hindi by Gillian Wright, Gurgaon: Penguin Books.

Smith, Adam (1759) [1976], *The Theory of Moral Sentiments*, as vol. 1 in D. D. Raphael and A. L. Macfie (eds), *The Glasgow Edition of the Works and Correspondence of Adam Smith*, Oxford: Clarendon.

——— (1776) [1976], *An Enquiry into the Nature and Causes of Wealth of Nations*, as vol. 2 in R. H. Campbell, A. S. Skinner, and W. B. Todd (eds), *The Glasgow Edition of the Works and Correspondence of Adam Smith*, Oxford: Clarendon Press.

Smith, Matthew (2012), 'Demand-led Growth Theory: A Historical Approach', *Review of Political Economy*, vol. 24, no. 4, pp. 543–73.

Solow, Robert (1956), 'A Contribution to the Theory of Economic Growth', *The Quarterly Journal of Economics*, vol. 70, no. 1, pp. 65–94.

——— (1987), 'Growth Theory and After', Nobel Memorial Lecture, 8 December, available at https://www.nobelprize.org/prizes/economic-sciences/1987/solow/lecture/, accessed 25 June 2020.

Sraffa, Piero (1960), *Production of Commodities by Means of Commodities*, Cambridge: Cambridge University Press.

Stirati, Antonella (1991) [1994], *The Theory of Wages in Classical Economics: A Study of Adam Smith, David Ricardo and Their Contemporaries*, translated from the Italian by Joan Hall, Vermont: Edward Elgar.

Stone, Richard (1951), *The Role of Measurement in Economics*, Cambridge: Cambridge University Press.

——— (1984), 'The Accounts of Society', Nobel Memorial Lecture, 8 December, available at https://www.nobelprize.org/uploads/2018/06/stone-lecture.pdf, accessed 25 June 2020.

The Royal Swedish Academy of Sciences (2018), 'Integrating Nature and Knowledge into Economics', *The Prize in Economic Sciences 2018: Popular Science Background*, available at https://www.nobelprize.org/uploads/2018/10/popular-economicsciencesprize2018.pdf, accessed 25 June 2020.

Vinodini, M. M. (2013), 'The Parable of the Lost Daughter', translated from the Telugu by Uma Bhrugubanda, in K. Satyanarayana and Susie Tharu (eds), *The Exercise of Freedom: An Introduction to Dalit Writing*, New Delhi: Navayana, pp. 164–77.

Weintraub, E. Roy (2002), *How Economics Became a Mathematical Science*, Durham: Duke University Press.

Wheen, Francis (2006) [2008], *Marx's Das Capital: A Biography*, New Delhi: Manjul Publishing House.

Xaxa, Abhay (2011), 'I Am Not Your Data', available at http://roundtableindia.co.in/lit-blogs/?p=1943, accessed 25 June 2020.

Index

Here is an unexpected exercise: look up India's National Classification of Occupations (NCO), published by the Directorate General of Employment, and identify the group under which the producer of this book's index—the indexer—is listed. Also, do you think that the listing is appropriate?

foreign institutional investors (FIIs), 61,
  79, 112, 188
foreign trade. *See* international trade
forex. *See* foreign exchange
forex rates, 59
Foundation for Agrarian Studies (FAS),
  137
four-sector economy, 81
  macroeconomic equilibrium in, 82
Frank, Andre Gunder, 110
free trade. *See* international trade
free trade area (FTA), 80
Friedman, Milton, 7, 174
fuel inflation, 179
full employment, 6–7, 10, 15, 27, 35, 62,
  69–70, 74, 77–8, 83, 88, 93–4, 96,
  112, 124, 136, 138, 151, 156, 159,
  161–3, 174, 178, 188, 191
functional income distribution, theories of,
  92, 125. *See also* profit; wage

Galbraith, John Kenneth, 7, 47
game theory, 7, 82, 153. *See also* marginalist
  economics
Ganguli, B. N., 162
Garegnani, Pierangelo, 95, 114
GDP deflator, 170
gender
  economic growth, 1, 147
  employment, 129, 138–9
  in fiction, 2, 137, 194. *See also* fiction for
    economists
  labour mobility, 13, 112
  land ownership, 11, 35, 129
  macroeconomy, 21
  mesoeconomy, 32. *See also* meso
    approach
geopolitics, 80–1, 83, 88, 113, 190
Georgescu-Roegen, Nicholas, 180
Ghosh, Amitav, 30
gig economy, 141
Global Financial Crisis (2008), 49, 89

Global Findex Database, 43
global value chains, 111
glut, 74. *See also* aggregate demand
gold, 5, 21, 61
Goods and Services Tax (GST), 34, 80–1,
  154
government
  anti-cyclical policy, 159
  counter-cyclical policy, 159
  and employment policy, 43, 138, 159,
    191
  and fiscal policy, 178–9, 184
  Five Year Plan. *See* Five-Year Plan of
    India
  of Indian, 41, 50, 75
  and inflation policy, 183, 191
  macroeconomic management, 60
  pro-cyclical policy, 159
  and productive capacity creation, 61
  role of, 146, 151, 152–6
government bonds. *See* sovereign bonds
government borrowing, 60, 125, 151, 154,
  156, 191
government debt. *See* public debt
  sustainability
government expenditure, 7, 16, 27, 67–8,
  75–7, 81, 96, 124–5, 153–6, 155,
  161, 179, 189
Government of India, 41, 50, 75, 146. *See
  also* Ministry of
government, role as
  entrepreneur, 2
  provider of employment
    MGNREGA, 121, 160
  provider of unemployment insurance,
    24
government, role of
  austerity, 124, 152, 159
  employment policy, 43, 138, 159, 191
  inflation policy, 183, 191
  private sector, relative to, 16, 38, 75, 154
  public debt, 41, 151, 153–4, 156
  relative to private sector, 16, 38, 75, 154

INDEX

money (*continued*)
money creation, 54
in an open economy, 58–62
operation of monetary policy, 184
quantity theory of money (QTM), 173, 183
supply of, 53–4
theories of, 52–7, 126
velocity of circulation of, 174
money flows, 27, 31
moneylenders, 40, 43, 45, 62
moneylending, 132
money market, 42, 51, 55–6. *See also* financial architecture of India
money wages, responsiveness of, 175
monopolistic competition. *See* imperfect competition
monopoly. *See* imperfect competition
monopsony, 127
moral sentiments, 30–1. *See also* Smith, Adam
Morgan, Mary S., 120
Mukherjee, Siddhartha, 136
multiplier, 75–6, 82, 94, 96, 101, 153, 155, 161
Mun, Thomas, 5
Muqaddimah (Ibn Khaldun), 5, 22
mutual benefit financial companies (MBFCs), 42
mutual funds, 27, 34, 40, 42, 49, 51–2, 58

Naoroji, Dadabhai, 23
Narayan, R. K., 44
National Accounts Statistics (NAS), 23, 25, 67
National Bank for Agriculture and Rural Development (NABARD), 43
National Bank of Egypt, 107
National Campaign on Adivasi Rights, 16
National Commission on Enterprises in the Unorganised Sector (NCEUS), 130

National Housing Bank (NHB), 46, 170
national income accounting (NIA), 23, 158
national income accounts, 139
development of, 23
estimation of, 23
'green' accounts, 24
in India, 23
National Sample Survey Organisation (NSSO), 102
All India Debt and Investment Survey (AIDIS) report, 43
Employment and Unemployment Situation of India (2014), 140
National Stock Exchange (NSE), 42
National Thermal Power Corporation (NTPC), 41
natural environment, 36, 37, 107, 180, 193
natural resources, 84, 87, 101
rate of utilisation of, 24
regional distribution of, 129
necessaries, 158, 172. *See also* wage
Neelima, Kota, 128–9, 137
neoclassical economics. *See* marginalist economics
net investment, 99. *See also* investment
new growth theory, 115. *See also* marginalist growth theory
*nidhi*s, 42
Nobel Prize, 23, 113
non-banking finance corporations (NBFCs), 42–3
non-banking financial institutions, 42
non-capitalist sector, 131
non-capitalist societies, 66
non-competitive economies, 14
non-economics journals
Accounting Review, The, 27
Political Quarterly, 162
non-farm business, 131
non-farm enterprises, 141
non-financial sectors, 79
non-renewable resources, 108

226

Made in the USA
Las Vegas, NV
14 July 2023

74738921R00144